Seeking Good,
Speaking Peace

THE LIBRARY OF SEPHARDIC HISTORY AND THOUGHT

edited by
Marc D. Angel

Seeking Good,
Speaking Peace

Collected Essays of

Rabbi Marc D. Angel

edited by

Hayyim J. Angel

KTAV Publishing House, Inc.
Hoboken NJ

Library of Congress Cataloging-in-Publication-Data

Angel, Marc
  Seeking good, speaking peace : collected essays of Rabbi Marc D.
  Angel / edited by Hayyim J. Angel.
  p. cm.
  ISBN 0-88125-241-7
  1. Orthodox Judaism. 2. Judaism--20th century. 3. Sephardim--United
States. I. Angel, Hayyim J. II. Title.

BM45.A53   1994
296'.8'32--dc20

                                                    94-10452
                                                    CIP

In Honor of Maria (Manya) Wallach

In Loving Memory of:
Lillian Ruth Illoway
Bernard Samuel Illoway
Jacob Wallach
Miriam Ruth Phillips
Elward Jonas Phillips
Rabbi Bernard Illovy
Abraham (Adi) Donner
Rabbi Abraham Mordechai (Mutik) Blum
Simon Ellenberg

CONTENTS

ACKNOWLEDGEMENTS

by Rabbi Marc D. Angel

A wise rabbinic teaching is that *bera mezakeh abba*, a son brings merit to his father. I am pleased and honored beyond words that our son Hayyim has edited this book with love, diligence and talent. He is a young *talmid hakham* of remarkable perception and sensitivity. I thank him for undertaking this project and for doing it so well.

A number of the articles in this volume have appeared over the years in various publications. Each of them has been edited for this volume, and a number of them include revisions from the originals. This book also includes some previously unpublished lectures and addresses. I thank Mrs. Hennie Imberman for her role in preparing the manuscript and her great assistance.

I express profound gratitude to my wife, Gilda, and to our daughters Ronda and Elana who—together with Hayyim—have played a significant role in the development of the material in this book. Over the years, we have discussed issues of Jewish thought, Jewish law, the Sephardic experience, and issues in contemporary Jewish life. The insights and inspiration gained from them have been beyond measure.

I thank Mr. Bernard Scharfstein and his staff at Ktav Publishing House for the wonderful cooperation and expertise that was given to the production of this volume. Bernard

Scharfstein has not only been a good publisher, but also a good friend.

This collection of essays and addresses has been prepared in honor of my 25th anniversary of service at Congregation Shearith Israel, the historic Spanish and Portuguese Synagogue of New York City. We have a large and diverse congregation. Our family has been blessed over the years with many wonderful friendships within the congregation and we thank all those congregants who have made our experience at Shearith Israel a fulfilling and meaningful one.

The suggestion to prepare this volume came from our good friend Mr. Alvin Deutsch, Segan of Congregation Shearith Israel. Mr. Ronald P. Stanton, Chairman of the congregation's Ministerial Committee, was instrumental in moving this project along. I thank both of them for their support, encouragement, and constant friendship. I wish to thank the following members of Congregation Shearith. Israel who have contributed towards this volume: Mr. Henri Bengualid, Mr. & Mrs. Marc Bengualid, Dr. Victoria Bengualid, Mr. & Mrs. Norman Benzaquen, Mr. & Mrs. Victor Capelluto, Mr. & Mrs. Alvin Deutsch, Mr. Helmut Friedlaender, Mr. & Mrs. Arthur Goldberg, Mr. & Mrs. Simon Haberman, Mr. Joseph Maleh, Mr. Jonathan de Sola Mendes, Mr. & Mrs. Edgar J. Nathan, 3rd, Mr. & Mrs. David Nathan, Mr. & Mrs. Avery Neumark, Mr. & Mrs. Morris Pinto, Mr. & Mrs. Jack Rudin, Mr. Ronald P. Stanton, Mr. & Mrs. Ezra Zilkha, and the Shearith Israel League.

I express heartfelt gratitude to the Almighty who has brought us to this milestone. I pray for the continued good health and happiness of our family, our congregation, our community. May we speedily witness genuine peace for the people of Israel and the world.

INTRODUCTION

Rabbi Yehoshua ben Perahia (Avot 1:6) enjoins every Jew, *aseh lekha rav*, "make for yourself a teacher." Sensitive to the central role of this dictum in Jewish tradition, Rabbi Hayyim David Halevi, the current Sephardic Chief Rabbi of Tel Aviv–Jaffa, wrote a nine-volume series of responsa entitled *Aseh Lekha Rav*. The very first responsum (1:1) examines the nature of what it means to have a *rav*, or teacher. Rabbi Halevi begins with the standard explanation of the mishnah in Avot, that people must select a rabbi well versed in Jewish law (halakhah) to answer queries pertaining to Jewish observance.

Rabbi Halevi continues, however. He writes that there is another dimension to a *rav*, and that this component is probably more important than his ability to give halakhic counsel: a *rav* is someone who is a personality, who presents a sound and all-encompassing worldview. One imbued with Jewish tradition knows that Judaism affects one's every action, both in the religious and the secular spheres. Jewish law and values pervade the spirit of such individuals, so that they react naturally and spontaneously to every situation with Jewish ethics as their guiding force. Through conscientious association with a *rav*, people will discover not only which foods are kasher and how to observe Shabbat; they will learn how to be Jews in all facets of their lives.

How does one select a *rav*, a teacher? If the *rav*'s sole function were as a halakhist, then the decision would be simple. Objective tests could be administered to determine who best

knows the Talmud, Rambam's *Mishneh Torah*, Rabbi Yosef
Karo's *Shulhan Arukh*, and the vast halakhic literature on every
topic in Jewish law. But according to Rabbi Halevi's analysis of
the function of a *rav*, such a criterion alone is insufficient. To
be sure, a *rav* must have an excellent grasp of halakhic literature to function as a rabbi; yet he also needs a "Torah personality," through which he may serve as a living model of
Judaism.

Once a person has selected a competent *rav*, a new question
arises: how much should one rely on his or her *rav*? Does the
rav assume complete authority over his adherents' lives, or
should he support their preconceived ideas? In the religious
realm (and, for that matter, the secular realm also), absolutes
are often simpler and more alluring than multi-faceted positions. An authoritarian approach to Judaism often sounds
appealing: it provides one with a sense of security; it gives a
person a reliable authority figure who makes his or her decisions. On the other side, a self-sufficient approach supports
the notion of human freedom, whereby a *rav* may give advice,
but ultimate decisions fall into the responsibility of the individual.

Although both practices have some meritorious features,
they both fall short of the Jewish ideal. The blind following of
an authority figure deprives the individual of any freedom of
thought, and effectively reduces him or her to an observant
automaton. Conversely, the *rav*less, autodidactic tactic can and
almost must lead to the irresponsible violation of the boundaries of Judaism. It is both naive and self-deceptive to believe
that one can lead a sound Jewish life without the guidance of
an expert.

A competent *rav* must sensitively synthesize both
approaches. On one side, there *are* absolute boundaries in
Judaism; if one steps beyond them, it no longer is Judaism. It
is therefore incumbent on the *rav* courageously to guard the
bounds of Jewish tradition. Within these confines, however,
there is room for innovation, creativity, diversity. In fact, these

differences are encouraged within Judaism. There is a special blessing recited upon seeing large numbers of Jews, *Barukh Hakham ha-razim*, "Blessed is the wise One, cognizant of all that is hidden." This blessing glorifies Israel, which is composed of a multitude of differing voices, each with an insight, an outlook, and an understanding of Judaism which nobody else shares. Each Jew has the duty to share his or her views with others, and to study various opinions of great Jewish thinkers, so that the Jewish people as a whole can thrive as a united group of distinct individuals.

Thus, the job of the *rav* is to direct his adherents in the path of Judaism. But he must not attempt to create mindless clones of himself; rather, he must provide for others the basis for self-development and fulfillment within their sacred and ancient tradition. Likewise, the student of the *rav* must straddle the delicate balance between mindless mimicry of the *rav*, on the one hand, and the hazard of innovation without responsible guidance, on the other. Thus, *rav* and student work together in developing each other's worldview and behavior patterns. By combining both approaches, one maturely recognizes that he or she *needs* a teacher in order to thrive spiritually; but each person remains an individual—with innate responsibility and self-respect.

My father has been my *rav* for my entire life. In addition to his role as a father, he has guided and continues to guide my religious life. He is truly *avi mori*, my father and my teacher. He has touched the lives of a vast number of people, and has been a *rav* for many of them. He has served as rabbi of Congregation Shearith Israel, the historic Spanish and Portuguese Synagogue of New York City (founded in 1654), for the past twenty-five years. He has been a leading spokesman for Orthodoxy in America, and has served in many positions of communal leadership. He has lectured widely to diverse audiences throughout North America and beyond. In addition to his public life, he has authored significant books and numerous articles, in order to share his knowledge with the reading public.

In preparing this volume, I selected those articles which best represent my father's religious outlook, his positions on various halakhic issues, and his view of how to live all aspects of life from a Jewish perspective. (In the back of this volume is a bibliography of most of my father's books and articles for further reading.) A central theme in all of my father's writings is that contemporary Jews must draw wisdom from the post-1492 Sephardic diaspora. It is from these communities and their religious leaders, all too often ignored in general Jewish scholarship, that profound insight for living a sensible religious life in the modern world derives.

Although books cannot substitute for an actual *rav*, this volume offers more than abstract ideas—it presents my father's personality as a religious model to all who read it.

Hayyim J. Angel

New York, N.Y.
Rosh Hodesh Adar, 5754
February 12, 1994

I
Jewish Thought

1

HESED VE-EMET—COMPASSION AND TRUTH: TENSIONS WITHIN ORTHODOXY

*C*ompassion and truth are basic elements of religion; yet these elements are often in dialectic tension. They pull in opposite directions.

The talmudic sage, Rav Ashi (Taʿanit 4a) taught: "Any *talmid hakham* [rabbinic scholar] who is not as hard as iron is no *talmid hakham*." One who understands the religious tradition must recognize its absolute truth as the word of God. This certainty is an overpowering force in his life, and everything else must be measured against this truth. A religious person must stand strong in his convictions; he should not bend under the weight of external pressure.

Several lines later on the same page of the Talmud, though, we find the opinion of Ravina, who—although agreeing that a rabbinic scholar must be strong in his convictions—stated: "Even so, a person must teach himself the quality of gentleness." A religious person must be compassionate, empathetic, humble. He must not only be hard as steel; he also must know when to bend, when to be soft.

Address at the installation of officers of the Chicago Rabbinical Council, November 20, 1986, at the Sephardic Synagogue, in honor of Rabbi Michael Azose, new President of the Chicago Rabbinical Council.

3

Both truth and compassion are essential ingredients in religious life; they must be kept in delicate balance. To push to the extreme of truth leads to religious fanaticism, even warfare. To push to the extreme of compassion leads to the dissipation of religious traditions altogether. The spiritual climate of a Jewish community might be measured by the way these two tendencies are handled.

The Torah itself presents a striking illustration of how truth and compassion can create different styles. The example is the story of the golden calf. When Moshe came down from Mount Sinai and found the Israelites dancing around the golden calf, he became enraged. He cast down the tablets of the law, so that they shattered. His attitude was one of righteous indignation. Hard like steel, Moshe had the perpetrators of this crime executed, so that thousands of Israelites were slaughtered as just punishment for their transgression. Moshe stood for the truth. He could not brook such a heinous crime against truth. His response was quick, forceful, and well justified.

But the story of the golden calf also includes the character of Aharon. While Moshe was still on the mountain, the people of Israel became impatient waiting for their leader. They called upon Aharon to make an idol for them to worship. Aharon, being pliable and conciliatory, attempted to stall the people off. But seeing their insistence, he collected gold from them and personally assisted in the creation of this golden calf. Although Aharon did receive some rebuke, God did not strip Aharon of the high priesthood, in spite of his ostensibly ignoble behavior during the golden calf incident.

Moshe and Aharon reflect two different personalities. Moshe, the personality of truth, was consumed with his passion for truth. This man, who saw God face to face, could not tolerate his people worshipping a false god. Aharon, the personality of compassion, went to the extreme of conciliation and compromise, sacrificing truth for the sake of the immediate needs of the people. Aharon's overwhelming tendency towards conciliation allowed the people of Israel to have their golden calf.

When the great talmudic sage, Hillel, suggested a role model for the Jewish people, he chose Aharon. In the first chapter of the Pirkei Avot (1:12), Hillel is quoted to say: "Be among the students of Aharon, loving peace and pursuing peace; loving your fellow beings and bringing them closer to Torah." Thus, instead of being castigated in Jewish tradition, Aharon is idealized. His reputation has passed through the generations with honor, as a man of peace and compassion.

Aharon loved peace and therefore pursued it. He loved his fellow beings and therefore reached out to them to bring them closer to Torah. There are famous Midrashim which portray Aharon as one who would do anything, even lie, in order to bring peace between husband and wife, between two quarreling friends. In giving us the model of Aharon, Hillel teaches that it is not enough merely to have pious sentiments of unity, peace and conciliation; love of peace means actually working for it, and love of Torah means actually reaching out to bring people closer to it.

It is well known that the school of Hillel and the school of Shammai represent different points of view in Jewish law. The school of Shammai tended to be stricter; the school of Hillel tended to be more lenient. The Talmud (Eruvin 13b) teaches that a heavenly voice announced that both schools represented the voice of the living God—but that the law should follow the school of Hillel. In other words, both positions have validity. Faithfulness to absolute truth, following that truth regardless of consequences—this is a respectable position, reflected by the school of Shammai. Recognizing that law affects people's lives directly and that people's feelings must be taken into consideration—this is a legitimate position, reflected by the school of Hillel. The heavenly voice decided in favor of the latter approach. Abstract Truth must give way to practical personal love and compassion.

Rabbi Hayyim David Halevi writes (*Aseh Lekha Rav*, 5:48) that the halakhah follows the school of Hillel because they were more sensitive to the human predicament, sympathetic to human weaknesses and inadequacies, considerate of the difficulties of life which affected people's behavior. Reality does not always conform to theoretical ideas as to how humans should conduct themselves. Rabbi Halevi points out that his teacher, the late Rishon le-Tzion, Rabbi Bentzion Uziel, was a model of a *posek* (halakhic decisor) in the tradition of Bet Hillel. And this is the model we need to follow today.

Rav Yohanan states (Bava Metzia 30b) that Jerusalem was destroyed only because the people established the law according to the precise meaning of the law—but did not go beyond what the exact law required—*lifnim mi-shurat ha-din*. Rabbi Eliezer Papo, one of the great sages of the last century, comments that they did not demonstrate enough real piety, sensitivity, compassion. They were content to be strict legalists, without seeing the broader implications of Torah teachings. Rabbi Papo reminds us that *be-middah she-adam moded modedim lo*, the same standards by which we judge others will be used by the heavenly court when we ourselves stand to be judged. If we are emphatic about *emet* (truth), then we can expect the heavenly court to be equally strict in applying the standard of *emet* to the way we live our lives. If we are filled with *hesed* (compassion), we can expect God to be compassionate with us. In a real sense, then, the way we view and judge others is the way in which we ultimately will be viewed and judged.

Religious life demands a balancing of the demands of truth and the demands of compassion—but the tilt must be in favor of compassion. This is not to say that compromise is always good or always right. Nor does it mean that one should not fight with all his strength for those principles which he knows to be absolutely true. A true religious personality is constantly involved in balancing these two vital dimensions of religious life. This endeavor is not an easy task; it is not without risks, and one person's judgement will differ from that of another as to where one must be hard as steel and where one must be pliable.

In recent years, it appears that the models of Aharon and Hillel have suffered a decline in respect. The rise of religious extremism no longer can be ignored or explained away as a fringe element in Jewish life. Religious extremism is a problem in Israel and in the Diaspora. It is more fashionable now in the Orthodox world to fight for the "truth" at all costs, and to consider lenient or moderate positions as being examples of lesser piety, even of cowardice or heresy. Right-wing "triumphalism" is the product of people who know the "truth" and who will not listen to any opinion which questions or denigrates that truth.

Recently, we have seen a number of unfortunate examples of extremism at its worst. A Reform rabbi was buried in the cemetery on the Mount of Olives. Some religious extremists wanted the body disinterred, arguing that the Reform rabbi should not be buried in the same cemetery with pious, Torah-observant Jews. When the authorities decided that the body should remain in its grave on the Mount of Olives, some religious zealots were reported to have put a fence around the grave, so as to separate it from the rest of the cemetery. As would have been expected, this episode created a furor in the Israeli press, and tensions between "religious" and "secular" Israelis worsened.

Such behavior on the part of religious extremists is repugnant not only to non-Orthodox Jews, but to many Orthodox Jews as well. One would think that even religious fanatics would have the sense to evaluate the consequences of their behavior on the general population. Is the burial of a Reform rabbi in the cemetery the place to draw a spiritual battle line for what they consider to be the ultimate truth? Don't they need to consider such Jewish notions as compassion for fellow Jews, decency, desecration of God's name? Shouldn't religious people be dominated by the love of peace and of fellow Jews so that they pursue peace and graciously lead their less-observant counterparts closer to Torah?

When a leading rabbi exclaimed that Israeli children were killed in an accident because a movie house in Petah Tikvah had opened on the Shabbat, did he believe that he would win an appreciation of Torah values from his listeners? Does that rabbi know for a fact what God thinks and how God acts and why God does what He does? And even if the rabbi believes his statement to be absolutely true, should he not have taken into consideration the quality of compassion before having made a public statement on such a sensitive issue?

And, of course, we have the classic stories of "ultra-Orthodox" Jews throwing rocks at cars driven through their neighborhoods on Shabbat. In serving the Lord so energetically, do these religious extremists believe that more people are likely to become observant of Shabbat? Or more respectful of Torah learning? Or more sympathetic to the moral lessons of Shabbat?

The *Jerusalem Post* international edition (week ending February 22, 1986) reported on a poll taken among "secular" Israelis. Only 19 percent of the respondents described Orthodox Jews favorably. Twenty-five percent thought that Orthodox Jews were "opportunists, liars and charlatans." Twenty-two percent described Orthodox Jews in terms of religious coercion and extremism. Thirteen percent identified Orthodox in terms of unique style of dress. Nineteen percent believed that Orthodox Jews were "moral, well-educated and proper." Amazingly, only 25 percent identified Orthodox Jews with a commitment to observe mitzvot. Obviously, our impressions of ourselves are not shared by the non-Orthodox. We have not succeeded in living the Torah in such a way as to gain respect. Outspoken extremists have been hard like iron, but they have not shown enough compassion or gentleness.

On a recent visit to Israel, I spoke with a highly educated woman in Haifa who told me that she had a "custom" to buy pita from a Druze village for Pesah. I asked her if she could not survive seven days without bread in order to observe the festival in the traditional manner. She told me: "I hardly eat bread all year long. But for Pesah I must buy bread, simply to declare that I want no part of Orthodoxy. I consider myself a traditional Jew—but I will not be coerced!" Those pious Jews who put a fence around the grave of a Reform rabbi in order to fight for "truth" do not realize that there is a correlation between their action and a woman in Haifa eating bread on Passover. Their behavior is not without consequences.

Modern, compassionate Orthodoxy, represented by such organizations as the Chicago Rabbinical Council and the Rabbinical Council of America, must speak out clearly and decisively against religious extremism, and not be intimidated by pressures from the right. The Orthodoxy of calm wisdom can serve as a mediating element in Jewish religious life. We are as concerned with truth as are the extremists, but we also have the virtue of sincerely loving peace and pursuing peace. Our Orthodoxy must reassert its spiritual leadership, not for our sake, but for the sake of the honor of the Torah. We need to show by our lives and deeds that Torah is sweet, beautiful, enlightening, pleasant, wise, compassionate. We need to have a clear understanding that our attitudes and actions do not exist in isolation. They influence others, they repel others, they bring people closer. We should not merely speak of harmony; we must work together harmoniously. We should not love peace merely in the abstract; we must work directly for it. We need not sacrifice our devotion to truth. We simply must give predominance to compassion.

It is said that Rabbi Yitzhak Luria would begin his morning prayers by saying: "Behold, I accept upon myself the commandment: 'You shall love your neighbor as yourself.'" Before opening our mouths in prayer to God, we need to have a full and loving appreciation of all Jewish people.

May the Almighty give strength and success to the officers, members and supporters of the Chicago Rabbinical Council. May you be hard as iron in your commitment to Torah values, may you demonstrate gentleness and compassion in all your sacred work on behalf of our people.

2

AUTHORITY AND DISSENT:
A DISCUSSION OF BOUNDARIES

*D*iversity of opinion is a reality well recognized in Jewish tradition. The Talmud (Berakhot 58a) records the ruling that one is required to make a blessing upon seeing a huge crowd of Jews, praising God who is *Hakham ha-razim*, who understands the root and inner thoughts of each individual. "Their thoughts are not alike and their appearances are not alike." Just as no two faces are exactly the same, so too no two people think in exactly the same way. God created each individual to be unique; He expected and wanted diversity of thought.[1]

The recognition that each person thinks differently leads to a respect for the right of a person to express his opinion. This notion is underscored dramatically in the laws relating to a *zaken mamre*, a rebellious elder. The elder (rabbinic scholar) is not deemed guilty for teaching opinions contrary to the rulings of the Great Court; he is punishable only if he instructs people to defy those rulings (see Rambam, *Hilkhot Mamrim*). It is also reflected in the talmudic practice of recording minority opinions, even though the law follows the consensus of the majority.[2] Even rejected opinions are entitled to respect.

Yet, although Judaism respects diversity of opinion and allows considerable freedom of expression, it also sets some boundaries beyond which a person may not trespass. One may not believe in the divinity of idols. One must believe that the

Originally published in *Tradition*, vol. 25 (Winter 1990).

Torah is from Heaven. Indeed, Rambam lists thirteen principles of faith which a Jew must accept, or else lose his portion in
the World to Come.[3] We are not free to follow our intellect if it
leads us to incorrect beliefs. Our intellectual freedom, thus, is
limited by the authoritative beliefs taught by the Torah and
our sages. Within the boundaries of normative Judaism, dissent is respected and even encouraged. But beyond those
boundaries, dissent is not tolerated. Intellectual freedom gives
way to the authority of tradition.

A problem arises. What exactly are the boundaries established by tradition? A variety of attempts have been made over
the centuries to establish the principles of Judaism from which
one may not deviate.[4] There are certain tenets of faith which
may not be denied. Yet, within the framework of Jewish law
and thought, there is considerable room for responsible differences of opinion. When the right to express responsible opinions is negated, Judaism suffers.

In a fascinating responsum, Rabbi Naftali Tzevi Yehudah
Berlin—Netziv—writes that during the Second Temple
period, the Jewish people were divided between the Pharisees
and Sadducees. Competition between the groups was intense.
The situation became so bad that Pharisees branded as a Sadducee anyone who deviated even slightly from prevailing
practice. To dissent from the predominant opinion led to one's
being ostracized. Netziv applies the lesson to contemporary
times:

> It is not difficult to imagine reaching this situation in our
> time, Heaven forbid, that if one of the faithful thinks that a
> certain person does not follow his way in the service of God,
> then he will judge him as a heretic. He will distance himself
> from him. People will pursue one another with seeming jus-
> tification (*be-heter dimyon*), Heaven forbid, and the people of
> God will be destroyed, Heaven forfend.[5]

The Netziv was concerned that self-righteous individuals
were attempting to suppress the opinions of others. In the
name of Torah, they sought to discredit others—even brand-

ing them as heretics. Yet, Jewish tradition respects the right and responsibility of individuals to express opinions which are based on proper Torah authority—even when those opinions differ from those popularly held. Rabbi Yehiel Mikhel Epstein, author of the *Arukh ha-Shulhan,* notes that differences of opinion among our sages constitute the glory of the Torah. "The entire Torah is called a song (*shirah*), and the glory of a song is when the voices differ one from the other. This is the essence of its pleasantness" (Introduction to *Hoshen Mishpat*).

The boundaries of dissent and authority are not always obvious. Let us consider two specific issues, one in the realm of halakhah and one in the realm of aggadah.

THE REALM OF HALAKHAH

The *Shulhan Arukh* rules (*Yoreh De'ah* 242:2, 3) that one who dissents (*holek*) from his rabbi is as one who dissents from the Shekhinah (God's Presence). The *holek al rabbo* is defined as one who establishes his own yeshivah and sets himself up as teacher without getting his rabbi's permission. Rama adds: "but it is permissible for him to dissent from (his rabbi's) ruling or teaching if he has proofs and arguments to uphold his opinion that the law is according to him (rather than his rabbi)."

This halakhah deals with the balance between authority and dissent.On the one hand, a student must respect the authority of his teacher and not try to establish himself as an authority on his own. This would undermine the status of his teacher. On the other hand, if the student has strong proofs to support a halakhic ruling against his teacher, he may disagree with him. Rabbi Hayyim Yosef David Azulai, in his *Birkei Yosef* (Y.D. 242:3), cites the opinion of Radbaz that a student may disagree with a ruling of his teacher but should not publicize the disagreement nor write a contrary *pesak* (ruling) for distribution. The students of each generation had disagreements with their teachers, and did present their proofs and refutations to them. To be sure, students are *obligated* to present their cases respectfully and reverently. Their purpose must be to establish the truth, not to aggrandize themselves nor demean their rabbis. Moreover, we are speaking of students who themselves have reached a very high level of Torah learning, and whose opinions deserve serious consideration.

Rabbi Hayyim David Halevi (*Aseh Lekha Rav*, 2:61) has stated: "Not only does a judge have the right to rule against his rabbis; he also has an obligation to do so (if he believes their decision to be incorrect, and he has strong proofs to support his own position). If the decision of those greater than he does not seem right to him, and he is not comfortable following it, and yet he follows that decision (in deference to their authority), then it is almost certain that he has rendered a false judgment (*din sheker*)." Likewise, Rabbi Yaakov Emden (*She'elot Ya'avetz*, 1:5) rules that students should question their rabbis' teachings as best as they can. In this way, truth is clarified.

Rabbi Hayyim Palachi writes that

> the Torah gave permission to each person to express his opinion according to his understanding. . . . It is not good for a sage to withhold his words out of deference to the sages who preceded him if he finds in their words a clear contradiction. . . . A sage who wishes to write his proofs against the kings and giants of Torah should not withhold his words nor suppress his prophecy, but should give his analysis as he has been guided by Heaven. [In this situation] one does not give honor to the rabbi, for this is Torah and I must study it.

Rabbi Palachi notes that even though Rambam wrote with Divine inspiration, many great sages of his generation criticized his work. There are numerous examples of students refuting their teachers: Rabbi Yehudah ha-Nasi disagreed with his father; Rashba disagreed with Ramban. The Tosafists disagreed with Rashi. Respect for authority does not mean that one may not hold opposing opinions. (See *Hikekei Lev*, vol. 1, O.H. 6 and Y.D. 42.)

Rabbi Moshe Feinstein, in one of his responsa (*Iggerot Moshe*, O.H. 1:9), expresses disagreement with an opinion of Rabbi

Shelomo Kluger. In rejecting that opinion, Rabbi Feinstein writes: "But it is certain that I am right (*ha-tzedek iti*) and that the words of Rabbi Shelomo Kluger—with all due respect— are nothing (*enam kelum*). One must love truth more than anything." In another responsum (*Iggerot Moshe*, Y.D. 3:88), Rabbi Feinstein replied to a rabbi in Benei Berak, who worried because he sometimes taught opinions contrary to those of the Hazon Ish, who had previously been the rabbi of that vicinity. Rabbi Feinstein points out that it was not at all disrespectful for the rabbi to study and quote the words of the Hazon Ish, even if he disagreed with some of them. On the contrary, that approach shows honor to the Torah—that the words of great scholars are taken seriously and evaluated seriously. It could not have occurred to the Hazon Ish that there would never arise rabbis who would disagree with his teachings. Rabbi Feinstein concludes by saying that one certainly is allowed to question and disagree with the sages of our generation, even the greatest sages, as long as one does so respectfully, and with proper halakhic justification.

Rabbi Yosef Hayyim of Bagdad (Ben Ish Hai), in the introduction to his *Rav Pe'alim,* stresses the need to be exceedingly respectful of the sages of previous generations. He admits that even great sages make errors. Yet, when one offers a critique or correction of the words of sages, he should not do so with any sense of personal pride or vanity. He should be humble, aware that even great sages may overlook a source or miss a particular point.

From this discussion, we see that responsible and respectful disagreement is a legitimate and necessary aspect of the halakhic system. Views that can be properly substantiated, even if they conflict with views of greater and earlier authorities, deserve to be heard. One cannot properly be called an *apikores* (heretic) simply because he holds a position which differs from others. On the contrary, his position should be evaluated carefully. If it is wrong, it should be criticized and rejected. If it is right, it should be accepted in spite of the greatness of authorities who held a different opinion. The boundary of legitimacy is not what one individual or group defines it to be. Rather, one may offer his insights and opinions as long as they do not go beyond universally accepted principles of Jewish faith, and as long as they are properly and correctly substantiated by authoritative sources. The halakhic system depends on intellectual inquiry, receptivity to the positions of others, devotion to truth, humility, respect for authority. It is not appropriate to outlaw responsible and respectful criticism of authorities nor to discredit those who offer properly substantiated opinions, even when those opinions dissent from leading authorities.

THE REALM OF AGGADAH

The balance between authority and dissent may also be considered in the realm of aggadah. One opinion prevalent in rabbinic literature is that all the words of our talmudic (and even later) sages are true and must be upheld. Another position is that the words of our sages must be treated with respect, but we are not bound to believe that all their aggadic teachings are without error. Does the authority of our sages preclude the possibility of legitimate disagreement with their aggadic teachings? Is someone who questions or rejects some of those teachings an *apikores*?

In Pirkei Avot 6:6, we are taught that the Torah is acquired in forty-eight ways. One of them is *emunat hakhamim,* trust in the sages. Rabbi Yosef Yaavetz, one of the rabbis at the time of the expulsion of Jews from Spain, explains that one must not hasten to criticize the words of our sages. If he does not understand or agree with their words, he should attribute the problem to his own intellectual weakness. "He should suspect his own intelligence, not the intelligence of our sages and their words, which were spoken in truth" (*Kol Sifrei Rabbi Yosef Ya'avetz*, vol. 2, p. 149).

Following this attitude, Radbaz, a younger contemporary of Rabbi Yaavetz, writes that the aggadah is true and essential, "given from Heaven like the rest of the Oral Torah. And just as the Torah is interpreted with thirteen principles, so the aggadah is interpreted with thirty-six principles. And these principles were transmitted to Moshe our teacher at Sinai" (*Teshuvot Radbaz*, 4:232). Rabbi Moshe Hagiz wrote an important essay on *emunat hakhamim* (acceptance of rabbinic authority), in which he argued forcefully against questioning the validity of any of the words of our sages. He believed that an attack on rabbinic dicta ultimately would lead to a general rejection of rabbinic authority. This would undermine religious observance and belief (*Mishnat Hakhamim*, sec. 23).

Rabbi Hayyim Hizkiyahu Medini, in his *Sedei Hemed* (vol. 1, p. 192), states unequivocally: "We must believe in all that is stated in the aggadot of our sages." Rabbi Zvi Hirsch Chajes follows this assumption when explaining that

> there are several subjects in the Gemara whose meaning cannot be taken in a literal sense, because the text expounded literally would depict God as a corporeal being, and would also at times involve an act of blasphemy. We should be, and we are, indeed, duty-bound to believe that the transmitters of the true *kabbalah* (tradition), who are known to us as righteous and saintly men and also as accomplished scholars, would not speak merely in an odd manner. We must therefore believe that their words were uttered with an allegorical or mystical sense and that they point to matters of the most elevated significance, far beyond our mental grasp.[6]

The demand that one must believe all the words of our sages in the aggadah came into question in the famous disputation in Barcelona in 1263. Ramban was challenged by his Christian opponent with an aggadah that stated that the Messiah was born on the day that the Temple in Jerusalem was destroyed. Ramban responded: "I do not believe in this aggadah at all." He went on to explain that Jewish religious writings are divided into three traditional categories: Bible, Talmud and Midrash.

The first we believe entirely . . . ; the second we believe when
it explains laws. We have yet a third book which is called
Midrash, sermons so to speak . . . ; and this book, if one
wishes to believe it he may, and one who does not believe it
does not have to. . . . We call it a book of aggadah, which is to
say discourses, that is to say that it merely consists of stories
which people tell one another.[7]

This explanation of Ramban was rejected by those who
insisted on maintaining the truth of all the words of our sages.
Some argued that Ramban never meant what he said, that he
only said it to deflect the challenge of his opponent. The Sedei
Hemed wrote that it is forbidden even to think that Ramban
meant what he said. Writing over two centuries after the disputation, Rabbi Yitzhak Abarbanel strongly disavows the statement of Ramban because "it opens the gates to undermine all
rabbinic authority when we consider any of their words as
errors or foolishness."[8]

Those maintaining the above position assume that respect
for our sages demands that we not dissent from nor find fault
in their words. Should we do so, we undermine their authority. If we find some of their aggadic teachings problematic, we
should not reject them; rather, we should assume that we have
not understood their true meaning.

But there is another position, also well-rooted in authoritative rabbinic sources. Rabbi Hai Gaon teaches that the
aggadah should not be considered as Divinely revealed tradition. The authors of aggadah were stating their own opinions,
and "each one interpreted whatever came to his heart."
Therefore, "we do not rely on them (the words of aggadah)."
Rabbi Hai Gaon maintains that aggadot recorded in the Talmud have more status than those not so recorded—but even
these aggadot need not be relied upon.[9] Rabbi Sherira Gaon
teaches that aggadah, Midrash and homiletical interpretations
of biblical verses were in the category of *umdena*, personal
opinion, speculation.[10] Another of the Geonim, Rabbi
Shemuel ben Hofni, states: "If the words of the ancients con-

tradict reason, we are not obligated to accept them."[11] This position also is expressed by Rabbi Shemuel ha-Naggid in his introduction to the Talmud. He writes that aggadah represents the personal opinions and interpretations of our sages.

Rabbi Avraham, son of Rambam, in an important essay concerning aggadah, maintains that one may not accept an opinion without first examining it carefully.[12] To accept the truth of a statement simply on the authority of the person who stated it is both against reason and against the method of Torah itself. The Torah forbids us to accept someone's statement based on his status, whether rich or poor, whether prominent or otherwise. Each case must be evaluated by our own reason. Rabbi Avraham states that this method also applies to the statements of our sages. It is intellectually unsound to blindly accept the teachings of our rabbis in matters of medicine, natural science, and astronomy. He notes:

> We, and every intelligent and wise person, are obligated to evaluate each idea and each statement, to find the way in which to understand it; to prove the truth and establish that which is worthy of being established, and to annul that which is worthy of being annulled; and to refrain from deciding a law which was not established by one of the two opposing opinions, no matter who the author of the opinion was. We see that our sages themselves said: if it is a halakhah (universally accepted legal tradition) we will accept it; but if it is a ruling (based on individual opinion), there is room for discussion.

This is not to say that the words of our sages should not be taken seriously. On the contrary, statements of great scholars must be weighed carefully and be respected. But they also may be disputed, especially in non-halakhic areas.

In his introduction to *Perek Helek*, Rambam delineates three groups of people, each having a different approach to the words of our sages. The majority group, according to Rambam, accepts the words of our sages literally, without imagining any deeper meanings. By taking everything literally—even when the words of the sages violate our sense of reason—they actually disparage our rabbis. Intelligent people who are told that they must accept all Midrashim as being literally true will come to reject rabbinic teaching altogether, since no reasonable person could accept all these teachings in their literal sense.

> This group of impoverished understanding—one must pity their foolishness. According to their understanding, they are honoring and elevating our sages; in fact, they are lowering them to the end of lowliness. They do not even understand this. By Heaven! This group is dissipating the glory of the Torah and clouding its lights, placing the Torah of God opposite of its intention.

Rambam describes the second group as also taking the words of the sages literally. But since so many of the statements of the rabbis are not reasonable if taken literally, this group assumes that the rabbis must not have been so great in the first place. This group dismisses rabbinic teachings as being irrelevant, even silly. Rambam rejects this point of view outright.

The third group, which is so small that it hardly deserves to be called a group, recognizes the greatness of our sages and seeks the deeper meanings of their teachings. This group realizes that the sages hid profound wisdom in their statements, and often spoke symbolically or in riddles. When one discovers a rabbinic statement that seems irrational, he should seek its deeper meaning.

While Rambam argues forcefully for a profound understanding of aggadah and Midrash, he does not argue that all rabbinic statements are of Divine origin. Rather, they are worthy of serious study because they represent the thinking of great sages. Presumably, his son Avraham carries his argument further. When one finds rabbinic statements to be unreasonable or incorrect—even after much thought and investigation—he is not bound to uphold them.

Rabbi Shimshon Rephael Hirsch echoes the opinion of Rambam and his son. He writes that "aggadic sayings do not have Sinaitic origin . . . they reflect the independent view of an individual sage." Rabbi Hirsch goes on: "Nor must someone whose opinion differs from that of our sages in a matter of aggadah be deemed a heretic, especially as the sages themselves frequently differ." He rejects the opinion that the authority of aggadah is equal to the orally transmitted halakhah. Indeed, he thought this was "a dangerous view to present to our pupils and could even lead to heresy."[13]

CONCLUSION

Rabbinic tradition, thus, has two valid approaches to the authority/dissent issue in the realm of aggadah. Rabbi Hayyim David Halevi (*Aseh Lekha Rav*, 5:49) has written a responsum which offers a balance between the two positions. He notes that there are Midrashim where sages disagree with each other. For example, the Torah records that following the death of Yosef, a new Pharaoh arose over Egypt. Rav interpreted this verse to mean that an actual new Pharaoh arose. Shemuel, though, maintained that it was the same Pharaoh who now made new decrees against the Israelites (Sotah 11a). It is impossible for both of these opinions to be objectively correct. Obviously, each offered an interpretation, based on his own understanding of the text. Moreover, there are topics about which the sages spoke-—not relating specifically to the Torah and its interpretation—in which they expressed their own opinions. The statements of our rabbis concerning natural science, for example, were not Divinely revealed traditions. In fact, our sages admitted that the wise men of the non-Jews had greater knowledge than the Torah sages in some scientific matters (Pesahim 94b).

Rabbi Halevi writes:

> If it becomes clear through precise scientific methodology that a specific idea expressed by our sages is not entirely cor-

rect, this does not mar their greatness, Heaven forbid, and their greatness as sages of Torah. Their words relating to Torah were stated with the power of the holiness of Torah, with a kind of Divine inspiration; but their other words on general topics were stated from the depth of their human wisdom only.

In non-halakhic matters, we should recognize that the sages spoke with great wisdom, although not with Divine inspiration. Therefore, there were disputes among them such as the one concerning the new Pharaoh, where it is clear that one side is wrong. While respecting the authority and wisdom of our sages, we also must recognize the possibility that some of their non-halakhic statements and interpretations are incorrect. To say this does not make one an *apikores*; on the contrary, one who says this displays a great respect towards the rabbis by weighing their words carefully.

It is clear, then, that there is room for dissent and criticism within the halakhic and aggadic systems. This dissent and criticism must be based on great reverence for our sages; on properly substantiated and argued positions; on commitment to the Divine origin of Torah. Dissent may not go beyond the universally accepted principles of our faith. But within this boundary, freedom of inquiry, analysis and criticism must be respected—and encouraged.

NOTES

1. See also Bemidbar Rabbah, Pinehas 21:2; Tanhuma, Pinehas 10. An excellent discussion of intellectual freedom in Jewish tradition was written by Menahem Elon in *Piskei Din Shel Bet ha-Mishpat ha-Elyon le-Yisra'el,* vol. 39, section 2, Jerusalem, 1983, pp. 291–304.

2. See Tosefta on Eduyot 1:4 and 1:5; and Eduyot 5:6.

3. Rambam, Introduction to Perek Helek; a good discussion of the medieval understanding of principles of faith is by Menachem Kellner, *Dogma in Medieval Jewish Thought,* Oxford University Press, New York, 1986.

4. See Kellner's book, *Ibid.*

5. *Meshiv Davar,* Warsaw, 5654, no. 44. A contemporary author,

the Debrocziner Rav, in his *Be'er Moshe,* nos. 3 and 6, has written that it is forbidden to study Torah from a rabbi who is a Zionist or who has studied at Yeshiva University. For him, the boundaries of faith are quite limited, and exclude a considerable number of pious and righteous scholars. His responsa reflect the problem which the Netziv described, and are testimony to the spiritual troubles in which Orthodoxy finds itself.

6. *The Student's Guide to the Talmud,* London, 1952, p. 201. See also his discussion on pp. 208 f.

7. See C. Chavel's edition of the Vikuah in *Kitvei Rabbeinu Moshe ben Nahman,* 1963, vol. 1, pp. 306–8.

8. *Yeshu'ot Meshiho,* 1812, p. 9b.

9. See *Otzar ha-Ge'onim,* ed. B. M. Lewin, Jerusalem, 5692, vol. 4 (Hagigah), pp. 59–60.

10. *Ibid.,* p. 60.

11. *Ibid.,* pp. 4–5.

12. The *Ma'amar Odot Derashot Hazal* is printed in the introductory section of the *En Ya'akov.*

13. See Joseph Munk, "Two Letters of Samson Raphael Hirsch, a Translation," *L'Eylah,* April, 1989, pp. 30–35.

OTHER THOUGHTS ABOUT JEWISH PLURALISM

*P*luralism is a popular catchword in modern Jewish religious life. It implies that Judaism is composed of various "streams," e.g. Orthodox, Conservative, Reform, Reconstructionist, and perhaps others; and that each of these "streams" has a right to be respected as a legitimate form of Judaism. Members of one stream need not accept the positions of members of another stream, but they should be respectful to one another. They should be able to admit that they may not have the entire truth of Judaism and that the other streams may have truth in them.

Pluralism as a catchword has a genuine appeal to American Jews, since we have been raised to be respectful of differing opinions and religious views. Pluralism offers us a framework for being Jewish in an overwhelmingly non-Jewish society. Religious denominations must be tolerant of others, must accept in some way the legitimacy of others. Proponents of Jewish pluralism point to religious fanaticism and intolerance perpetrated by Jews of one stream against Jews of other streams. You see, pluralism is necessary. It is respectful, civil and proper. The lack of pluralism leads to feuding, to power politics, to exclusion of some Jews from certain areas of religious authority.

I would like to suggest an alternative model to pluralism. Indeed, it may be argued that the existence of "streams" in

Originally published in *Midstream*, January 1990.

Judaism is unfortunate and pragmatically destructive. Before offering this model, let us think a bit more about pluralism.

Many Jews are attached institutionally or ideologically to one of the major Jewish religious movements. We support separate rabbinical schools, day schools, synagogue organizations, Zionist organizations, rabbinical associations, youth movements. Orthodox, Conservative, and Reform Jews lead their Jewish lives along separate tracks. Various organizations exist where Jews of different denominations work together for common causes; but generally, serious religious discussion and dialogue are avoided. Our religious differences are too great to bridge; talking about these differences is painful and usually unproductive.

Each movement promotes its own institutions and ideals. Since the movements have different institutions and ideals, they inevitably come into conflict. One group attacks the others; one group tries to out-maneuver the others; one tries to suppress the others. In all this institutional and ideological fury, where is God? Where is the Torah? Does the existence of separate denominations bring the Jewish people closer to God and Torah, or does it—at least in some important ways—distract us from Jewish spiritual life, from a unified Jewish religious vision?

If we could turn the clock back 200 years and if we had the power to shape Jewish history, would we *ab initio* divide Judaism into separate ideological and institutional movements? Knowing what we do of contemporary American Jewish life, would we direct history willingly and eagerly in order to splinter Jews into religious "streams"? Would we create a setting which demanded pluralism? Or would we nip the process of development of different religious movements in the bud? Would we try to find an alternative?

Much of the ugliness and unpleasantness in Jewish religious life today stems directly from the existence of "streams." The argument for pluralism, to a large extent, is an attempt to idealize and justify the status quo. Yet, the status quo is seriously deficient and is even harmful. Confusion as to "who is a Jew" is the product of controversy among "streams" which use different definitions and standards. The Reform movement considers many thousands of people to be Jews (either because of patrilineal descent or because of Reform conversion) whom the Orthodox and Conservative movements do not consider to be Jewish.

Everyone should agree that when different "streams" use different definitions and standards on the most basic aspects of Jewish identity and family life—this leads to confusion, divisiveness, rancor. It is an unhealthy situation which threatens the fabric of Jewish peoplehood. We are now eating the fruits of serious historic mistakes which were made 150–200 years ago in Europe and later in the United States. Let us consider some elements in the development of the rift between Reform and Orthodox Judaism, as illustrations of the problems facing us.

REFORM REJECTION OF CERTAIN HALAKHOT

The Reform statement concerning patrilineal descent states that "this issue arises from the social forces set in motion by the Enlightenment and the Emancipation." Indeed, Reform Judaism can be understood only in the context of modern Western European/American culture. Jews at last had the opportunity to participate openly and with legal equality in Christian society. Reform was a response to Enlightenment and Emancipation. It sought to make Jewish religious life more acceptable and appropriate for Western Jews striving to live as integral members of Western countries.

Reform sought to remove those elements in traditional Judaism that seemed to impinge on the Jews' ease in participating in non-Jewish society. The Pittsburgh Platform stated bluntly:

> We hold that all such Mosaic and rabbinical laws as regulate diet, priestly purity, and dress, originated in ages and under the influence of ideas altogether foreign to our present men-

tal and spiritual state. They fail to impress the modern Jew with a spirit of priestly holiness; their observance in our days is apt to obstruct rather than to further modern spiritual elevation.

A Reform responsum of 1913 opposed major Jewish mourning customs. It was claimed that the ancient practices of tearing the garment, sitting on the ground during the seven-day mourning period and similar observances have been "dropped by the people as militating against the spirit of modern times." Subsequently, the Reform movement abrogated these traditions. A responsum of 1955 stated that a number of Jewish wedding traditions were no longer appropriate. For example, the custom of the bridegroom breaking glass after the marriage ceremony is described as a "crude dramatic performance [which] tends to distract rather than to inspire, to mar rather than to enhance the impressiveness of the occasion."

Early Reformers were anxious to treat Judaism as a religion—a modern, civilized religion with a universal humanistic message. The Judaism of the Prophets represented a highly ethical religion dedicated to social justice and human dignity. Reformers rejected the classic Jewish notion that the Jews are in fact a nation, a chosen people promised a chosen land. This rejection is evident in a Reform battle cry: "Berlin is my Jerusalem." In other words, Jews were Germans, or Frenchmen, or Englishmen, or Americans—of the "Mosaic persuasion." They had no national aspirations. They were simply adherents of a religion, an enlightened religion at that.

Reform had many unkind things to say about traditional Judaism. Often, Reform was described as being modern, creative and spiritual. Orthodoxy, on the other hand, was described as being antiquated, rigid, and legalistic. A Reform responsum of 1922 charges that "Orthodox Judaism rests upon laws of conformity . . . whereas Reform Judaism releases the individual and enables him to realize his own nature, and therefore allows him to contribute whatever there is implanted within his soul and mind in humanity."

A Reform responsum of 1982 claims that conversion to Reform Judaism emphasizes instruction and understanding; traditional Judaism, it claims, stresses the ritual more than the instruction. A 1952 responsum criticizes the Orthodox laws of Shabbat observance. It states that many Jews might be true Shabbat observers in the spiritual sense "if we could but rescue the Sabbath from the host of unreasonable restrictions which mar its character and weaken its appeal to the modern mind." Israel Bettan wrote in 1950 that "of course, we liberal rabbis have always claimed the right, in the interest of a progressive faith, to modify rabbinic law and to remove what we regard as an obstacle in the advance of the spirit."

The teachings of Reform Judaism originated and flourished among 19th and 20th century Western European and American Jews. Clearly, these teachings are tied to the social and cultural context of modern Western Jewry. Many of the practices of Reform were adopted to make Jewish religious practice conform to modern Western European/American mores. The Reform movement did not arise earlier than the 19th century and did not emerge outside the Western European/American context.

ORTHODOX OPPOSITION TO REFORM

Not at all surprisingly, the Reform movement was greeted with hostility by traditional Jews who believed in the Divine origin of the Torah and halakhah. According to traditionalists, Reform sold out classic Jewish beliefs and observances in order to conform to Western society. Furthermore, traditionalists claimed that Reform undermined Jewish law, disregarded the authority of our sages, eliminated Jewish nationalism. The antinomianism of Reform may have been considered as a modern parallel to early Christianity. For traditionalists, Reform was not Judaism at all; it was a perversion of Judaism.

The Hatam Sofer, one of the leading halakhic authorities of the 19th century, wished he had the power to separate the Reformers from the Jewish community. He compared the latter to Sadducees and Karaites.

Maharam Shik urged traditional Jews not to marry Reformers, since they do not adhere to halakhic laws of marriage and divorce. He ruled that one should not even associate with Reformers. A modern-day halakhic authority, Rabbi Eliezer Waldenberg, stated that the Reform leaders are guilty of blinding the masses, leading them along the wrong path; Reform must be fought as a basic threat to the integrity of classic halakhic Judaism.

Rabbi Moshe Feinstein, one of the foremost halakhic authorities of the 20th century, ruled that one should not respond "Amen" to a blessing recited by a non-Orthodox rabbi, since the non-Orthodox deny God and His Torah. When they say God's name, they are not referring to the same God we worship—the God Who gave us the Written and Oral Torah. Rabbi Feinstein rejects the validity of any conversion performed by a Reform rabbi by definition. Reform rabbis are not valid witnesses, since they deny the Divinity of Torah. The very fact that they call themselves "Reform" is proof enough that they do not observe the mitzvot properly.

In rejecting Reform, Orthodoxy placed an even higher premium than ever on the need to hold to tradition. The more changes were instituted by Reform and Conservatism, the more the Orthodox perceived these movements as threats to authentic Judaism; and the more the Orthodox responded by attacking non-Orthodox movements.

European/American Orthodox Jews reacted strongly against encroachments on traditional Jewish beliefs and practices. The anti-Reform and anti-Conservative rhetoric, though, can be understood only within the context of the 19th and 20th centuries, and only within the worlds of European and American Jewry. The battles among the Orthodox, Conservative and

Reform did not take place before the 19th century and did not take place outside the Christian world.

THE SEPHARDIC APPROACH

While European and American Jews followed the process of degeneration into ideological movements in many ways hostile to each other, Asian and African Jews—as well as European Sephardim—followed a different path. Indeed, it is among these Jews, whom we shall call Sephardim, that an alternative model to pluralism may be found.

Most Sephardim lived in Muslim rather than in Christian lands. Their political, sociological, and psychological situations were different from those of the Ashkenazic Jews of Europe and America. Whatever reasons one may suggest, the fact remains: Sephardic communities did not splinter themselves along ideological lines. They did not create movements or "streams." They did not evolve a context which required the apologetics of pluralism.

This does not mean that there were no serious differences of opinion among Sephardim, nor that Sephardim were untouched by religious controversy. Indeed, the 19th century witnessed the rise of a strong secular literature among Sephardim; the emergence of vocal anti-clericalism; the decline of traditional Jewish observance among the more "enlightened" Jews.

Sephardic leaders and intellectuals were well aware of the currents of Enlightenment and Emancipation. Rabbi Eliyahu Benamozegh (1822–1900) of Livorno was steeped in both religious and general literature. He was a professor of philosophy and theology, and his books reflect an impressive awareness of classic and modern Jewish and non-Jewish sources. Although he was thoroughly at home in Western Jewish and non-Jewish literature, Rabbi Benamozegh respected and supported traditional halakhic/kabbalistic Judaism.

His biblical commentary (*Em la-Mikra*) quotes from biblical scholars and commentators, Christian sources, archaeological and philological research. He believed in the value of studying general wisdom and of applying modern insights to Judaism. Although he was as "enlightened" as any intellectuals in the Ashkenazic world, Rabbi Benamozegh posited the classic Sephardic attitude: faithfulness to tradition, commitment to halakhah, tolerance for different points of view.

Rabbi Israel Moshe Hazzan (1808–1863), a leading Sephardic figure, also was open to secular knowledge and was keenly aware of the contemporary intellectual currents. He was a staunch defender of tradition. When he was in London, he energetically opposed the innovations of Reform. He argued in his writings that Jews must be faithful and loyal to the age-old teachings and traditions of Judaism. He wrote that Jews should adhere to their own laws, even in matters of wills and legacies. Jews should preserve their own system of law; indeed, the Christian world did not ask Jews to relinquish their legal system. Why then would Jews willingly abandon the ways of the Torah?

Rabbi Hazzan also criticized the extremism which he characterized as European. The Sephardic attitude was to maintain normative traditional Jewish standards and procedures. If individual Jews had dissenting theological views or if their level of religious observance was less than total, they were still part of the community. They did not have cause to establish new synagogues or movements to conform to their individual beliefs. Rather, they recognized the necessity of a unified communal religious system.

Rabbi Yehudah Yaakov Nehama was a leading intellectual figure in 19th century Salonika. His published letters show his vast erudition and his openness to modernity. Similar to other Sephardic intellectuals, he was a proponent of maintaining the traditional halakhic framework of the Jewish community. He was critical of those who wanted to reform the practices of

Judaism, blaming this tendency on those Ashkenazic Reformers of Europe.

Indeed, the Sephardic spiritual elite of the 19th century which was open to secular culture consistently favored loyalty to Jewish tradition. They saw in the Enlightenment and Emancipation serious threats to the integrity of Jewish autonomy. They simply concluded that the Jewish people should not sell out their religious beliefs and traditions. Jews are happiest when they live as Jews, faithful to their own heritage. When Jews abandon Judaism in order to "Europeanize" or to "modernize," they deprive themselves of their own authenticity as Jews. At the same time, however, the rabbis did not oppose studying secular knowledge; they were not isolationists.

The model which prevailed in the Sephardic world, then, was one which fostered the maintenance of a traditional, halakhic communal structure. Halakhah defined and governed the Jewish people. Individuals who did not believe in all the traditions or who did not observe all the mitzvot still felt that they belonged to the community. A spirit of tolerance was fostered. Religious extremism, to be sure, was not entirely absent from the Sephardic world, but religious tolerance was widespread. Sephardim innately felt (and I think most still feel) that Judaism is characterized by compassion, openness, tolerance, generosity of spirit. The ideological battles which characterized Ashkenazic Jewry and which resulted in the creation of religious "streams" were not part of the Sephardic experience.

So we have an alternative model to pluralism: the Sephardic model. This model posits that Jews should be governed formally by halakhah and by traditional halakhic authorities. There should be no movements or ideological groupings which undermine the central authority of halakhah. On the other hand, Jews must be tolerant and gracious even to those whose actual observance of mitzvot is less than total.

The beauty of the Sephardic model is that it provides a unified communal structure to which all Jews agree to adhere. If we had this structure today, we would not have controversies on "who is a Jew"; we would not have problems about what constitutes valid marriages and divorces and conversions. On the other hand, the Sephardic model allows for tolerance of individuals whose religious behavior is not entirely in conformity with halakhah.

To follow the Sephardic model, though, requires the individual to recognize his subservience to the total community. If he personally does not agree with or understand or approve of traditional halakhic norms, he must yet agree to live within the system of classic Jewish law. What he thinks or does privately is his own business. But he has to be humble enough and thoughtful enough not to want to create an institution or movement which will undermine the age-old communal structure.

This is not to say that the Sephardic model is perfect and easily applicable to modern Jewish life. Nor could one argue that Sephardic communities of the 19th century were devoid of controversies. Yet, we do find a real alternative to pluralism; and it is an alternative which seems to be more capable of maintaining Jewish unity and religious harmony.

If all the religious "streams" in America suddenly would decide to follow the Sephardic model, I think American Jewry would benefit dramatically. Yet, this is not a likely eventuality. Too many American Jews are tied too deeply to their "movements." Moreover, each of the movements is involved in its own power politics; each is fighting for greater control and influence. The situation in the United States is so deeply entrenched that there may be no way out of our morass for the foreseeable future. For many years to come, American Jews are likely to be identified not simply as Jews, but as adjective Jews (Orthodox, Conservative, Reform, etc.).

But what about Israel? Israel still has not taken the route of splintering into religious "streams." Yet, the dangerous tendency is in its incipient stages. A militant and authoritarian Orthodoxy evokes antagonism from "secularists" and from non-Orthodox Jews. Conservative and Reform movements are building themselves institutionally and are making greater demands for pluralism. If things continue along the present course, Israel ultimately will suffer the problematic fate of the European/American Jews—religious movements, ideological warfare, religious disunity, alternative definitions of Jewishness. Pluralism leads to more intolerance, more feuding, more institutionalism.

Can we dare hope that Israel's Jews will avoid the pitfalls of Western Jewry? Will people seriously consider the Sephardic model as an alternative to the future development of religious life in Israel? The problems inherent in this suggestion are, of course, enormous. But perhaps there is room for hope if thoughtful people will think beyond their "movements" and consider the universal needs of the Jewish people. Also, shouldn't we remember that more than half of the Jews in Israel are of African/Asian background—Jews who had no historical connection with the emergence of the "streams"? Isn't it a form of cultural and religious colonialism to try to draw these African/Asian Jews into movements which are a product of 19th–20th century Europe and America? Why not let them live according to their own historical model?

It is easy to dismiss the thesis of this essay by saying it is too simplistic, too unrealistic. Readers who have been reared on the idea of pluralism and who are committed to their "movements" will not want to consider the Sephardic model too readily. There are a whole host of reasons and emotions which may make it difficult for people to open themselves to another possibility in the evolution of Jewish religious life.

Yet, we are at a crossroads in our history. Israel is at a religious turning point. We require tremendous courage and openness and selflessness. What is at stake is not the success or failure of the "streams," but the viability of a powerful unifying Jewish religious vision. By agreeing to adhere to halakhic norms for public and communal life, and by agreeing to be tolerant of individuals whose beliefs and practices do not conform to halakhah—we create a framework for a harmonious and unified Jewish people.

4

THOUGHTS ABOUT PRAYER

PARADOX AND PRAYER

If we think carefully about prayer, we arrive at a significant paradox in human existence. Does it not seem arrogant, preposterous, for finite human beings to address an infinite and eternal God? What claim can any of us have on God's concern? How do we dare assume that our lives are so significant that we have a right to ask God to heal us when we are sick, to give us strength when we are weak, to provide us with our needs and wants? Moreover, how can we find adequate words of praise for God? Inevitably, our words must fall far short of their goal; we cannot even begin to enumerate God's greatness with our feeble and inadequate utterances.

And yet, we pray. In spite of the above questions, we feel perfectly natural in bringing our petitions and praises to God. And the Bible itself is our precedent. Our ancestors prayed and they were answered. We pray, then, not from a rational philosophical justification, but from a deeply felt natural human need. And, as Jews, our emotional commitment to prayer is bolstered by our most ancient traditions, going back to the Bible itself, where we see that prayer is natural and acceptable.

Originally published as a pamphlet by Sephardic House at Shearith Israel, 1984.

36

Rambam (*Hilkhot Madda* 2:2) discusses the two emotions which tie human beings to God: love and reverence (*ahavah ve-yirah*).

> When a person contemplates His great and wondrous acts and creations, obtaining from them a glimpse of His wisdom which is beyond compare and is infinite, he will love and glorify Him promptly, longing exceedingly to know the great Name of God. As David said: "My whole being thirsts for God, the living God" (Tehillim 42:3). And when he ponders these very subjects, he will be afraid and will recoil, knowing that he is a lowly and obscure creature . . . as David said: "As I look up to the heavens Your fingers made . . . what is man that You should be mindful of him?" (Tehillim 8:4–5).

The spiritual context of religion—and therefore of prayer—is dynamic. It fluctuates between feelings of love and feelings of fear, awareness of the spiritual greatness of human beings and awareness of our ultimate insignificance.

This spiritual tension is an essential feature of our prayer service. The morning service (Shaharit) and the evening service (Arvit) both include the recitation of the Shema, the classic biblical text affirming the unity and uniqueness of God. The Shema is preceded by two prayers, each of which culminates with a blessing of God. Although the actual texts differ from Shabbat and holidays to weekdays, their themes are identical. The first blessing praises God as Creator, the Almighty Being who oversees the entire universe, whose power is overwhelmingly awesome. This blessing evokes fear and reverence in us. We are humbled by our own smallness in relationship to the Almighty God.

The second blessing, however, focuses on God's love of Israel. It evokes within us a feeling of closeness to God. Its mood contrasts sharply with that of the previous blessing.

After having experienced both moods—fear and love—then we say the Shema, illustrating that God is One. Our contrasting experiences of God, first as the Almighty Creator and then as a loving compassionate God, merge into our greater perception of God's unity. The structure of our prayers helps us to recognize the surprising tensions inherent in prayer as well as the surprising satisfaction from unifying dissonant perceptions.

FEELING THE NEED TO PRAY

When does a person feel the need to pray? Ideally, people should always feel that need. Every moment of our lives presents a need to pray, if we have the spiritual sensitivity.

The reality, though, is that most people spend little time on spiritual reflection in the course of their everyday lives. Usually, it is during a crisis that people spontaneously pray. People call out to God when they, or someone they love, are desperately ill. People pray when confronted with death, be it their own or that of a loved one.

Likewise, people may be moved to prayer when seeing extreme beauty—an overwhelming sunset, a majestic mountain, a thundering ocean, a star-filled night. Recognizing the spiritual power of the beauties of nature, some mystics of 16th century Safed recited their prayers outside, on the hills. They chanted the Kabbalat Shabbat (service receiving the Shabbat) as they watched the sun set. The sacred words of the Psalms blended with the dramatic setting of the sun.

PRIVATE PRAYER

We offer spontaneous words to God at moments of crisis, when we are filled with strong emotions. But there may be other times, too, when we utter private prayers—asking God to continue His kindness to us, thanking God for the good things we have, etc.

The Talmud (Berakhot 16b–17a) lists a number of private prayers composed by great rabbis. Some of these prayers, though originally private, have been included in our prayer book. For example, we conclude each Amidah with a prayer composed by Mar, the son of Rav Huna. It begins with the words: "My God, guard my tongue from evil and my lips from speaking deceit. Let my soul be silent to those who reproach me, let my soul be lowly to all as the dust. Open my heart through your Torah that my soul may follow your Commandments." Rabbi Yehudah ha-Nasi recited a personal prayer at the end of his daily prayers, and it too has found a place in our liturgy (in the early morning blessings). It begins: "May it be Your will, Lord my God, and God of my ancestors, to deliver me from the shameless and from insolence; from a bad person, from any mishap."

It is desirable for one to offer private prayers in his or her own words. Such prayers can be said spontaneously, whenever and wherever one wants.

PUBLIC WORSHIP

Aside from private prayer in which each of us is free to engage, Jewish law prescribes a set ritual of prayer three times a day. Preferably, these prayers should be recited in public (with a *minyan*). If one is unable to recite them with a *minyan*, then one is still obligated to say them on his own. The morning prayer is known as Shaharit; the afternoon prayer as Minhah; and the evening prayer as Arvit.

Rambam suggests the following explanation of the development of our communal prayers in Hebrew (Laws of Prayer 1:4):

> When the Jewish people were exiled in the days of wicked Nebuchadnezzar, they mixed with Persians, Greeks and other nationalities. Children were born to them in foreign lands. The language of these children was confused, a mixture of many languages. They were unable to express themselves adequately and accurately in any one language. . . . When any one of them prayed, his Hebrew vocabulary was too limited to express his needs or to praise God without mixing Hebrew with other tongues. When Ezra and his council took notice of this, they instituted the Eighteen Blessings (Amidah) in their present order: the first three

contain praise to God; the last three thanksgiving; the intermediate blessings contain petitions for the most essential
needs of the individual and the community. They were to be
uttered by everyone's lips and learned, so that those of inar-
ticulate speech might offer prayer as clearly as those who
speak an eloquent Hebrew. For this reason, they instituted
all other blessings and prayers which are arrayed on the lips
of all Israel, to make each blessing readily available to one
who is unfamiliar with the language.

Since Hebrew is the language of our people, it is fitting that
we pray in this sacred tongue. The prayers were arranged in
clear Hebrew for the benefit of all Jews, especially those who
do not know Hebrew. The Hebrew prayers were prepared,
therefore, to make it easier and more comfortable for Jews to
pray to God.

Yet, praying from a fixed text has certain problems. Praying
by formula or by rote strikes us as being absurd, parallel in
some ways to automatic prayer wheels. But, there is a profundity about this kind of prayer. We recognize our limitations.
Whatever we say is inadequate. We cannot have confidence in
our own abilities to generate proper prayers. By using a fixed
text, we recognize our inability to say all that we want and all
that we feel. Prayer by a fixed text must be understood not
merely for its content, but as a symbol of our recognition of
our limitations.

Answer the following questions honestly. When you last
attended synagogue, did you pray to God? Did you feel God's
presence? Did you have any personal religious experience, a
feeling that you approached God? If you answered yes, you
are very fortunate and very sensitive. If you answered no, we
need to understand how it is possible to spend hours in a synagogue reciting prayers and still not feel as though we have
prayed.

Public prayer is highly ritualized, surprisingly mechanical.
Our services are almost entirely predictable from beginning to
end. It is possible to follow the ritual and never once feel the

presence of God. It is possible to be concerned for the forms of prayer without allowing ourselves the spiritual freedom of praying. There is another problem. Think of your favorite poem. Think of being obligated to read it three times a day at fixed times, every day, forever, without changing a word of it! Once in a while you may respond to some of its words, but sheer repetition takes away its freshness and its mystery. In a similar manner, repetition of our prayers three times a day can create spiritual problems, in spite of the fact that these prayers also provide us with many advantages.

Public prayer must be understood in its communal context. It is not a substitute for private religious experience. It is not the exclusive domain of Jewish spirituality. Nevertheless, communal prayer does fulfill a number of important roles.

For one thing, it provides communal continuity. A Jew may attend services in any traditional synagogue in the world and be able to follow, to feel part of the service. The very regularity of these services serves to unite all Jews everywhere with a religious bond.

Moreover, there is a sacredness that comes with historical association. By reciting the same prayers which our parents and grandparents—and ancestors going back for generations—have recited, we feel the sanctity of our tradition. We do not offer our prayer to God merely as individuals; rather, we pray as members of the historic and ancient people of Israel. We draw strength from our historical memories.

If you look carefully through our prayer book, you will find that a large portion of the text does not consist of prayers to God. Rather, many pages serve as instruction to us. We have passages from the Bible and the Talmud. The Shema itself is a collection of three passages from the Bible. The purpose of these readings is to instruct us in proper values and behavior patterns. The Torah reading, which occupies a central position in many of our services, also serves to instruct the public in the word of God. Communal services, then, serve to instruct and inspire us, as well as provide us a means of praying to God.

If we had no public prayer, no fixed prayer book, we as a community would have lost our religious identity long ago. The fixed ritual has served to unite Jewish people everywhere and through all the generations. It has maintained us as a religious community, not merely as a conglomeration of individuals.

It is permissible to say the public prayers in any language one understands (*Shulhan Arukh, Orah Hayyim* 101:4). Our prayer book provides an English translation for the benefit of those who cannot understand Hebrew. Obviously, it is helpful to understand Hebrew, since our prayers are in Hebrew. Yet, not understanding the words of the prayers does not necessarily mean that it is impossible to have a proper religious experience. Prayer is devotion of the heart. It is not a rational intellectual pursuit. A mourner may say the Kaddish without knowing at all what the words mean, but still feel religiously moved. The hallowed sounds of the words are mysterious and sacred. Indeed, the words of our public prayers and the melodies of our services are aimed at our spiritual/emotional selves. They evoke images and feelings conducive to spirituality.

CONCENTRATION IN PRAYER

When reciting our public prayers, we must have proper concentration on what we are doing. We must realize that we are in the presence of God. This is especially so when we recite the Shema and the Amidah.

Rambam writes: "Any prayer uttered without mental concentration is not prayer. If a service has been recited without such concentration, it must be recited again devoutly" (Laws of Prayer, 4:15).

Rambam provides an explanation of what is to be understood by concentration of the mind *(kavvanah)*. He states:

> The mind should be freed from all extraneous thoughts, and the one who prays should realize that he is standing before the Divine Presence. Therefore, he should sit awhile

before beginning his prayers so as to concentrate his mind and then pray in gentle tones, beseechingly, and not regard the service as a burden which he is carrying and which he will cast off before proceeding on his way. Likewise, he should sit awhile after concluding the prayers, and then leave. The ancient pious ones used to pause and meditate one hour before the service, one hour after the service, and take one hour in its recital.

STRUCTURE OF THE SHABBAT MORNING SERVICE

It is our custom, in fact, to introduce the Shaharit service with blessings, biblical passages, Psalms, and other texts, all of which help us attune our mind to pray. The best way to understand the structure of our prayers is to study them directly. The service begins with blessings and sacred passages (biblical and talmudic), bringing us into the framework of thoughtfulness, study, awareness. Next, we begin Zemirot, a series of poetic passages, mainly from the Psalms, designed to awaken our spirituality. The Zemirot conclude with the chanting of the Song of Moshe and the children of Israel after they crossed the Red Sea during their exodus from Egypt. It is a song of victory and of thanksgiving, a prayer which recognizes the greatness of God and His providence.

The Shaharit then begins and is introduced by passages praising God's power and His compassion. These praises help to awaken within us an awareness of God's role in our lives.

Barehu, a call by the reader to the congregation, introduces the main part of the morning service. The congregation responds with a short sentence, indicating that everyone is prepared to say the prayers.

The following pages include the two blessings before the Shema, each with its own theme, as discussed earlier. The Shema is followed by a series of passages praising God's intervention in Jewish history and concludes with a blessing of God as the redeemer of Israel. This leads into the Amidah. The Amidah is recited first silently, and then is repeated by the *haz-*

zan. Originally, the repetition was instituted for the benefit of those who could not read the prayer themselves. By listening to the *hazzan* recite the Amidah, they could say "Amen," and thus fulfill their obligation. It is appropriate for everyone to listen to the recitation of the *hazzan* carefully and to respond at the appropriate places with "Amen." During the repetition, the Kedushah is recited by the *hazzan* with the congregation responding with the appropriate verses.

The next main point in our service is the reading of the Torah portion of the week. This is preceded by prayers for the government, for the congregation, and for the State of Israel. The Torah is taken from the ark and brought to the reader's desk as the *hazzan* and congregation sing special verses.

The Torah is divided into weekly portions so that it is read in its entirety during the course of each year, culminating on the festival of Simhat Torah. The purpose of the public reading is to teach the words of the Torah to the entire congregation. The sacred text of the Jewish people is not the private reserve of a few learned individuals; rather, it belongs to everyone, and everyone has equal access to it. The Torah reading is, in fact, a public study session. If one attends synagogue services each week, he or she will have had the opportunity to study the entire Torah over the course of a year. If this is done year after year, one will deepen his or her knowledge considerably. Therefore, it is quite important that congregants follow the Torah reading carefully. For those who cannot follow in Hebrew, it is recommended that you read the Torah portion in English.

After the Torah is read and returned to the ark, it is customary for the rabbi to deliver a sermon. The purpose of the sermon is also educational—to explain a passage from the Torah reading, to apply the words of the Torah to our lives, to help make us aware of the Torah's message to us.

The sermon is followed by the Musaf, an additional Amidah recited on Shabbat and Festivals, in remembrance of the fact that an extra sacrifice was offered in the ancient Temple in

Jerusalem on Shabbat and holy days. The service concludes with several talmudic passages dealing with the importance of studying Torah, the En Ke-lokenu, the Alenu, and the chanting of Adon Olam. It is customary to recite Kiddush following services, but Kiddush should be chanted also by each individual family at home prior to the Shabbat meal following services.

THE STRUCTURE OF THE AMIDAH

The Amidah is the main prayer of each service. It is recited while standing, facing east towards Jerusalem. Each Amidah begins with the same three paragraphs and ends with the same three paragraphs. The first three blessings consist of praises of God, while the last three are blessings of thanksgiving. On regular weekdays, the intermediate blessings are petitions for the things we need as individuals and as members of the community. We pray in the plural, asking God's blessing on all Israel. It is a good idea to study the daily Amidah carefully to understand its contents and its style.

On Shabbat, the first three blessings and last three blessings are the same as on weekdays. However, instead of the many petitions which characterize the weekday Amidah, the Amidah prayers of Shabbat substitute paragraphs relating to the theme of Shabbat.

It is interesting to examine the central paragraphs of the Friday evening, Shabbat morning and Shabbat afternoon Amidah prayers. Each is distinctive and each relates to a different theme of Shabbat.

On Friday night, the theme of the Amidah is Creation. Since God created the world in six days and ceased working on the seventh, God ordained Shabbat from the very beginning of Creation. (The Kiddush of Friday night, too, begins with the paragraph from Bereshit which states that God rested on the seventh day after He finished creating the universe.)

When we think of God as the Creator, we are immediately compelled to stand in awe of Him. We are dramatically shaken from our everyday complacence. Shabbat is here. God, who created the universe, created Shabbat. Just as God separated one day for Shabbat from the other six days, so are we expected to do likewise.

The central paragraph of the Shabbat morning Amidah relates to God's revelation at Mount Sinai. Shabbat was included among the commandments God revealed to Moshe and Israel at Sinai. Shabbat is a sign between God and Israel forever; it is a unique day which no one observes in the same way that we do.

The Shabbat afternoon Amidah has the theme of redemption. We dream of a messianic time, a world blessed with peace and security, when God's unity will be recognized by everyone. On Shabbat afternoon, as Shabbat is beginning to slip away from us, we pray for a world where the meaning of Shabbat will be understood and appreciated.

MEMORIAL PRAYERS, OFFERINGS

It has become customary for individuals to ask the Torah reader to recite a memorial prayer in memory of a loved one whose death anniversary is being observed. It also has become customary to offer a contribution to the synagogue in memory of the deceased. Many congregants make contributions to the synagogue at the Sefer or in front of the ark after the Sefer has been returned. These contributions are given in thanksgiving, to honor someone on a happy occasion, to wish someone good health, etc.

Announcement of such contributions is permissible on Shabbat. The *Shulhan Arukh* (*Orah Hayyim*, 306:6) rules that one may make business calculations on Shabbat for the purpose of a mitzvah, such as assigning charity. Some individuals have the custom of specifying the amount they are contributing, while others prefer to leave the amount of their contribution unspecified. This is a matter of personal judgement.

A custom which has arisen over the years is that a person who is called to the Torah has a memorial prayer and offering recited after the reading of his portion. This custom becomes quite problematic when there are many people in the synagogue who want to be called to the Torah in order to have these prayers recited. Although the Torah reading ordinarily is divided into seven portions, it is sometimes necessary to break the reading into smaller parts and even to repeat sections in order to accommodate those who wish to be called. This practice is disruptive of the Torah reading, and it hampers the concentration of the congregation.

It would be preferred if individuals who were observing an anniversary of the death of a loved one would not insist on being called to the Torah. Appropriate prayers can be said in front of the ark after the Torah reading.

SYNAGOGUE CUSTOMS

Each synagogue observes customs, some which may be specific to that congregation, while others may be part of a more widespread tradition. It is important to be a careful observer of synagogue services, since in that way you will become familiar with the customs.

Sephardic congregations in general observe a number of common customs. For example, the entire service is read aloud by the *hazzan*, so that congregants can chant along with him. Parts of the service are sung by the *hazzan*, with congregants responding at the appropriate points. Sephardic services are characterized by the involvement of congregants and the *hazzan*. The service is definitely not an occasion for the *hazzan* to put on a performance. Rather, his task is to lead the service gracefully and properly, enabling the congregants to participate actively.

Sephardic congregations place much stress on accuracy during the Torah reading. We insist that the reading be excellent—words properly pronounced and accented, musical notes chanted correctly. Since the Torah reading is so important, it should be read only by those who are skilled and knowledgeable of their responsibility. It is considered a great honor to be able to read the Torah portion.

When a person is called to the Torah, it is customary for his younger relatives to stand in his honor when he reads the blessings before and after the Torah reading. In some congregations, the custom is to remain standing for one's older relatives also while the Torah is read. This custom fosters respect for elders.

Most synagogues have melodies which are used only on holidays and on other special occasions. These melodies add another level of experience to our services. Just by hearing a certain melody, we are filled with the emotions associated with the holiday. Congregation Shearith Israel in New York, for example, has special melodies which are sung on the High Holy Days, on the first day of each festival, on the last day of the festivals, on Shabbat–Rosh Hodesh, Shabbat-Nahamu, Shabbat-Zakhor and a number of other occasions. Aside from the specific melodies for these services, there also are visual changes for many circumstances. On Rosh ha-Shanah, Yom Kippur, and Hosha'anah Rabbah, the Torah scrolls are covered with white cloaks, and the *tevah* (reader's desk) is covered with a white cover. On festival days and special Shabbatot, the Torah scrolls are covered with cloaks of different colors, while on regular Shabbatot the cloaks are all red. When the Ten Commandments are included in the Torah reading of the day, a special silk Torah covering is placed on the *tevah* which features an embroidered version of the Ten Commandments. There are a number of other similar variations throughout the course of the year, all of which help broaden one's experience of the day. Customs and symbolism become meaningful when we are so aware of them that they become natural to us.

BEING OPEN AND AWARE

Your appreciation of the synagogue service depends on your sensitivity, your understanding of the service, and your willingness to be alert and open to the synagogue experience. You will find that the more you attend synagogue services, the more meaningful they will become to you. If you study the text of the prayer book, you will enhance your own appreciation of the services you attend.

From one perspective, it is not easy to pray. It requires study, thoughtfulness, sensitivity and openness. But from another perspective, prayer is the natural language of a sincere and thoughtful person. As our rabbinic tradition has taught, prayer is "the service of the heart" (Ta'anit 2a).

5

A JEWISH PHILOSOPHY OF DEATH: A JEWISH PHILOSOPHY OF LIFE

Death is not an evil. It is a perfectly normal event which occurs to every living thing.

Death is not the opposite of life. Rather, life and death are interrelated parts of a continuum of existence, an eternal rhythm. Religious people believe in a life after death. But do we ever ask whether we experienced life before we were born into this world? Where does our existence begin? Where does it end? These are mysteries for which we offer no answers. But merely asking these questions helps us to broaden our view of what our life actually is.

The Torah teaches (Bereshit 1:31) that when God finished creating the world, He looked at it and saw that it was very good. The Midrash in Bereshit Rabbah explains that the words *hinneh tov me'od* ("behold, it was very good") refer to death. That is, God examined His creation, realized that death was a feature of it, and declared that the creation was excellent. Rabbi Moshe ben Nahman (Ramban) comments on this verse that the world is essentially good, despite the existence of death, suffering and other apparent evils. And yet, in our society, death certainly is not seen as being *tov me'od* ("very good"). On the contrary, death is perceived as an evil, and our doctors work diligently to delay and defeat death as much as

Originally published in *Proceedings of the Association of Orthodox Jewish Scientists*, vols. 8–9 (1987).

humanly possible. In our dislike of death, we do not even like to say that someone has died. Rather, we use euphemisms such as: someone has passed away, or passed on, or—if we want to sound scientific—someone has expired.

In our society, people are afraid to become old. The aging process is associated with the dying process. Americans spend billions of dollars a year on cosmetics, dyes, medical procedures and other vanities—all of which attempt to camouflage the fact that we are aging. Youth is idealized; old age is dreaded.

Elias Canetti, in his book, *The Torch in My Ear,* has expressed the deep repugnance for death which is shared by many of us:

> The aim is not to parrot the banality that so far all human beings have died: the point is to decide whether to *accept* death willingly or stand up against it. With my indignation against death, I have acquired a right to glory, wealth, misery, and despair of all experience. I have lived in this endless rebellion.

Canetti's words strike a resonant chord within many of us. Somehow, although we understand that death is natural and normal, we rebel against this knowledge. We idealize heroes who defy death or who scorn death: even if they themselves die in the process. This is one of the ironies of human existence: life is an obstacle course which, if we run it very successfully, we will die of old age.

In a recent lecture, Rabbi Maurice Lamm has described the Jewish attitude on death as "death defying." Our tradition emphasizes the sanctity of life, the need to preserve life even when it entails violating other religious precepts such as Shabbat. A person who is ill should not lose hope or give up hope of recovery. Even the confession to be recited before death is a conditional one. The *Shulhan Arukh* (*Yoreh De'ah* 338:2) records the text of the confession:

> I admit before You, God, my God and God of my ancestors, that my cure and my death are in Your hands. May it be Your will that You heal me with a complete healing. And if I

die, may my death be an atonement for the iniquities, transgressions and violations which I have transgressed and violated before You. And place my portion in the Garden of
Eden, and let me merit the World to Come reserved for the
righteous.

This form of confessional is indicative of the tenacity of our
tradition in emphasizing life. Even when it appears obvious
that a person will die, the person first asks God to heal him.
Only reluctantly does the individual consider the alternative
that he might not recover.

Jewish legal sources emphasize the need to help the ill person in his battle against death. For example, the *Shulhan Arukh*
(*Yoreh De'ah* 337) rules that we should not tell a very ill patient
the news of the death of one of his close relatives. Such news
would break his heart and reduce his ability to resist his sick-
ness. Even if a relative died over whom the ill person is obligated to mourn, we still may not inform him of the death, nor
tear his garments, nor cry, nor eulogize in his presence. The
commentary known as the Bah comments that we should not
tell an ill person of the death of anyone, even one who is *not*
related to him. By mentioning someone else's death, and by
showing our sadness over that death, the ill person may
become frightened that maybe he too will die.

Even when we inform a dying patient that he should say his
confession, we do so in a fashion that will not frighten him. We
tell him: "Many have confessed but have not died, and many
who have not confessed have died. And many who are walking
outside in the marketplace confess. By the merit of your con-
fessing, you live. And all who confess have a place in the World
to Come." The Bah comments that we may not tell an ill person to confess unless in fact he is obviously in the process of
dying. But if he is not at that last stage yet, we do not tell him
to confess since that would break his heart, and it would lead
to his giving up his fight for life.

Jewish reverence for life is also evident in the laws concerning a *goses*, a dying person in his last hours of life. Jewish law

prescribes that we are not allowed to move such a person, since even the slightest disturbance might cause him to die. In fact, someone who does move, or even touches a *goses* is equated in halakhah to one who has shed blood. The message is clear: death must not be hastened. Life is sacred (Semahot 1:1 ff.; Shabbat 152–153).

The Jewish defiance of death shows itself even after a person has actually died. During the mourning period we recite the prophetic verses beginning with the words *Billah ha-mavet la-netzah:* God "will utterly destroy death forever; and the Lord God will wipe the tear from every face . . . your dead shall live again, the mortal being shall rise up; awake and sing joyously, you who dwell in the dust, for as the reviving dew on grass shall be your dew, when the earth shall bring forth her dead."

Ultimately, then, death itself will be defeated by God. The implication is that death is bad, it is a flaw in the world that will one day be corrected. Belief in resurrection of the dead and in the "destruction" of death certainly contributes to the notion that the Jews have a death-defying culture. This conclusion emerges in spite of the midrashic interpretation which claims that death is very good, a necessary part of God's creation.

The contemporary Jewish discussions of death tend to echo Rabbi Lamm's sentiments. The halakhic literature tends to corroborate this point of view. Yet, I think that the notion that Jewish tradition defies death is only partially true. In fact, Jewish tradition is strikingly accepting of death.

When we think of cultures which are death-accepting, we generally think of Eastern religions. We think of a fatalistic attitude about reality, an attitude which sees this world essentially as an illusion or a dream. Death is accepted, since life itself is seen as transient and illusory. Life and death really do not matter. They are nothing to get excited about. Things are as they are.

When I say that Jewish culture is death-accepting, I do not mean to imply that we have the same outlook as Eastern religions. I do mean to say that Jewish tradition does *not* have the same point of view about death as does Western civilization. I also mean to say that Jews seldom are made aware of the deep tradition of death-acceptance within our teachings.

Think for a moment of the heroes in the Torah. Which of them expresses a fear, a dislike, a defiance of death? Actually, they lived quite at ease with the idea of dying. When Avraham died, the Torah tells us that he had lived a good life, he was old and satisfied, and he was gathered unto his people (Bereshit 25:8). When we are informed of Avraham's death, we do not feel sad. We do not even feel that Avraham was sad. On the contrary, he lived a good and full life. Since death is inevitable, we are glad that Avraham was able to live so long and so well before he died. Ramban comments on this verse, saying that God shows the righteous the reward they will receive in the World to Come. This information satisfies the righteous as they are dying. In other words, they do not resist death, they welcome it.

The pattern continues in the Torah. When Yitzhak is old and expects that he will die, he plans to bless his son (Bereshit, chapter 27). When Yaakov nears death, he calls Yosef and tells him to arrange his burial in the land of Canaan (Bereshit 47:29). Ramban comments that Yaakov felt that his powers were diminishing and that his weakness was increasing. He was not ill, but he knew he would not live too much longer. When he came to this recognition, he called Yosef, blessed his grandsons, and left his last words to his children. The Torah does not record that Yaakov was trying to defy death in any way. Rather, he seems to have accepted the reality and was giving his last words to his family (Bereshit, chapter 49).

The pattern continues with Yosef. Before he dies, he candidly tells his brothers that he is about to die and informs them that God will remember them and bring the children of Israel back to the land which He had promised to Avraham, Yitzhak and Yaakov. He also leaves instructions that his bones should be brought out of Egypt when the children of Israel leave (Bereshit 50:24–25).

The Torah offers a description of the death of Aharon on Mount Hor. God informs Moshe and Aharon that Aharon will be gathered unto his people (Bemidbar 20:22–29). Aharon's priestly clothes are removed and given to his son Elazar. In all this description, we find no evidence of resistance on the part of Aharon. There is an interesting Midrash that Moshe did not inform the people of Israel about Aharon's approaching death. He feared that, since they loved Aharon so much, they might attempt to prevent God's decree from being carried out by praying for Aharon's life. In this way, they would be acting contrary to God's wise plan (Yelammedenu in Yalkut I, 764).

Even the death of Moshe is consistent with this pattern of acceptance. Moshe did not ask for immortality, he did not ask God to conquer death for him: Moshe asked only for the privilege of living just long enough to enter the Promised Land. The tragic quality of the demise of Moshe is not directly concerned with death itself, but with the lack of fulfillment of Moshe's work on behalf of his people.

Because the characters of the Torah accepted death, this does not mean that they thought their lives were unimportant or lacking in meaning. It is apparent that none of them wanted to die prematurely; they did fear violent death. Consider for example Yaakov's behavior in his confrontation with Esav. Indeed, he did view life as something worth preserving. But when the end came, he accepted it calmly, as something that had been expected.

There is much evidence in rabbinic literature which also reflects this attitude. A Midrash tells us that Avraham mourned the death of Sarah, as did all the people of the country. The weeping and lamenting over her were so universal that Avraham, instead of receiving consolation, had to offer consolation to others. Avraham told the mourning people: "My children, take not the death of Sarah too much to heart. There is one event unto all, to the pious and impious alike. I pray you now, give me a burying-place with you, not as a gift, but for money" (Ginzberg, *Legends of the Jews,* Vol. I, pp. 287–88).

Philo *(De Abrahamo,* 44) wrote that Avraham mourned only a short time for Sarah, since the wise should not feel overly sorry when restoring to God the deposit entrusted to him. The same idea finds expression in Avot de Rabbi Natan, chapter 14. Students of Rabbi Yohanan ben Zakkai came to console him on the death of his son. Only Rabbi Elazar ben Arakh was able to console him properly. He said:

> I will give you a parable to what the matter should be compared: To a man who was given an object to watch by the King. Each day, he would cry and scream. He would say: "Woe unto me! When will I peacefully be free of this object?" So it is with you, Rabbi. You had a son who learned Torah, Prophets and Writings, Mishnah, halakhot, aggadot, and he has been freed from this world without iniquity. Shall you receive consolations when you have returned intact the object entrusted to you?

The Talmud, Berakhot 10a, reports that King David sang a special song *(shirah)* five times: in his mother's womb; when he was born and saw the stars; when he was nursed by his mother; when he saw the wicked destroyed. Finally, he sang a song when he looked at the day of death. What song did he sing? *Barekhi nafshi.* "Bless the Lord, O my soul. Lord my God, You are very great, You are robed with glory and majesty" (Tehillim 104:1).

A striking Midrash *(Eliyahu Rabbah* 16:81) states that the day of Adam's death was celebrated by his descendants as a festival. They rejoiced that man is mortal, for otherwise he would not do the will of his heavenly Father. Life would lack intensity, and one's service of God would be diminished. In other words, death is not only accepted; it is greeted with song and festivity. Death really is *tov me'od.*

The ultimate meaning of human life is bound inextricably to the fact that human beings die. Mortality provides life with intensity, deep emotion, and profundity. Ultimate meaning is not measured by the number of years one lives on this earth.

Rabbi David Ibn Zimra (Radbaz) considers the question: How could Adam follow Havvah's advice to transgress after he had been so well-treated by God (*Responsa of Radbaz*, 1:256)? He answers: It is well understood that everything ultimately returns to its origin. This is true of all living things, including humans. This knowledge was clear to Adam. When God told Adam not to eat from the tree of knowledge of good and evil, He threatened Adam with the punishment of death. This referred to an essential death, not a natural death. Adam realized that his natural death was inevitable; he did not think he was immortal. Adam knew that there was a tree of life in the Garden of Eden, but he did not know where it was. The snake's argument to Havvah, which was then conveyed to Adam, was that the humans should eat from the tree of knowledge in order to be like God—eternal, understanding the difference between good and evil. Adam believed that if he ate from the tree of knowledge he would gain the information as to where the tree of life was. He could then eat from that tree and serve God eternally like the angels. He reasoned that it would be satisfactory to transgress once and then repent, since in the final analysis, he would better be able to serve God if he were immortal. Although he was punished for his transgression, Adam ate from the tree of knowledge with good intention. He desired to be like one of the angels who serve God continually. Since he did not know the time of his own death and did not know how long he would live, Adam was anxious to gain eternal life without delay.

The interesting feature of this interpretation is that it again emphasizes that death is a necessary part of human existence. Seeking immortality, as Adam did, may strike us as being a pious gesture. But it was a gesture which was rejected outright by God. If He had wanted us to be deathless like the angels, He would have created us that way.

A death-defying culture is troubled by death. It basically is in constant struggle against the natural demise of all living things. A death-accepting culture is at ease with the idea of dying, and may come to the conclusion that life itself is not very important. The Jewish tradition balances these two attitudes. The death-defying aspects of Jewish tradition heighten our concern for the value of life. The death-accepting aspects of our tradition allow us to face death with wisdom and realism. When we understand how to die, we also understand how to live.

The Talmud, in Berakhot 17a, records a statement by Rabbi Yohanan, who, when finishing his study of the Book of Iyyov, said:

> The end of a human is to die and the end of an animal is to be slaughtered and everything stands ready for death. Happy is the one who was raised in the Torah and whose involvement was in the Torah; and he brings pleasure to his Creator. He was raised with a good name and he died with a good name from the world. About such a one, Shelomo said: "Better is a name than precious oil, and the day of death than the day of birth" (Kohelet 7:1).

It seems to me that Rabbi Yohanan presents a classic Jewish perspective to death and life. Death is natural and inevitable. But this does not mean that life is merely a dream, an illusion without meaning. Rather, one should live his life dedicated to Torah. A person should earn a good name, a good reputation. The day of death is better than the day of birth, in the sense that the struggle through life has been completed. Looking back at a complete life, it is possible to evaluate if it was lived well, in accordance with the values of the Torah. Death is accepted with wisdom, not with despair. The awareness of the inevitability of death does not demoralize a person; it makes him think more carefully about the life he lives.

DEATH FROM THE PERSPECTIVE OF THE ONE WHO IS DYING

Usually, death is discussed and contemplated by "outsiders."

We seldom stop to think of dying from the perspective of the one who is actually undergoing the experience. In recent years, there have been some studies which have tried to understand death from the perspective of individuals who are themselves dying.

Dr. Elisabeth Kubler-Ross has contributed important insights derived from her work with the terminally ill. She describes how the dying patient passes through stages in dealing with his illness and ultimate death. He may deny the fact that he is ill; he may visit one doctor after another hoping for a positive diagnosis. He may hide the fact of his illness from his friends and family. A dying patient will then enter a stage of anger; why me? He may bargain with God for an extension of life, promising to be better if only he recovers. Then, he will try to put his house in order—to make sure his will is drawn, and that all unfinished business is handled.

When a dying patient realizes that he really is dying, he may sink into a state of depression. He begins to mourn his own impending death. He may withdraw into silence, showing little interest in those who visit him. Finally, once he has passed through these stages, he will come to a stage of acceptance. At this stage, the dying patient has moved beyond grief and sorrow, beyond his own depression and sadness at reaching the point of death. With acceptance, the person is ready to die.

Rabbi Hayyim David Halevi discusses life after death extensively in the second volume of his *Aseh Lekha Rav*. His discussion focuses on recent research as well as on Jewish mystical texts which describe the experience of death. Based on these sources, Rabbi Halevi concludes that death is actually a marvelous experience, filled with light, glory, and satisfaction. Interviews by psychologists of people who have seemingly died but who have then been resuscitated indicate that these individuals experienced death uniformly as a wonderful happening. And this evidence corresponds to the notion that death really is *tov me'od*.

The thoughtful scientist, Lewis Thomas, has written: "We may be about to rediscover that dying is not such a bad thing to do after all." Drawing on the research concerning people who seemed to die but then were resuscitated, Thomas notes that "those who remember parts or all of their episodes do not recall any fear, or anguish. Several people who remained conscious throughout, while appearing to have been quite dead, could only describe a remarkable sensation of detachment." Sir William Osler took a similar view: he disapproved of people who spoke of the agony of death, maintaining that there was no such thing.

Death, then, is not experienced by the dying person as something bad. If a person is ready for death, it apparently is a beautiful experience. A talmudic aphorism (Ketuvot 103b) is: "One who dies from the midst of laughter—this is a good sign for him. One who dies from the midst of crying—this is a bad sign for him." Death-acceptance brings a happy death. Death resistance brings tears and suffering.

Reaching a level of acceptance of death may be the most profound experience a person can have in his whole life. It allows a person to see his life from the perspective of one who is about to leave this world. This period provides a person with insight and understanding; it is as though he receives the key to solving the riddles and enigmas of life. If you have had the experience of spending time with a person who has reached this level of death-acceptance, you will know the depth of wisdom, serenity, and love which characterizes this stage of life.

If reaching this stage of acceptance is so important to an individual, do we have the responsibility of rushing a dying patient along so that he will realize this stage as soon as possible? Put in another way, should we inform a terminally ill patient that he is dying?

As we have seen earlier, the Bah forbids us from discussing even the death of someone else in the presence of one who is very ill. The very thought of death may frighten the individual and deprive him of strength to fight his illness. Within the halakhic tradition, this definitely is the prevailing attitude. Dr. Kubler-Ross also maintains that no patient should be told that he is dying. Patients should not be forced to face their own death when they are not yet ready for it. Rather, they should be told that they are seriously ill, but that we are doing everything possible to help them. Each patient will relate to his illness in a different way, and move from stage to stage in the dying process according to his own pattern. Our task is not to rush the patient through the stages; rather, we must be sensitive to the stages as he undergoes them. Certainly, we should not deny death-acceptance when it finally arrives. We should not tell a patient who has achieved acceptance of death that he will become better, that God will give him a speedy recovery. Sometimes, a dying person accepts death long before his relatives and friends do so. The point is, we do a tremendous disservice to a dying person if we are not sensitive to what he or she is experiencing and thinking.

A Midrash (Bemidbar Rabbah 19:17) states that the righteous are informed of the day of their death so that they can transfer their crown to their children. This statement refers to Aharon, the High Priest, who was told when he would die so that he could transfer his authority to his son. The Tanhuma, Vayhi, reports that not one of our forefathers—Avraham, Yitzhak, and Yaakov—hoped that he would not die. Rather, each knew that he was dying and said so with his own mouth. The point of these midrashic texts may be that truly wise and righteous people reach the level of acceptance of death without much trouble. They may be informed of their impending death without that knowledge causing them any harm. But such people are clearly exceptional, especially in a society which is itself not death-accepting.

Considering death from the perspective of the dying helps us to appreciate the wisdom of our Jewish tradition in seeing that death was *tov me'od*, very good. Since we value life, we want to live as long and as well as possible. But since we also value death, we accept it when the time comes. Death-defiance may respond to some of our emotional needs. But death-acceptance provides us with wisdom.

There is a peculiar talmudic passage (Tamid 32a) which describes ten questions which Alexander of Macedon asked a group of rabbis. Two of the questions and the rabbis' response to them are: Question: What should a person do in order to live? Answer: He should make himself die (*yamit et atzmo*). Question: What should a person do in order to die? Answer: He should make himself live (*yehayyeh et atzmo*).

This enigmatic dialogue is explained by our commentaries in different ways. Rashi and Rabbenu Asher, for example, take the words allegorically, not referring to actual life and death. Yet, perhaps the rabbis were answering Alexander's question in a more direct way.

What should a person do in order to live? He should make himself aware of his own impending death. He should imagine himself to be dying. In this way, he will appreciate the value of every minute of life. He will see things with an intensity and a love which can only be experienced by someone who appreciates that he is about to lose what he has. In other words, in order to live a meaningful life, one must recognize his mortality.

What should a person do in order to die? He should make himself live. He should live his life fully, without fear of death. He should avoid becoming melancholy over the reality of death. If one gives himself fully to life, he can give himself fully to death when the time comes.

MOURNING

If death is so good, and if we are supposed to accept it as a positive feature of creation, why do we mourn our dead? Why are funerals so somber? Why do we associate death with crying, wailing and lamenting?

These questions bring us back to the balance which the Jewish tradition strikes. Our religious culture is not totally death-accepting, although we recognize the wisdom of death-acceptance. We place so much emphasis on life that we cannot fully reconcile ourselves to death. This ambivalence is well expressed in the statement of Rabbi Yaakov (Pirkei Avot 4:22) who said: "Better is one hour in penitence and good deeds in this world than all the life of the World to Come; but better is one hour of spiritual repose in the World to Come than all the life of this world."

Philosophically speaking, we probably should not mourn for our dead. In fact, we probably do not mourn for them even when we think we do. According to our tradition, we believe in the immortality of the soul. A person who has died—certainly a good person—will receive magnificent rewards from God in the World to Come. Moreover, the one who has died is now free from all the turmoil, pain and confusion of this world. No, we do not cry for the one who has died. We cry for ourselves.

We mourn because we will miss the presence of the loved one who has died. We will miss his/her relationship in our lives. We feel lonely, deprived of love, encouragement, wisdom, etc. We mourn because we feel sorry for ourselves.

These are legitimate feelings. Even though we philosophically might affirm death as a wonderful facet of creation, we still are pained by the loss of someone we love. Philosophy is one thing, emotional reaction is quite another. And both reactions must balance each other. Jewish tradition requires us to mourn—even if we philosophically have accepted death. But Jewish tradition forbids us from mourning too much—since we must recognize that death is part of God's plan.

The Jewish laws of mourning balance emotionalism and philosophical wisdom. Mourners are supposed to cry and are expected to participate in burying the dead themselves. There is no camouflage of death. There is no attempt to deny the starkness and fearfulness of what has happened. Mourners tear their garments, sit on the floor for seven days, and—in a sense—withdraw from their normal social context of life. They are free to be angry, upset, guilt-ridden. But, Jewish tradition prescribes that mourning is not simply a private matter. During the seven days of mourning, friends and relatives visit the mourners and offer consolation. In fact, the mourners—who ostensibly want privacy in order to grieve their loss—are placed into an active social context. They see friends and relatives whom they may not have seen for quite some time. People come with kind words, gifts of food, and messages from friends and relatives out of town. Even as the mourners feel the desire to be alone in their sadness, they also feel drawn to the many well-wishers who come to share the experience with them.

Jewish tradition is realistic. It teaches us to accept death, but recognizes our desire to defy death, and to mourn our dead. It provides a brilliant balance between acceptance and death-defiance.

The blend of Jewish wisdom and Jewish realism is apparent in a talmudic discussion (Berakhot 46b) which deals with the question: What should people say when they come to a house of mourning? The opinion of our sages is that they should say *Barukh ha-Tov ve-ha-Metiv*, "Blessed is God who is good and does good." Rabbi Akiva says that visitors should recite the blessing: *Barukh Dayyan ha-emet*, "Blessed be the true Judge." The opinion of the rabbis implies that we should accept death as a positive good so that we recite a blessing praising God's goodness when we visit a house of mourning. Rabbi Akiva, though, provides a voice of realism. The blessing he suggests is filled with resignation, not cheerfulness. It would seem to be more appropriate for a house of mourning. The Talmud concludes that both blessings are to be recited. And, in fact, we do incorporate both ideas in the blessing following the mourners' meal after a funeral. We say: "You are good and You do what is good. You are the God of truth and Your decree is just. You take back our souls in Your universal rule, doing according to Your will, and we are Your people, Your servants. Whatever befalls, we must acknowledge You and bless You." But after making these philosophical statements accepting God's goodness and His justness, we change moods: "May He who gives strength to the bereaved, in His compassion give solace in this bereavement to us and all His people Israel." We recognize the claim of a grieving human heart, just as we recognize the claim of a wise human mind.

Death is not an evil. It is a perfectly natural event which occurs to every living thing.

Death is not the opposite of life. Rather, life and death are interrelated parts of a continuum of existence, an eternal rhythm. A Jewish philosophy of death is also a Jewish philosophy of life; a Jewish philosophy of life is also a Jewish philosophy of death. Our tradition balances wisdom and emotionalism. It is practical and profound. Because we understand how to die, we understand how to live.

6

WHEN A GENERATION GOES

*I*n quiet, meditative moments, we ponder the eternal rhythm of life and death. "A generation comes, a generation goes; and the earth abides forever. . . . There is nothing new under the sun" (Kohelet 1:4, 9). We sense the profound and universal truth that every living being dies, that all humans are mortal, that the continuum of life and death is an absolute feature of existence. We accept and understand this on a philosophical level. Just saying the words makes us feel wise.

A parent dies. In the normal course of events, that is a natural and expected occurrence. "A generation comes and a generation goes." Yet, when we are confronted with the death of our own parent, it seems that there *is* something new under the sun. Initially, we find it difficult to see this event as part of a universal rhythm. Our philosophical wisdom becomes strikingly inadequate. Our parent dies and we cry; the death seems like a new and unique phenomenon, as though no one else before had ever been confronted with this crisis.

My mother died of cancer in May 1983, after several years of fighting the disease. She had undergone surgery, chemotherapy, radiation therapy; nevertheless, the cancer continued to spread. During the last four months of her life, her condition deteriorated rapidly. I remember her telling me: "I don't understand what is happening to me. I feel that I am the same person inside. I don't feel old. And yet my body is dying."

Originally published in *Hadassah Magazine*, October 1989.

I spent as much time as I could with my mother, traveling each month from my home in New York to visit her in Seattle. It was obvious that she was dying. She knew it and was not afraid of this knowledge. On my last visit to her at the end of May, I found her calm and radiant, overflowing with pure love and inner peace. She gave all of us her blessings. On Thursday morning, I gave her breakfast—she was too weak even to hold a spoon. Before leaving, I told her that I would be returning in June with my wife and children. She looked at me wistfully; we kissed good-bye. When I left her room, I found myself crying. I went to the airport and traveled back to New York. That Saturday night my father called to tell us that Mom had died.

On a rational, philosophical and practical level, her impending death was understood and accepted. Yet, when my father told me that Mom had died, I felt stunned. Death is so final, so absolute. Was it possible that I would never be able to speak to her again, or hear her wonderful voice? Was it possible that our family had lost its matriarch forever?

Again I found myself traveling to Seattle, this time to attend my mother's funeral. I remember thinking that I was having a bad dream, that everything would soon return to normal, that Mom would still be alive. But it was not a dream. Things would never return to the way they were.

Being a rabbi, I officiated at the funeral. During the eulogy, I found myself saying, "Now I am an orphan. My brothers and sister are orphans." Even as I said those words, I felt that they were surprising. The word orphan usually connotes helplessness. But I, my brothers and sister were married, had families of our own. We were not helpless. We were adults in the middle of our own lives. Nevertheless, I felt orphaned. And years later, I still feel so. The death of a parent changes one's life in practical and abstract ways. I don't think that one stops missing a deceased parent.

Freud has described the "work of mourning" as the process of reconciling oneself to reality. Although one knows that a loved one has died, he does not want to accept this fact. The initial stages of mourning find one feeling as though he were dreaming, engulfed by some sort of numbness. Many have told me that when they began the mourning process, they felt that this was happening to someone else, that they somehow were not really there. The work of mourning, then, takes the mourner from the stage of shock and numbness to the stage of realistic acceptance. The process is painful. It takes time. Some handle it better than others.

THE LAWS OF MOURNING

The Jewish laws and ceremonies associated with mourning help the adult orphan—and all mourners—through the process of the work of mourning. Before the interment, the mourners are considered in a state of *aninut* (deep distress), and they are exempt from a number of religious responsibilities such as prayer. This is a stage of alienation, during which one is struggling with illusions and reality.

Then comes the burial itself. Jewish tradition considers it a mitzvah to participate in the burial of the dead. As mourners and friends fill the grave with earth, the absolute reality of the situation becomes very clear. I vividly remember shoveling the earth into my mother's grave and saying good-bye to her again. It was then that I was jolted out of dream-like illusions. Her death had become real to me.

The week of mourning, popularly known by the Hebrew word for seven, *shivah*, is a period of adjustment for the mourners. The ancient Jewish traditions are filled with profound wisdom and spiritual power. They understand human nature and human needs to a remarkable degree. The rules of the *shivah* reflect the conflicted mental state of mourners. On the one hand, mourners feel pain, anger and guilt. They want to isolate themselves from life, from the social graces. In deference to those feelings, the laws of mourning require mourners to tear their garment, to sit on the floor, to abstain from shaving and from physical pleasures, to avoid greeting others according to the usual social conventions.

On the other hand, the mourners need to adjust to their new lives; they need to look ahead. In recognition of these needs, Jewish law prescribes a mourners' meal upon returning from the cemetery after the burial. It is as if to say: "We know you are grieving, that you feel the world has caved in on you, but you must eat. Life goes on. This is a difficult time; but you have the strength and capacity to go on with your lives."

The Talmud records an interesting debate concerning what blessing should be recited in the house of mourning (Berakhot 46b). The sages state that mourners should say *Barukh ha-Tov ve-ha-Metiv*, blessing "[God] who is good and who does good." Rabbi Akiva says that the appropriate blessing is *Barukh Dayyan ha-emet*, blessing "[God] who is the true Judge." The sages seem to take a philosophical stance, appealing to the mourners' intellectual understanding that death is natural. Since God created death and since He is good and all-knowing, we must accept death and acknowledge God's goodness.

Rabbi Akiva's opinion gives more weight to human emotions. Even if we can accept this death intellectually, we still feel bereaved. We mourn our loss. Therefore, the blessing he suggests is a blessing of resignation. The talmudic discussion concludes with the ruling that both blessings are to be recited. Indeed, the grace after the mourners' meal includes both aspects—a blessing which acknowledges God's goodness and which recognizes God as the true Judge. Thus, Jewish tradition teaches people to accept death, while still respecting the feelings of a grieving heart.

During the *shivah*, friends and family visit the mourners. It is appropriate to discuss the life of the deceased who is being mourned. When I was observing *shivah* for my mother, I was fascinated by the many reminiscences of visitors—each of whom knew my mother in a different context. All the various stories and anecdotes taught me things about Mom which I had not known; they demonstrated her influence on so many people in so many different ways. What also interested me were the different memories of Mom expressed by my father, my brothers and sister, my family members and close friends. The *shivah* period gave all of us the opportunity to bring together fragments of Mom's life and to understand her life more fully. By the end of the *shivah*, when I returned to New York, I realized that the Jewish traditions had helped me considerably with the work of mourning. I had moved from a feeling of illusion to a greater recognition of reality.

When a parent dies, his or her relationship with the children does not cease. Each of us continues to live with "the parent within." Many years ago, I attended a dinner honoring a prominent philanthropist who was then about 70 years old. When he received a plaque, his first words of response were: "I wish my father were here to see this. He would have been so proud." His father had died long ago; yet, this distinguished and influential man still was influenced profoundly by his father.

Parents continue to live within us in our memories, our attitudes, even in our gestures and mannerisms. As time passes, the initial pain and confusion of mourning lessens; a deeper, wiser understanding emerges.

ACCEPTING THE LOSS

As long as our parents are alive, we feel that they are our connection with the past. They tell us stories of their childhood, of their parents, of their grandparents. They give us the traditions and the historical context of our own lives. We enjoy seeing photographs of them as children. We are intrigued by the world in which they lived, a world which has changed so dramatically and so quickly. The Israeli poet Amnon Shamosh wrote a poem describing how his mother, who came from Syria, would visit him each summer in his kibbutz in Israel. She told him endless stories, to which he paid little attention. One summer his mother did not come. She had died. Shamosh found himself trying to reconstruct the stories his mother had told him. He put them to paper and only then began to discover his mother's world, a culture departed. But now his mother could neither tell him any new stories nor correct any of the old stories the poet remembered.

When a parent dies, a source of our civilization dies. We are cut off. We are startled by how many things we wanted to ask but never got around to asking; by how many things we heard, but never paid careful enough attention to. No longer can we draw on the parent's memories. Our past seems to shrink or to freeze.

We begin to feel a subtle transition. *We* are now the older generation. We have the responsibility to transmit our culture to our children and their generation. This sense of destiny is more evident when one has suffered the loss of both parents. In describing their feelings at the death of their second parent, a number of mourners have told me: "Now there is nothing between me and eternity. My parents were buffers between me and the next world. Now that they are gone, I am to my children what my parents were to me."

This realization can make one more thoughtful and sensitive. Rabbinic tradition teaches that although we are intellectually aware of the existence of death, we live our lives oblivious to this awareness. We feel as though we will live forever. Indeed, if we were constantly to keep in mind the possibility of dying, we would not be able to live a healthy and enjoyable life. We would be morose, frightened, self-centered. On the other hand, pondering the day of death makes us appreciate the importance of living our lives thoughtfully and righteously. It is often the death of a parent which makes us think more carefully about the meaning of life.

Jewish tradition prescribes that children recite the Kaddish doxology during the first year of mourning, as well as on the anniversary of the death of parents. The Kaddish expresses praise of God and does not refer directly to death or mourning. Its recitation reflects the mourners' acceptance of God's will and demonstrates a commitment to carry on with life in a spirit of wisdom and righteousness. The power of the Kaddish, for many people, does not come from the literal meaning of the words, but from the recitation itself. There is a certain mysterious ring to the words, an echo of generations of children who have mourned the deaths of their parents. We become part of the eternal rhythm of history. As we recite Kaddish, we link ourselves with the generations past—and sense our own personal mortality. But we also praise God, recognizing that it is He who created life and death. We trust in His wisdom.

"A generation comes and a generation goes. . . . There is nothing new under the sun." A parent dies, and it seems as if there were indeed something new under the sun. We grieve, we mourn, we learn, we look back, we look ahead. A parent dies, and the adult orphan suddenly grows older and more thoughtful. We begin to understand the mystery of the generations.

7

IN SEARCH OF PEACE

Gadol ha-Shalom: "Great is peace." This well-known rabbinic dictum is not only a pervasive theme in Jewish thought, but it reflects the deepest hope and aspiration of the Jewish people. This is an obvious truism, as anyone who reads our prayer book will understand.

The classic Jewish idealization of peace is encapsulated in the messianic idea. Rambam (*Hilkhot Melakhim* 12:4–5) writes that our prophets and sages yearned for messianic times, not so that the Jewish people would rule over others, nor for any material benefits; rather, they desired an age of peace and prosperity, when everyone could turn his attention to Torah study and fulfillment without disturbances. In the messianic era, there will be no famine, no war, no jealousy or strife. Instead, all people will be engaged in pursuing the knowledge of God and will attain their greatest human potential.

The messianic ideal is the goal towards which we strive. Our perennial faith in the ultimate redemption of Israel by the Messiah is a clear testimony to the innate optimism of our people. No matter how problematic human events may be, no matter how many wars and conflicts—we believe unflinchingly that peace and harmony ultimately will prevail. Regrettably, though, until the messianic era arrives, we find ourselves in a world in which war is "normal." The history of humankind is

---

Lecture given at the Torah Retreat of the New York Region of the Orthodox Union, May 1991.

saturated with the blood of endless wars. And the Jewish people have not been exempt from this phenomenon.

Our tradition speaks of mandatory war (*milhemet mitzvah*) and permissible war (*milhemet reshut*). In both cases, though, halakhah prohibits going to war unless one first has sued for peace (Rambam, *Hilkhot Melakhim* 6:1).

The Mishnah in Sotah (8:7) describes the process of preparing for war. In a mandatory war, everyone must go out to battle, even brides and grooms. Since the mandatory war is one of self-defense, no exemptions are allowed. The very security of the nation is at stake, and each person must do his or her share to protect Israel. But when it comes to a permissible war, certain exemptions are allowed, following biblical instructions. Thus, a person may ask to be excused from military service if he was newly married, or if he planted a new vineyard, or built a new home. He could ask to be excused simply because he was afraid.

Rabbi Hayyim David Halevi offers an interesting discussion on the military exemptions (*Aseh Lekha Rav* 3:58). Exemptions were allowed in order to slow down the process of going to war. Since it was fairly easy to come up with an excuse for not going to battle, the leader of the country could not commit a nation to war without first winning the support of the public. For example, if he decided to wage a permissible war, but the vast majority of the people did not agree with that decision, they simply could excuse themselves by saying they were afraid, or by utilizing one of the other exemptions. In effect, this could preclude the possibility of waging the war. In other words, a permissible war could occur only after adequate consultation with the people, and after enough of them felt it was worth the risk. The very nature of this process favored arriving at peaceful solutions to problems, delaying the waging of war until there was no other viable alternative.

In another responsum (*Aseh Lekha Rav* 4:1), Rabbi Halevi offers two explanations to the verse: "The Lord will give strength to His people, the Lord will bless His people with

peace" (Tehillim 29:11). One way of understanding this statement is that first the people of Israel need to be strong. Once
they are strong, then they will be blessed with peace. According to this interpretation, peace is the result of strength. A second interpretation, though, derives a different lesson from the
verse. The verse may be seen as a historical description. That
is, God has blessed His people with strength in the past; we
have witnessed many victories and great successes. Now the
time has arrived when He will bless His people with peace.
Referring to the State of Israel, Rabbi Halevi applies the interpretation as follows: Just as the Almighty has given us strength
during recent wars, so may He bless us now with the ability to
know how to make peace. Rabbi Halevi adds that it is quite
plausible to argue that "it is easier to wage war than to attain
real peace; therefore, we are dependent upon the blessing,
that the Almighty will bless His people with peace."

Although war is permitted and even mandated in certain circumstances, the general Jewish desire has always been to
attain peace. Although we recognize and praise the valiance of
heroic Jews who fight and have fought on behalf of our people, we also must recognize the clear tendency of peacefulness
and non-violence which has characterized our people over the
generations. When Jews were oppressed by enemies, they
often reacted not by perpetrating violence against the oppressors, but by accepting the violence against them as being the
will of God. After the expulsion of Jews from Spain, for example, Rabbi Yosef Yaavetz—himself among the expelled Jews—
wrote a number of works, none of which called for self-defense
or acts of violence against the oppressors of the Jews. On the
contrary, Rabbi Yaavetz explained the expulsion as being a
punishment from God for various transgressions of the Jewish
community. He also extolled the virtue of *yissurin*, chastisements, since they have the power of strengthening Jewish
faith. Chastisements lead Jews to repentance, to a deeper
sense of reliance upon God. This attitude of Rabbi Yaavetz is

evident in the teachings of many other sages throughout the generations.

Rabbi Aaron Samuel Tamaret (1869–1931), who was renowned as the "Maltsher illui," served as the rabbinic leader of Mileitchitz. His writings were characterized by a concern for non-violence. In one of his Pesah sermons, he stated that the Torah "suggests that Egyptians could never have succeeded in dominating and oppressing the Jews, had not the Jews themselves deteriorated morally. Constantly seeing the violence and cruelty of their Egyptian masters, they themselves began to esteem the power of the fist and to grant it the right and privilege of persecuting and crushing their own oppressed." He argued that every act of violence begets more violence. "Evil actions poison the atmosphere, and a man's evil acts pollute the air until finally he himself breathes the poisonous vapors, and such poisons flow from all the actions of a man, whether physical or mental." The Israelites did not fight against the Egyptians; they were told to stay in their homes when the tenth plague struck the Egyptians. Their abstention from participation in vengeance upon Egypt prevented the plague of vengeance from stirring up within the Jews themselves. He concluded: "The children of Israel, then, must derive this lesson from the events of that Pesah eve: Not to put their trust in wealth, and not to put their trust in might, but rather in the God of truth and justice, for this will serve to defend them everywhere against those who would dominate by the power of the fist."

Judaism teaches us to maintain a delicate balance. On the one hand, we should strive mightily to achieve peace. We should favor non-violent ways of solving problems. On the other hand, there are times when using force is necessary and when war is justified. We need to strike a balance between pacifism and militarism.

Striking this balance is far from an easy enterprise. Different people have different tendencies: some tend to one extreme, some to the other. It is interesting to note that Orthodox Jews

are often viewed as being hawkish. The media portray Orthodox nationalists in Israel as being militant. On the other hand,
Peace Now is almost always depicted as a movement of left-
wing, secularist Jews. It has always seemed peculiar to me that
Orthodox Jews are not visibly identified with peace efforts and
peace movements. As people imbued with Torah wisdom, with
Torah attitudes—shouldn't our efforts be devoted to finding
ways of saving blood from being spilled? Shouldn't we be
guided by the principles of the Torah, whose ways are ways of
pleasantness and all of whose paths are peace? Shouldn't we,
more than anyone else, be attracted to activities on behalf of
peace? Shouldn't religious Jews, who profess a deep faith in
God, be more willing to sacrifice for peace, since we may rely
on God's help? And shouldn't it be more likely for the secularists—who do not rely on God's providence—to argue for militarism?

There are, of course, numerous reasons which might be
cited to explain the phenomenon of militancy among Orthodox Jews. There are significant halakhic arguments pertaining
to the return of land which color the Orthodox positions on
these matters. Nevertheless, it seems to me that Orthodox
Jews should be at the forefront of all peace efforts. It is precisely people of faith, people of Torah, who should believe in
peace and aspire to peace more than anyone else.

During the 1920's, a gun battle broke out in the Tel Aviv
area between Jews and Arabs. Rabbi Bentzion Uziel, who was
then the Chief Rabbi of Tel Aviv, went out to the battlefield in
his rabbinic attire. Both sides stopped firing. Rabbi Uziel went
to the Arab side and told them: We are brothers, the land is
big enough for all of us; why shall we fight and hurt each
other? Let us live in peace and harmony. We mean you no
harm and ask you not to harm us. The Arabs were moved by
this gesture of a great rabbi. They walked away, and the battle
was over.

Rabbi Uziel risked his life for peace and harmony. He might
very well have been shot. His words might very well have

fallen on deaf ears. People on both sides might have found good reasons to continue the battle in spite of Rabbi Uziel's words. Nevertheless, Rabbi Uziel prevailed. His actions and his words reflect the very best in Torah teachings, and they ought to be a model for all religious Jews. As Rabbi Hayyim David Halevi, himself a student of Rabbi Uziel, has suggested: it is easier to make war than to make peace. Although we certainly must be ready to fight if there is no alternative, our major efforts and concerns should be towards the achievement of peace. May the Almighty give us strength, may He bless us with genuine peace.

II
Jewish Law

8

MODERN ORTHODOXY
AND HALAKHAH: AN INQUIRY

In his book, *The Perspective of Civilization,* Fernand Braudel utilizes a concept that he calls "world-time." Braudel notes that at any given point in history, all societies are not at the same level of advancement. The leading countries exist in world-time; that is, their level of advancement is correlated to the actual date in history. However, there also are countries and civilizations which are far behind world-time, whose way of life may be centuries or even millennia behind the advanced societies. In this year of 5745, for example, the advanced technological countries exist in world-time while underdeveloped countries lag generations behind; some societies are still living as their ancestors did centuries ago. In short, everyone in the world may live at the same chronological date, but different societies may be far from each other in terms of world-time.

Braudel's analysis also can be extended to the way people think. Even though people may be alive at the same time, their patterns of thinking may be separated by generations or centuries.

The characteristic of modern Orthodoxy is that it is *modern,* that it is correlated to the contemporary world-time. Being part of contemporary world-time, it draws on the teachings of modern scholarship, it is open to modern philosophy and literature, and it relates Jewish law to contemporary world reali-

Originally published in *Journal of Jewish Thought,* 1985.

ties. On the other hand, "non-modern" Orthodoxy does not operate in the present world-time. Its way of thinking and of dealing with contemporary reality are pre-modern, generations behind contemporary world-time. Thus, there are deep mental gulfs of time between such Orthodox people as Rabbi Joseph Soloveitchik and the Satmar Rebbe, or between many members of the Rabbinical Council of America and many members of the Agudath ha-Rabbanim. It is not that one is more Orthodox than the other: their belief in God, *Torah min ha-Shamayim* (Divine revelation of the Torah) and the sanctity of the Oral Law are shared commitments. The differences between so-called right-wing Orthodoxy and modern Orthodoxy are not differences in sincerity or in authentic commitment. Rather, the differences stem from different world views, from living in different world-times.

A modern Orthodox rabbi does not wish to think like a medieval rabbi, even though he wishes to fully understand what the medieval rabbi wrote and believed. The modern Orthodox halakhist wishes to draw on the wisdom of the past, not to be part of the past.

The philosophy of modern Orthodoxy is not at all new. Rather, it is a basic feature of Jewish thought throughout the centuries. In matters of halakhah, for example, it is axiomatic that contemporary authorities are obligated to evaluate halakhic questions from their own immediate perspective, rather than to rely exclusively on the opinions of rabbis of previous generations. Rambam (*Hilkhot Mamrim* 2:1) writes: "A great court—*bet din gadol*—when interpreting the Torah with one of the hermeneutic principles, found that the law on a certain matter was such-and-such, and then another court came afterwards and found a reason to reject the ruling of the first court—the second *bet din* rejects the ruling of the first *bet din* and rules according to what it deems correct. As it is said (Devarim 17:9) 'To the judge who will be in office at that time'—you are not obligated to go except to the *bet din* of your generation." The well-known phrase that "Yiftah in his generation is like Shemuel in his generation" (Rosh ha-Shanah 25b) expresses the need to rely on contemporary authorities, even if they are not of the stature of the authorities of previous generations. We are obligated to be "modern Orthodox," to recognize present reality and to participate in contemporary world-time.

Rabbi Hayyim David Halevi (*Aseh Lekha Rav,* 2:61) deals with the case of a judge who had reached a certain halakhic conclusion and gave a ruling on it. The judge then learned that another judge greater than he ruled on the same case but came to another conclusion. Should the first judge change his decision and rely on the authority of the greater one, or is he obligated to maintain his own position if he truly believes it to be correct? Rabbi Halevi quotes Rambam (*Hilkhot Sanhedrin* 23:9), who states the principle that *En le-dayan ella mah she-enav ro'ot*—"A judge has only what his eyes see." Rabbi Halevi states that the decision of a judge must be based solely on his own understanding of the case he is considering. "And no legal precedent obligates him, even if it is a decision of courts greater than he, even of his own teachers." Later in the same responsum, Rabbi Halevi writes: "Not only does a judge have the right to rule against his rabbis; he also has an obligation to do so (if he believes their decision to be incorrect, and he has strong proofs to support his own position). If the decision of those greater than he does not seem right to him, and he is not comfortable following it, and yet he follows that decision (in deference to their authority), then it is almost certain that he has rendered a false judgment (*din sheker*)."

The key principle here is that each judge must make a decision based on what his own eyes see. Obviously, a judge will want to understand the reasons why the greater rabbis and courts came to their conclusions. Perhaps by studying them, he will realize that he has erred and subsequently change his opinion. However, if after all his studying and analyzing the previous decisions he still maintains that his opinion is the correct one, he is then obligated to rule according to his own conclusion. He is not bound by precedent or by the weight of greater authorities.

One of the weaknesses of contemporary Orthodoxy is that it is not "modern" in the sense just discussed. There is a prevailing attitude that teaches us to revere the opinions of the sages of previous generations, and to defer to those contemporary sages who occupy a world-time contemporary with those sages. Who is addressing halakhic questions today on the basis of what his own eyes see? Who are the sages of the present world-time, who absorb the contemporary reality, the contemporary ways of thinking and analyzing?

It is a common lament among modern Orthodox Jews that modern Orthodoxy lacks courage. Modern Orthodoxy is intimidated by the so-called right-wing, by the group of Jews that is pre-modern. Modern Orthodox scholars are reluctant to express their opinions and rulings for fear of losing religious stature in the eyes of the more fundamentalistic Orthodox Jews. When a modern Orthodox scholar does express his own opinion, he often is criticized sharply by the pre-modern Orthodox, and he is not adequately supported by the modern Orthodox. The spiritual climate of today makes it very easy to remain quiet rather than risk lonely spiritual battle against forces that are more militant and more vocal.

We need to understand that the difference between modern Orthodoxy and pre-modern Orthodoxy is not one of religious validity. And we also must understand that being modern Orthodox or pre-modern Orthodox does not make our decisions necessarily right or wrong. To be modern Orthodox Jews means to accept our limitations, but it also means that we must accept our responsibility to judge according to what our own eyes see, according to our own understanding. It means to have the self-respect to accept that responsibility. Modern Orthodoxy and pre-modern Orthodoxy do not engage in intelligent dialogue because they operate on separate time-waves. They follow different assumptions.

In a recent discussion concerning the adoption of a pre-nuptial agreement to avoid the *agunah* (abandoned wife) problem, a pre-modern opinion has been expressed that we should not initiate a new procedure, since this would seem to say that we are more sensitive and creative than the sages of previous generations who did not initiate such a procedure. This kind of argument cannot be countered with a reasonable discussion. This is an argument from a different world-time. The argument, which is fairly widespread, is essentially ludicrous. Throughout the centuries, our sages have initiated *takkanot* (corrective decrees) in their communities to meet the contemporary needs of their people. Did they think it was an insult to their predecessors to be responsive to contemporary needs? Did Rabbenu Gershom slander all previous generations of rabbis by instituting his *takkanot*?

The fact is that rabbis in all generations have had to face the serious responsibility of leading their communities in the ways of Torah. They have drawn on the wisdom and holiness of our sages of previous generations, but they ultimately have had to rely on their own judgement and on what their own eyes saw. The sages of each generation are influenced by the social and political realities of their time. If many of our sages believed in demons and witches, if they thought that the sun revolved around the earth, or if they assigned inferior status to women and slaves—we can understand that they were part of a world that accepted these notions. We do not show disrespect for them by understanding the context in which they lived and thought. On the contrary, we are able to understand their words better, and thus we may determine how they may or may not be applied to our own contemporary situation. It is not disrespectful to our sages if we disagree with their understanding of physics, psychology, sociology, or politics. On the contrary, it would be foolish not to draw on the advances in these fields that have been made throughout the generations, including those of our own time. There is no sense in forcing ourselves into an earlier world-time in order to mold our ways of thinking into harmony with modes of thought of sages who lived several hundred or even several thousand years ago.

Modern Orthodoxy requires us to live in the present world-time, knowing full well that many of the notions which we consider true and basic may become discredited in future centuries. We do not want those future generations of rabbis to be limited in their thinking to what we are thinking and teaching today. We want them to be respectful of our teachings and to consider our words seriously; but it is they who must lead their generation. Our time is now, and only now. The Torah, which is eternal, requires Jews to go to the judge living and serving in their own time.

SPECIFIC EXAMPLES

If we take modern Orthodoxy seriously, then we will study talmudic passages and halakhic sources with an eye to understanding their historical and intellectual context. Sometimes we will come across texts that have broad halakhic implications but whose application to the contemporary situation is problematic. The following are several specific examples of the conflict that arises.

Shabbat Desecrators

There is a well-known rabbinic dictum: "One who desecrates the Shabbat in public is as an idol worshipper" (Hullin 5a). This statement underscores the importance of Shabbat in Jewish thought and practice. To desecrate Shabbat publicly is an open statement that one denies that God created the world in six days and ceased working on the seventh. By extension, one who blasphemes God as Creator by desecrating Shabbat is indeed like an idol worshipper—i.e., he does not recognize the one true God, Creator of heaven and earth (see Rashi, *ad loc.*).

Flowing from this statement are a host of halakhot. A *mehallel Shabbat* (Shabbat desecrator) is disqualified from serving as a *shohet* (ritual slaughterer). Even if he slaughters an animal entirely in accordance with Jewish law, the meat may not be eaten by Jews (Rambam, *Hilkhot Shehitah* 4:14). A *mehallel Shabbat* may not serve as a witness, since he is in the category of *rasha* (evildoer). If he touches wine, we may not drink it, just as if the wine were touched by an idol worshipper. Rabbi Hayyim David Halevi *(Aseh Lekha Rav,* 5:1) discusses the question whether a *mehallel Shabbat* may be counted as part of a *minyan*. He quotes the *Peri Megadim*, who stated that "A *mumar* (willful transgressor) to *avodah zarah* (idol-worship), one who desecrates Shabbat, or one who violates any commandment *le-hakhis* (willfully), behold he is as an idolater and is not included (in the *minyan*)." Moreover, following this principle to its conclusion, a *mehallel Shabbat* may not be given an *aliyah* to the Torah, just as we may not call an idolater to the Torah.

There are several options available to us on how to deal with this set of halakhot and the principle on which they are based.

We may accept the statement at face value that in fact a *mehallel Shabbat* is like an idolater, and is subject to the aforementioned disqualifications. To hold this position, we must posit that the talmudic statement and the halakhic development of that statement transcend all generations, and are as applicable now as when first stated. Consequently, we should maintain the ancient standard without compromise, regardless of ramifications. If the talmudic characterization of a *mehallel Shabbat* is equally applicable to our time, then we should fight heroically to defend the principle and the laws based on it. This is essentially the opinion of the "pre-modern" Orthodox.

The modern Orthodox position is that this statement simply cannot be taken at face value in our time. The number of Jews who violate Shabbat far exceeds the number of those who observe Shabbat.

One approach is to express loyalty to the original statement while finding extenuating circumstances so that the implications of the original statement need not be fully applied. For example, Rabbi Hayyim David Halevi was asked a question

(Aseh Lekha Rav, 5:1) that posed the problem of a small synagogue that had a *minyan* only if Shabbat desecrators were
included. Should the Shabbat desecrators be counted for *minyan,* even though this would be against the basic law? Or
should the synagogue be closed due to a lack of a proper *minyan?* Rabbi Halevi writes. "It is incumbent upon us to find a
way of being lenient." It bothers him that a synagogue should
have to close because of the technicality of the *mehallel Shabbat.*
He offers several arguments to justify his position. As an extra
point, he gives the following analysis:

> A *mehallel Shabbat* in public who is disqualified from being
> counted into a *minyan* of ten—this refers only to those early
> days when they understood and evaluated the seriousness of
> the prohibition (of Shabbat) and also nearly everyone was
> scrupulous in observing Shabbat according to the law, so that
> one who "breached the fence" was disqualified. But this is
> not true in our time. Our eyes see a multitude of Shabbat
> desecrators, and the overwhelming majority do not under-
> stand and do not realize the seriousness of the prohibition.
> Behold: they come to the synagogue and pray and read in
> the Torah, and do not understand and do not realize—they
> walk in darkness—and afterwards they desecrate the Shab-
> bat. And perhaps such as these are as a *tinok she-nishbah* (a
> child who was captured and then grew up among hea-
> thens—he is not held accountable for his transgressions, for
> he never knew any differently).

In another responsum *(Aseh Lekha Rav,* 3:16) Rabbi Halevi
deals with the question whether a Bar Mitzvah and his family
may be called to the Torah, if they come to the synagogue on
Shabbat in a car. His answer is that we must try to bring the
young boy and his family closer to the Torah, and not reject
them. He quotes his own earlier work, *Mekor Hayyim ha-Shalem*
(vol. 3, 122:20), where he wrote that even though—according
to the technicality of the law—those who desecrate Shabbat in
public should not be called to the Torah, yet,

> if there is a fear that this will cause bad feelings, then such
> people should be called to the Torah as *hosafot* (those called

to the Torah beyond the regular seven) since in our generation, an orphan generation, it is proper to be lenient in such
circumstances and it is our obligation to bring them closer
and not to push them away further, and God in His goodness will have mercy on us.

Rabbi David Tzevi Hoffmann (*Melammed Leho'il*, no. 29)
deals with the question of whether a *mehallel Shabbat* in public
may be counted in a *minyan*. He first lists sources that forbid
such a person from being counted. Then he goes on to say:
"In our time it is customary to be lenient in this, even in Hun-
gary, and certainly in Germany." He mentions the case of a
man who kept his business open on Shabbat who wanted to
serve as the *sheli'ah tzibbur* (leader of public prayer services)
during his mourning. He was allowed to do this in a synagogue even though the *gabbai* (one in charge of delegating
responsibilities during services) who let him lead the service
was a learned and God-fearing man. Rabbi Hoffmann asked
the *gabbai* why he did not prevent the man from leading the
service. The *gabbai* answered that it had long been the custom
not to prevent such people from leading services. Since the
rabbis of that synagogue were outstanding scholars and they
allowed this practice, Rabbi Hoffmann concludes that they
must have had a good reason. He suggests that perhaps they
relied on a responsum of *Binyan Tzion ha-Hadashot*, no. 23,
which stated that "*Mehallelei Shabbat* in our time are considered somewhat like a *tinok she-nishbah* (a child in captivity who
grew up among Gentiles; he is not held responsible for his
transgressions), since—due to our great iniquities—the majority of Jews in our country are *mehallelei Shabbat,* and it is not
their intention to deny the basic tenets of our faith."

Rabbi Hoffmann then writes that he was told by Rabbi
Meshulam Zalman Hakohen in the name of the author of
Sho'el u-Meshiv, who wrote: "The people in America are not
disqualified because of their *hillul Shabbat,* since they are as
tinok she-nishbah." Although it would be better to pray among

Jews who were all Shabbat-observant, there is enough precedent to be lenient in this matter.

Rabbi Hoffmann concludes by offering the following analysis: In our time, such people are not called "*mehallel Shabbat* in
public, because the majority of Jews violate the laws of Shabbat. If the majority of Jews were observant and a few of them
were arrogant enough to violate Shabbat, then this minority
would be guilty of denying the Torah and of committing a dis-
graceful act and of removing themselves from the community
of Israel. (This is obviously the original context of the talmudic
statement.) However, since the contemporary reality is that the
majority of Jews violate Shabbat, the individual does not think
that violating Shabbat is such a terrible crime. His public transgression today is equated to *be-tzinah* (transgressions of the
Shabbat done in private)." Rabbi Hoffmann concludes by
lamenting that in our times, those who observe Shabbat are
considered separatists, while the transgressors are considered
to be following the normal pattern.

Rabbi Hoffmann's concluding discussion makes it clear that
the original context of the talmudic statement equating a
Shabbat violator with an idolater cannot be applied to the contemporary situation. We cannot judge someone to be a desecrator of Shabbat if he does not realize the true sanctity of the
day. There are a great many Jews who transgress Shabbat
laws, but who consider themselves to be perfectly upright
Jews. They do not view themselves as denying God as Creator
or as blaspheming the basic principles of our faith.

The challenge of modern Orthodoxy is to review the true
status of Jews who violate Shabbat today. If someone had been
religious and had studied the laws of Shabbat—and then con-
sciously decided to violate Shabbat as a sign of his rebellion
against the Torah—then such a person fits into the talmudic
category and should be penalized accordingly. If, however, a
person never understood the sanctity of Shabbat, his violation
of the laws of Shabbat does not reflect heresy or hatred of
Torah. On the contrary, it reflects his ignorance and his being

part of a Jewish community that largely does not observe Shabbat properly. Such a person is like a *tinok she-nishbah,* and should not be subject to the penalties accorded to a true *mehallel Shabbat* in public. This position is stated not as a compromise with the authentic halakhah; this is *the* actual halakhah. The Talmud simply was not referring to the situation we have today. And we must judge according to the present world-time, according to what our own eyes see.

Another insight into this question may be drawn from the laws of *shehitah.* Rambam (*Hilkhot Shehitah* 4:14) rules that a *mehallel Shabbat* is disqualified from serving as a *shohet.* Even if he performs the *shehitah* perfectly in accordance with halakhah, and even if there are reliable religious Jews overseeing his *shehitah,* the meat is still not considered to be kasher. In halakhah 16, though, Rambam rules that a Sadducee or another person who denies the Oral Torah may not serve as a *shohet;* but if he does slaughter an animal in the presence of a trustworthy Jew, then the meat may be eaten. The Sadducee is not totally disqualified from performing *shehitah.* Yet, a problem arises. According to us, a Sadducee is definitely a *mehallel Shabbat.* Sadducees do not accept the Oral Torah; since many of the laws of Shabbat are known only from the *Torah she-be'al peh,* it is inevitable that a Sadducee will not observe Shabbat as we do. He will be transgressing rules that we consider basic to Shabbat observances.

It seems, then, that a Sadducee—though he violates the laws of Shabbat in public—does not become disqualified as a desecrator of Shabbat. His lack of observance is based on a lack of knowledge, or on misguided teachings he has received. But he does not perceive himself at all as one who desecrates the Shabbat, even though from our point of view he is violating many laws. The rulings pertaining to a *mehallel Shabbat* are applied only to an individual who recognizes the severity of his actions and who desecrates Shabbat as a sign of his rejection of God and Torah.

The Status of Women

Let us move on to another area of discussion. In several places (Kiddushin 80b, Shabbat 33b) we find the statement that *Nashim da'atan kalah*. Generally, this statement is translated to mean that women are temperamentally lightheaded or that women's understanding is light. We also have the remarkable statement of Rabbi Eliezer (Sotah 20a) that whoever teaches his daughter Torah teaches her *tiflut* (foolishness or obscenity). These statements reflect a cultural bias against women that was pervasive in ancient society, and which still can be found in less-advanced societies today. These statements reflect the world-time of their authors. From a literary or historical standpoint, it would be fairly easy to dismiss these—and similar comments—by arguing that they belong to a particular time and a certain way of thought.

The problem arises, though, in that these sentiments were not left merely as opinions of rabbis on the nature of women; they were incorporated into practical halakhah. The following is a quotation from Rambam, *Hilkhot Talmud Torah* (1:13):

> A woman who learns Torah receives a reward, but not the same reward as a man, since she was not commanded (to learn Torah); and anyone who does something for which he was not commanded does not receive reward on the same level as someone who was commanded and who performed it, but rather receives less than he. And although she does have a reward, our sages commanded that a man must not teach his daughter Torah since the intelligence of the majority of women is not geared to be instructed; rather, they reduce the words of Torah to matters of foolishness according to the poverty of their understanding. Our sages said: One who teaches his daughter Torah is as though he taught her foolishness. To what does this refer? To the *Torah she-be'al peh* (Oral Law) but as concerns the *Torah she-bikhtav* (Written Law), he should not teach her; but if he did teach her it is not as though he taught her foolishness.

Once talmudic statements are incorporated into halakhic codes, they transcend their own original world-time and become a factor in the thinking of all later generations. The modern sensibility that accords women equal intellect with men comes into conflict not only with ancient talmudic statements, but also with practical halakhah. How do we deal with this dilemma?

We may submit ourselves to the talmudic world-time. We may argue that the statements of our sages are true and binding on all future generations. Since Rambam himself rules that women may not be taught Torah and that their ability to learn is poor, we should see to it that our daughters receive no formal Torah education, except in the mitzvot that concern them directly. Moreover, when we teach girls, we should treat them as being intellectually inferior compared to boys, and therefore we should have different curricula for girls and for boys. This point of view is adopted by pre-modern Orthodox.

There are schools for girls where the girls do not learn *Torah she-be'al peh* and where their curriculum is different from that in boys' schools. There is no yeshivah for girls in the same sense as there are yeshivot for boys who wish to devote their days and nights to the study of Torah.

Among the modern Orthodox, though, there is a general recognition that our social situation is radically different from that of previous generations. The need to educate our daughters in Torah has been widely recognized, even though there is still great difference of opinion as to how they should be educated. Rabbi Ovadiah Yosef wrote a responsum (*Shanah be-Shanah*, 5743, pp. 157–61) in which he permitted the celebration of Bat Mitzvah for girls who have reached the age of twelve. In the course of the responsum, he quotes Rabbi Yehiel Yaakov Weinberg (*Seridei Esh*, 3:93), who wrote that it was perfectly proper to celebrate a Bat Mitzvah.

> And concerning those who argue against this because this was not practiced in previous generations: this is no argument at all, since in the generations before us they did not have to engage in the education of their daughters because every Jew was filled with Torah and *yirat Shamayim* (fear of

God), and the entire environment was filled with a pure spirit and the holiness of Judaism. . . . But now, due to our many transgressions, the generations have undergone a very great change. The influence of the street destroys and uproots all attachment to Judaism from the hearts of Jewish girls. It is incumbent upon us to rally all our strength for the education of girls: and to our joy, the *gedolei Yisra'el* (sages) of the previous generation already took a stand and established educational institutions of Torah and understanding for Jewish girls. . . . And if the distinction that is made between boys and girls (in terms of Bar or Bat Mitzvah) severely damages the human sensibility of the girl, it is permissible to have a party and celebration at home for girls who celebrate their Bat Mitzvah.

Since times and conditions have changed, we must adapt to the new realities.

The modern Orthodox approach calls on us to re-evaluate the original sources and the halakhot based on those sources. We need to determine whether those statements refer to us at all. If they do then we must follow them—regardless of the social consequences and implications. If they do not, then we have the freedom to deal with the reality before us without having to apologize.

The idea that women's intelligence is inferior, that girls should not learn Torah because it is too complicated for them—this is a notion that generally is discredited among intelligent people in our world-time. What possible value can there be in arguing in defense of untenable attitudes? General evidence in modern education shows that girls are perfectly able to learn and to make great intellectual achievements. If women can win Nobel Prizes, if they can become doctors and lawyers and judges and engineers—why should they be unable to tackle the complexities of Talmud and halakhah? Our eyes see that the understanding of women is not any lighter than that of men. We can understand why ancient and medieval rabbis wrote the way they did—because they lived in an environment where women generally were relegated to inferior status. But we cannot apply those outgrown attitudes to our contemporary life. We need to say: We are not "compromising" on halakhah by educating our daughters in Torah; rather, we are establishing the halakhah that women and girls must learn Torah commensurate with their abilities—which are equal to those of men and boys. (See R. Hayyim David Halevi, *Aseh Lekha Rav*, 2:52.)

It is difficult for modern Orthodoxy to muster the courage to deal with such cases in a straightforward way. It is easier to surrender to an earlier world-time; or even to work out gradual compromises, which take a long time and which create much dissatisfaction. It is easier not to assume the responsibility for our generation. Because of the extreme caution of Orthodoxy not to "insult" the rabbis of previous generations, there is a reluctance to make any changes or to move in new directions.

The Nahem Prayer

Let us consider one further example of the dissonance between ancient texts and contemporary reality. Rabbi Hayyim David Halevi initiated a change in a text of a prayer for Tisha b'Av—a change that was eminently intelligent. Yet he was criticized sharply by many people. On Tisha b'Av, we have the prayer that begins *Nahem*, which describes Jerusalem as a destroyed, humiliated and desolate city without its children. Rabbi Halevi said that the statement is no longer true. Jerusalem is filled with Jews, and is definitely *not* destroyed, humiliated and desolate. How, therefore, can someone recite the traditional prayer when in fact the prayer is false? To recite this text would make us guilty of reciting falsehoods before God. Therefore, Rabbi Halevi changed parts of the *Nahem* text to the past tense, asking God to console the city that *was* destroyed, humiliated and desolate (*Aseh Lekha Rav*, 1:14). Rabbi Halevi defends his position eloquently (*Aseh Lekha Rav*, 2:36–39). It is indeed amazing that his position should have been criticized at all, since it is so perfectly sensible and understandable. Yet, such is the fear of change, that many were ready to criticize this ruling. The same critics have no problem reciting a prayer to God that in fact includes an obvious lie: Jerusalem is not destroyed, humiliated, nor desolate of its children.

For modern Orthodoxy to succeed in meeting its responsibility, it will be necessary for us to recognize that we are part of the contemporary world-time. We should have a *va'ad* composed of modern Orthodox rabbinic scholars who will be willing to evaluate the above examples as well as so many others, and to come up with specific halakhic rulings for our generation. If we have the confidence and good sense to lead, we may be surprised to find that many people are ready to follow. It is up to us to bring Orthodoxy into the modern generation— and world-time.

9

A STUDY OF THE HALAKHIC
APPROACHES OF TWO MODERN
POSEKIM

*I*n the introduction to his first volume of responsa, Rabbi Bentzion Uziel described the goal and method of a halakhic decisor:

> The talmudic judge or *posek* may not say to himself or to his questioner regarding a question which comes before him— let me look at the book and I will decide the law according to whatever is already printed in the book. This is not the method of those who give halakhic decisions (*ba'alei hora'ah*). Rather, his obligation is to search the source of the halakhah, to clarify it, refine it, purify it, according to his relevant ideas, his proper logic and his straightforward reasoning, to judge a true judgment and to conclude the matter according to the halakhah. . . . In all my responsa I have not attempted to be lenient nor to be strict from my own mind or inclination. Rather, my intention and my goal were to search and find the truth.

Each *posek* of every generation attempts to establish the halakhah according to its real truth. He attempts to understand it deeply and accurately, and to follow the sources wherever they may lead, regardless of his own inclination. Yet, a study of responsa literature reveals a variety of different styles, attitudes and decisions of *posekim*. Although halakhic decisors rely

---

Originally published in *Tradition*, Spring 1988.

on the same classic rabbinic texts, they are influenced by the specific time and place in which they live, as well as by their own personal sensitivities and intellectual inclinations.

In this essay, I will focus on two great modern-day *posekim,* studying how they approach similar halakhic questions. Both are scholars of vast erudition, of wide influence; both have written and published many works. The two *posekim* to be discussed are Rabbi Moshe Feinstein and Rabbi Hayyim David Halevi.

Rabbi Moshe Feinstein, of blessed memory, certainly must be counted among the greatest rabbinic authorities of our generation. His volumes of responsa, *Iggerot Moshe,* are highly respected and widely studied. Rabbi Feinstein was raised and trained in Eastern Europe. When he came to New York, he continued the traditions which he learned from his father and teachers in Europe. He was part of the Yiddish-speaking Torah world.

Rabbi Hayyim David Halevi, who presently is the Sephardic Chief Rabbi of Tel Aviv–Jaffa, was born and raised in the Sephardic tradition. A student of the late Rabbi Uziel, Rabbi Halevi is part of the Sephardic Torah tradition which flourished in the Ottoman Empire.

Rabbi Feinstein was Ashkenazic, Yiddish-speaking, and lived in the Diaspora. Rabbi Halevi is Sephardic, Hebrew-speaking, and lives in Eretz Yisrael. A study of the halakhic decisions of these two men will shed light on the halakhic process. References in the text in the case of Rabbi Feinstein refer to *Iggerot Moshe,* and in the case of Rabbi Halevi refer to *Aseh Lekha Rav,* unless otherwise stated.

I would like to preface the analysis by saying that this article does not attempt to pit these two Torah luminaries against each other, nor to draw conclusions as to which follows a "better" method. Nor do I claim that this study is exhaustive, or that other examples than those which I cite could not have been chosen. I offer this analysis as a study of contrasts in outlook and halakhic decision-making, fully aware that others might handle this topic differently.

THE WORLD OF TORAH AND THE OUTSIDE WORLD

In studying the volumes of *Iggerot Moshe*, one finds a spiritual world in which Torah study and observance are the central reality of life. Non-observant Jews, especially those who identify as Reform and Conservative (particularly Reform and Conservative rabbis), are often categorized as *resha'im*, wicked people, or *koferim*, deniers of the true faith. The non-Jewish world is viewed as being essentially hostile towards Jews. Foreign ideas are dangerous and corrosive to true Torah knowledge. Rabbi Feinstein records with pride that he is not influenced by foreign ideas. "My entire world view stems only from knowledge of Torah without any mixture of outside ideas (*yedi'ot hitzoniyyot*), whose judgment is truth whether it is strict or lenient. Arguments derived from foreign outlooks or false opinions of the heart are nothing" (*Even ha-Ezer,* 2:11).

The spiritual world reflected in the responsa of Rabbi Halevi is also one which is totally committed to Torah; and it is open and inviting, unafraid of others. One finds a profound tolerance for those who do not understand or observe halakhah. There is a reluctance to categorize people as *resha'im* or *koferim*. Rabbi Halevi is open to wisdom from all sources, Jewish and non-Jewish. The responsa manifest a deep respect for the words of our sages, but also a flexibility in dealing with modern reality.

Let us turn to some specific examples. In one of his responsa (*Yoreh De'ah* 3:83), Rabbi Feinstein stresses the importance of learning Torah studies in the morning in yeshivot, relegating secular subjects to a time later in the day. This arrangement serves to highlight the importance of Torah studies, and to inculcate in the students the belief that the secular studies are not as important. Indeed, the main responsibility of a yeshivah is to teach Torah studies; secular studies are taught as a concession to the laws of the country. In another responsum (*Yoreh De'ah* 3:73), Rabbi Feinstein forbids teaching science from texts which deny that God created the world. If it is impossible to obtain science textbooks which conform to our religious belief, then the offensive pages in the textbooks should be torn out. Rabbi Feinstein rules that a teacher of Greek and Roman history may not read books written by ancient authors about their religions. But books written by authors who reject and scorn those religions and which point out their foolishness are not forbidden. If a teacher is required to teach about the religions of the Greeks and Romans, he should do so in such a way as to make it clear that he considers them to be foolishness and emptiness. There may even be a positive result of this teaching—students will realize that religions which once were thought to be true by so many people are actually quite foolish. Therefore, they should not be surprised that many people today believe in religions which are essentially false and nonsensical (*Yoreh De'ah* 2:52). For Rabbi Feinstein, then, secular knowledge is not highly prized. Secular knowledge which contravenes religious teachings is dangerous, and should not be taught, or be taught only with derision.

A different attitude towards secular knowledge emerges from the responsa of Rabbi Halevi. Obviously, his main concern is also Torah study. Yet, he recognizes the need for secular studies, and he himself draws on sources other than rabbinical. He was asked by a religious student if it was permissible to study secular subjects (history, literature, etc.) on Shabbat in preparation for examinations. Rabbi Halevi cites rabbinic authorities who forbid secular studies on Shabbat, as well as those who permit such study on Shabbat. Rabbi Halevi suggests that it is better to sanctify the Shabbat by studying holy texts rather than books of general wisdom. Nevertheless, not being allowed to study for examinations would cause the student suffering and anxiety. Therefore, we may rely on the opinion of those who permit such study on Shabbat. "According to this, it is permissible to study general studies during the period of examinations, and the principle is that all your deeds should be for the sake of Heaven" (1:36).

When Rabbi Halevi was asked a question about transcendental meditation (2:47), he consulted a student who was versed in the subject to discover exactly what it was. He also read a volume on the subject. Through his consultation and his reading, he determined that the initiation ceremony was idolatrous and that the mantras were the names of pagan deities. If one could study the methods of transcendental meditation without going through the initiation procedure, however, there would be no halakhic objection. Nevertheless, Rabbi Halevi states that a person who lives a life of Torah and mitzvot should find sufficient spiritual satisfaction so as not to need to resort to transcendental meditation.

In another responsum (2:2) Rabbi Halevi deals with the question of life after death, drawing not only on the teachings of the Zohar and other classic Jewish sources, but also on the findings of contemporary researchers of the topic. He quotes the work of a psychiatrist from the University of Virginia along with Jewish classical texts.

TRADITIONAL SOURCES AND CONTEMPORARY KNOWLEDGE

There are cases where halakhic practice has been long established; yet, modern research and discoveries may call for a reevaluation of the halakhic practice. There sometimes arises a conflict between traditional practice and contemporary knowledge.

An example in point is cigarette smoking. For many generations, halakhists did not forbid the smoking of cigarettes. With recent medical research, though, we have learned that cigarettes are in fact dangerous to one's health. Does the halakhah continue to maintain the permissibility of smoking cigarettes, since they were not forbidden in the past? Or does the halakhah take into consideration the new findings, and thus declare cigarettes forbidden? Rabbi Feinstein (*Yoreh De'ah* 2:49) states that since there is evidence of the danger to health caused by cigarettes, a person certainly should pay attention to this fact. Yet, he argues that one may not prohibit cigarette smoking on the basis of its health dangers, since so many people have smoked and do smoke, and since "the Lord protects the simple." In particular, writes Rabbi Feinstein, a number of Torah luminaries of past generations smoked, and a number of Torah sages in our own time also smoke. Therefore, it is obvious that halakhah does not forbid cigarette smoking (see also *Hoshen Mishpat* 2:76).

Rabbi Halevi, on the other hand, rules that cigarette smoking is forbidden according to halakhah (2:1). The new evidence concerning the health hazards of smoking is overwhelming and cannot be ignored. Rabbi Halevi argues that if the rabbis of the Talmud and the great *posekim* of earlier generations had known the scientific research which is available to us now, they certainly would have forbidden cigarette smoking. In another responsum (3:25), Rabbi Halevi deals with the case of a person who took a vow not to smoke, but now wants that vow to be annulled. He rules that one should not find a way to annul the vow, since smoking is itself a prohibited act. On the contrary, one should try to convince the person to uphold his vow, since this is in his own best interest (see also 6:58, 7:67).

Another example of traditional practice requiring reevaluation based on modern discoveries relates to kosher meat. According to classical halakhic sources, one should not leave meat unsalted for three days, since the blood in the meat will become congealed and will not be drawn out by the salting process. If, however, the unsalted meat is soaked in water within three days, then it can remain another three days (less half an hour). This law is based on the premise that the water keeps the meat fresh, so that the blood will not congeal. Thus, traditional halakhic practice has been to soak unsalted meat at intervals of less than three days. The question arises: since we now have freezers, may we place unsalted meat in them and rely on the cold to preserve the freshness of the meat—thereby not requiring the meat to be soaked every three days? Rabbi Feinstein ruled that one should not rely on freezers; rather, one must actually soak the meat at the regular required intervals. Although he agrees that according to logic, freezing the meat should be satisfactory, there are many who have required the soaking of the meat. Rabbi Feinstein rules that only after the fact, and only in case of great need, may one salt meat that has been frozen (and not soaked) for more than three days (*Yoreh De'ah* 1:27; 2:42).

On the other hand, Rabbi Halevi rules that meat which was kept in a freezer is permissible to be salted and cooked, even if it had not been soaked during the three-day period. This may be done even initially (*le-khathila*), "since our eyes see that . . . it is as fresh as the moment when it was placed into the freezer, and this is obvious and clear" (*Mekor Hayyim*, vol. 5, 261:26).

Both *posekim* deal with the issue of natural childbirth: is the husband permitted to be in the delivery room when his wife is giving birth to a child? Rabbi Feinstein states (*Yoreh De'ah* 2:75) that he would not advise this practice to anyone who asked him. He believes that labor pains are great, and that the presence of the husband is not able to turn the wife's mind away from her suffering. Nevertheless, if a woman wants her husband present in the delivery room, there is no prohibition, as long as the husband stands at her head and behaves modestly.

Rabbi Halevi (4:58) also expresses his generally negative attitude towards having the husband present during childbirth. Yet, he goes on to note that modern research has found that the husband's presence can be helpful to his wife during delivery. Although this is a relatively new finding, and our mothers and grandmothers were perfectly able to have children without their husbands being present, it is possible that contemporary women may feel the absolute need for their husbands to be present during delivery. Without their husbands there, the women of today may feel that they will suffer greater pain and will be in greater danger. Therefore, for women who feel this way, Rabbi Halevi believes that the husbands should be present in the delivery room since this is a matter bordering on *piku'ah nefesh,* saving another person's life.

WOMEN LEARNING TORAH

The question of the permissibility of teaching Torah to women is a pressing one in contemporary halakhic discussions. Rabbi Eliezer's statement that "whoever teaches his daughter Torah teaches her obscenity" (Sotah 20a) is well known and often quoted. Rambam (*Hilkhot Talmud Torah* 1:13) rules that one should not teach Torah to girls, since women have limited intellectual ability. Halakhah generally has permitted women to study only the written Torah as well as those specific laws which they need to govern their own lives. Until modern times, it generally has been regarded as forbidden to teach women the Oral Torah. Rabbi Feinstein (*Yoreh De'ah* 3:87) follows the classic halakhic position opposing the teaching of the Oral Torah to women. The administration and teachers of a certain religious school for girls wished to introduce the teaching of Mishnah. Rabbi Feinstein ruled that this should not be done, since our sages have established the halakhah that women should not be taught the Oral Torah. The only exception to this principle is the teaching of Pirkei Avot, since that work deals with ethical conduct and teaches proper behavior. But other tractates certainly are not to be taught.

Rabbi Halevi (2:52) cites the classic texts which forbid teaching Torah to women. However, he notes that our eyes see that women are in fact able to learn complicated subjects quite well. The original assumption that most women are not capable of learning Torah in a serious way is problematic, when we see how well women today are able to study many complex subjects on a very high and serious level. Rabbi Halevi posits that in olden times when women received no formal education, teaching them Torah—which is so sublime and elevated—was problematic. Girls simply did not receive the intellectual training to be able to handle the study of Torah in a proper fashion. However, since contemporary girls do receive general education, the situation is different. Therefore, those girls who are able to handle general topics may also be taught Torah, including the Oral Torah. Older girls, who have already shown their academic ability in studying other topics, may be taught the Oral Torah, which is a source of life for all who engage in it.

RESPONSIBILITY OF TEACHING TORAH

Since Torah education is a primary value of halakhah, the question arises whether Torah teachers have the right to go on strike if they are not satisfied with their remuneration. Rabbi Feinstein takes a dim view of such action. When asked whether a teacher was allowed to come to class late, arguing that since he was paid in such an unsatisfactory manner he was free to shorten the time of his instruction, Rabbi Feinstein rejected his claim (*Yoreh De'ah* 1:138). Indeed, a teacher of Torah is not allowed to waste even one minute of precious time that could be given to Torah education. In another case (*Yoreh De'ah* 3:74), Rabbi Feinstein deals specifically with the question of a strike of Torah teachers who have not been paid on time. He rules that, in essence, a strike by Torah teachers is forbidden except in the most extreme circumstances, where the teachers are so worried about their income that they are unable to concentrate on their teaching. It would be a rare circumstance when a strike by Torah teachers would be halakhically justified. (See also *Hoshen Mishpat* 2:59.)

Rabbi Halevi (3:23) approaches the question from a different perspective. He argues that the ultimate responsibility of teaching children Torah does not rest on teachers, but on parents. The Torah places the obligation on parents; if they are not able to teach their children, then they may appoint teachers as their agents to do the actual teaching. Therefore, if Torah teachers are dissatisfied with their remuneration, they may decide to stop working as the agents of the parents. In

that case, the responsibility reverts back to the parents themselves. Thus, if there is *bittul Torah* caused by a strike of teachers, then the responsibility is solely on the shoulders of the
parents, and not on the teachers. If the parents are anxious
that their children not lose time that should be devoted to
studying Torah, then let the parents take off work and teach
their own children. If they want the teachers to do this work,
then they must pay a satisfactory wage. This position is discussed and elaborated in another responsum (5:23).

CALLING NON-OBSERVANT JEWS TO THE TORAH

There are halakhic sources which would forbid calling non-
observant Jews to the Torah. Since they desecrate Shabbat or
otherwise break the laws of the Torah publicly, they have forfeited their right to the honor of being called to the Torah during prayer services.

Rabbi Feinstein (*Orah Hayyim* 3:12) explains that the blessing
of *koferim,* those who deny the faith, is no blessing and therefore one should not respond with "Amen" afterwards. This
refers only to those who actually reject faith in God; but if a
person transgresses the laws of the Torah, even the laws of
Shabbat, without considering himself a heretic, then his blessing is valid and may be answered with "Amen." Therefore, one
should not call to the Torah anyone who is a *kofer,* even if he
had been raised that way by his wicked parents. Since he does
not believe in the sanctity of the Torah, his blessing is not valid
and he should not be permitted to read from the Torah. Yet, if
he believes in God and His Torah, though he commits transgressions, he may be called to the Torah. The authorities,
though, should do as much as possible to diminish the opportunity for such people to be called. It would be preferable to
arrange things so that only observant Jews would be called. In
another responsum (*Orah Hayyim* 2:73), Rabbi Feinstein rules
on a case of a boy born of a Jewish mother who was married to
a non-Jewish man. May this young man be called to the Torah

on the day of his Bar Mitzvah? Rabbi Feinstein responds that even though the child is certainly Jewish according to hala-khah, since his mother continues to live in her wickedness, we should do all that we can not to call the boy to the Torah on his Bar Mitzvah and not to allow any celebration in the syna-gogue. Likewise, it would be well not to accept him as a stu-dent in the Talmud Torah. These measures are *migdar milta*— preventive measures to discourage others from following the mother's bad example. Once the mother separates from her non-Jewish husband, then the boy may be accepted into the Talmud Torah and may be called to the Torah and have a Bar Mitzvah celebration. If there is a definite expectation that accepting the boy into the Talmud Torah would create a bad influence on other children, then the boy is forbidden to be accepted in the school by law, not just because of *migdar milta*.

Rabbi Halevi (3:16) deals with a case of a Bar Mitzvah boy and his guests who came to the synagogue on Shabbat morn-ing in a car. Since they all have violated Shabbat publicly, may the boy and his guests be called to the Torah? Rabbi Halevi notes that we live in a time when, unfortunately, the majority of our people do not observe the commandments. We should not push them away; on the contrary, it is incumbent upon us to bring them closer, to speak pleasantly to them, to show them the beauty of the ways of the Torah and commandments. Although in this case we clearly know that the boy and his guests have violated the Shabbat in public, "in our generation, an orphan generation, it is proper to be lenient in such a case; and it is our obligation to bring closer, not to push away. And the good God will forgive." Similarly, in another responsum (5:1) Rabbi Halevi rules that a Jew who violates Shabbat may be counted as part of a *minyan,* even though there are halakhic sources which would oppose this view. "It is obligatory upon us to find a way to be lenient." Our situation today is very dif-ferent from the situation in which the halakhah was first stated—when all Jews were observant of Shabbat. In those days, if a Jew transgressed the Shabbat in public, that was his way of showing disdain for the Torah. Today, however, even people who consider themselves "good Jews" transgress Shabbat laws without even being aware of the implications of such transgressions. Although it would be preferable to have a *minyan* of properly observant Jews, a transgressor of Shabbat may be counted for a *minyan* if necessary.

THE RELIGIOUS SIGNIFICANCE OF ISRAEL

Rabbis Feinstein and Halevi differ significantly in their understanding of the religious significance of Israel. On the question of whether *aliyah* is a positive commandment incumbent upon us, Rabbi Feinstein rules that it is a mitzvah—but not an obligatory mitzvah. That is to say, if one lives in Israel, then he is fulfilling a mitzvah; but there is no special mitzvah in our time for someone living outside of Israel to go to settle in Israel (*Even ha-Ezer* 1:102). In contrast, Rabbi Halevi rules that it is quite obvious that a person who is able to make *aliyah* and has no serious obstacle which prevents him from doing so transgresses each day for living outside of Israel, for not fulfilling an obligatory positive commandment. He states that there is a mitzvah to settle in Israel in our own time, just as this mitzvah was operative in the past. Furthermore, in our time it is clear that the land of Israel is a center of Torah study and is an excellent place to raise children in the ways of Torah. There is no place in the world where it is easier to fulfill the Torah than in Israel. One with vision will understand that there is no spiritual future for Jews except in the land of Israel.

Rabbi Feinstein refers to those Zionists who established the Israeli state, most of whom were not religious, as being *resha'im* (*Orah Hayyim* 1:46). Rabbi Halevi (1:3) recognizes that many of the founders of the modern state of Israel were not observant of Torah; nevertheless, they played a vital role in the revival of the Jewish people. Many of the Torah-observant people of the last century were not receptive to working for and establishing a Jewish state. The Divine Providence called on the non-religious Jews to lead the way towards the redemption of Israel. Although they viewed themselves as nationalists, in fact they were tools in the hand of the Divine Providence which was moving the people of Israel to redemption. Rabbi Halevi's attitude thus ascribes a positive role to founders of Israel, even though many were not observant of Torah.

Rabbi Halevi writes at length and with great enthusiasm about the sanctity of Israel, and that the state of Israel represents the *athalta de-ge'ulah*, beginning of redemption (1:3). With the national revival of Israel, he believes that we should cut down on the chanting of elegies and dirges on the fast day of the 9th of Av. Although we must continue to observe the day in remembrance of past destructions and in awareness that complete redemption is not here, we should still make some indication in our observance that we are in the process of redemption. We should not continue the same pattern that existed prior to the establishment of the state of Israel (4:34).

Rabbi Halevi rules that we should emend the *Nahem* prayer, recited at Minhah of the 9th of Av. That prayer refers to Jerusalem as a city "destroyed, humiliated, and desolate without its children." The fact is that this description is no longer accurate. Jerusalem—while not fully restored—is not destroyed, nor humiliated, nor desolate of its children. How can we recite these words in our prayers to God when the words themselves are not true? He suggests that the text be emended to read that God should have compassion on the mourners of Zion and Jerusalem, the city which *was* destroyed, humiliated and desolate without its children. She *sat* with her head covered, etc. By placing the description in the past tense, we avoid speaking lies in our prayers to God. Rabbi Halevi was criticized for this emendation, but he responded forcefully and convincingly (2:36–39).

CONVERSION

There is a diversity of opinion among halakhic authorities on questions relating to conversion to Judaism. Rabbi Feinstein's responsa reflect considerable unhappiness with the contemporary situation. Since the majority of candidates for conversion are motivated by the desire to marry a Jewish partner, they are not usually committed to observing halakhah completely. He explicitly states that he does not approve of conversion for the sake of marriage, and even though he does not prohibit this practice, he expresses strong disapproval (*Yoreh De'ah* 1:159). In another responsum, Rabbi Feinstein discusses the case of a convert who did not observe the commandments after his conversion. Even if he had stated at the time of the conversion that he was going to accept the commandments, it is clear that he never intended to do so. Rabbi Feinstein states that a convert who did not accept the commandments is certainly not considered a convert at all, even *post facto* (*bedi'avad*) (*Yoreh De'ah* 1:157; see also *Yoreh De'ah* 3:106; *Even ha-Ezer* 1:27, 4:16).

Rabbi Halevi deals with the question of receiving converts in two important responsa (1:23 and 3:29). He reviews the halakhic literature on the topic and concludes that the halakhah of conversion is left to the discretion of the individual judges in each case. The Torah neither gave a commandment to convert non-Jews, nor did it give a commandment to reject converts. The rabbis of each generation and in each situation were given the obligation of deciding whether to be lenient or strict in matters of conversion. The Torah wished that the mitzvah of accepting converts should always be considered as a *hora'at sha'ah* (a spontaneous ruling, based on individual circumstances) with each judge deciding for himself whether to accept converts or not, depending on the specific conditions of his time and place. "Rabbinic courts which are lenient in conversion as well as those which are strict—all of them intend their actions for the sake of Heaven and work according to their pure understanding and conscience." Thus, Rabbi Halevi places the responsibility on the rabbis who accept converts to determine the sincerity of the desire to fulfill the commandments. There are public considerations as well as private considerations to be evaluated by the rabbis of the *bet din*.

CONCLUSION

In considering various responsa of Rabbi Moshe Feinstein and Rabbi Hayyim David Halevi, we have seen differences in attitude and in halakhic rulings. Since the purpose of this article was not to go through all the proofs and reasonings of these *posekim*, readers should not rely on this essay for actual *pesak*; rather, they should study the sources themselves. Moreover, there are many areas which have not been discussed in this article and which deserve study: e.g., questions of medical ethics and attitudes on halakhic methodology. By studying the responsa of two great *posekim*, representatives of different halakhic traditions, we can gain a deeper appreciation of the vitality and strength of halakhah. We may broaden our horizons of halakhic inquiry. We may find models of halakhic authority which can teach us, inspire us and guide us.

10

A DISCUSSION OF THE NATURE OF JEW-ISHNESS IN THE TEACHINGS OF RABBI KOOK AND RABBI UZIEL

*W*hen addressing a halakhic question, each *posek* (halakhic decisor) attempts to arrive at a decision which is objectively true. He will study and analyze the available halakhic literature, with the goal of understanding the halakhah as clearly and accurately as possible.

Yet, halakhic literature is characterized by a variety of decisions regarding the same questions. Different *posekim* arrive at different conclusions—even though they generally rely on the same source literature. Sometimes these differences are based on alternate readings or interpretations of the source texts. Or, one *posek* may attribute greater authority to certain halakhists, while another may prefer to depend on others. Differences in local conditions, halakhic traditions, educational backgrounds—these and many other factors may also result in different decisions from different *posekim*. So may differences in hashkafah (religious world-view).

The interrelationship of hashkafah and halakhah may be illustrated in how two recent *posekim*—Rabbi Avraham Yitzhak Kook and Rabbi Bentzion Meir Hai Uziel—dealt with issues involving the understanding of the nature of Jewishness.

A Lecture given at the Spanish and Portuguese Synagogue of New York City, Spring, 1993.

Rabbi Kook (1865–1935) was born in Latvia and studied at the yeshivah of Volozhin. In 1904, he migrated to Israel, where he became the Chief Rabbi of Jaffa. In 1919 he was appointed Ashkenazic Chief Rabbi of Jerusalem and in 1921 he became the first Ashkenazic Chief Rabbi of Eretz Yisrael. Rabbi Uziel (1880–1953) was born in Jerusalem and studied under the Torah scholars of the city, including his own father, Rabbi Yosef Raphael Uziel, who was the Av Bet Din (chief justice) of the Sephardic community. In 1911, Rabbi Uziel became Chief Rabbi of Jaffa, where he worked closely with Rabbi Kook. In 1921 he became Chief Rabbi of Salonika; in 1923 he returned to Israel to serve as Chief Rabbi of Tel Aviv; and in 1939 he became Rishon le-Tzion, the Sephardic Chief Rabbi of Eretz Yisrael.

Both Rabbi Kook and Rabbi Uziel were strong advocates of religious Zionism. They were outstanding communal leaders, teachers, and scholars. Both were prolific writers who left major contributions in the fields of halakhah and hashkafah.

Yet, despite these external similarities, their attitudes towards several crucial issues are radically different. Their disparate understandings of the nature of Jewish peoplehood are manifested in a number of their halakhic decisions.

CONVERSION

Let us begin with a discussion of how they dealt with the question of conversion to Judaism. How does a non-Jew enter the Jewish fold? What is the nature of the Jewishness which the convert accepts?

Rabbi Kook and Rabbi Uziel had before them the same talmudic and rabbinic sources. That their rulings were diametrically opposed to each other reflects their different hashkafot, their different understanding of the nature of Jewish peoplehood.

Both dealt with the serious problem of what to do with individuals who requested conversion to Judaism, even when it was believed that the converts were not likely to observe all the mitzvot. For the most part, such converts were interested in *gerut* (conversion) for the sake of marrying a Jewish person, and were not motivated by theological concerns. Obviously, neither Rabbi Kook nor Rabbi Uziel thought that such converts represented the ideal. On the contrary, everyone would agree that it was preferable for converts to choose to join the Jewish people from a belief in the truth of Judaism and a total commitment to observe the mitzvot. However, a great many converts do not come with these ideal credentials.

Rabbi Kook was adamant in his opposition to accepting converts who did not accept to observe all the mitzvot. Even if a convert followed the technical procedure for conversion, but lacked the absolute intention to observe the mitzvot, his conversion is not valid. When the Talmud states (Yevamot 24b) that *kulam gerim hem* ("they are all converts"; this passage refers to individuals who converted for the sake of marriage or because of other external factors), this refers only to those who *did* have the intention to accept the mitzvot. Rabbis who receive for conversion those candidates who come for worldly reasons, but who will not fulfill the mitzvot, are making an error. Much evil will befall such rabbis. They are guilty of bringing thorns into the house of Israel.

Rabbi Kook argues that rabbis who accept such converts are transgressing the prohibition of *lifnei ivver* (placing a stumbling block in the path of a blind person; by extension, this prohibition includes acts of misleading others). If the conversions are not halakhically valid, then the rabbis are misleading the Jewish public by calling such individuals Jews when in fact they are not Jewish. Such negligence will lead to many problems, including possible intermarriage. On the other hand, if these individuals are to be considered valid converts, then the rabbis are misleading them by not stressing how they will be subject to punishment for violating the mitzvot.[1]

In another responsum, Rabbi Kook again emphasizes that converts who do not commit themselves to keep the mitzvot should not be accepted. If unqualified individuals (*hedyotot*) accepted them, no rabbi should perform weddings for them even after they have been converted in this way. "And happy is the one who stands in the breach to guard the purity of Israel, may a good blessing come to him."[2]

For Rabbi Kook, then, the acceptance of mitzvot is the essential ingredient in Jewishness. One who does not accept mitzvot simply cannot become part of the Jewish people, even if he or she were to go through the technical rituals of conversion. And even if one were to find halakhic justification to validate such conversions, we still should not allow such converts to marry full Jews.

Rabbi Uziel also wrote a number of responsa dealing with would-be converts whose commitment to observance of mitzvot was deficient. While acknowledging that it was most desirable that converts accept all the mitzvot, Rabbi Uziel noted that in our times many individuals seek conversion for the sake of marriage. Instead of disqualifying such conversions, however, Rabbi Uziel actually encouraged them. He felt that it was necessary for us to be stringent in matters of intermarriage, i.e., we should do everything possible to prevent a situation where a marriage involves a Jew and a non-Jew. If we can convert the non-Jewish partner to Judaism, then we have preserved the wholeness of that family for the Jewish people, and we can hope that their children will be raised as Jews. Given the choice of having an intermarried couple or performing such a conversion, Rabbi Uziel ruled that it is better to perform the conversion. He, of course, believed that rabbis should do everything in their power to break off the projected intermarriage. They should resort to conversion only when it is clear that the couple would not be dissuaded.[3]

In another responsum, Rabbi Uziel explains that the obligation of rabbis is to inform candidates for conversion of *some*, not all, of the mitzvot (*Yoreh De'ah* 268:2). It is impossible for a *bet din* to know with certainty that any convert will keep all the mitzvot. Conversion, even initially, does not require that the

convert accept to observe all the mitzvot. Indeed, the procedure of informing a non-Jew about the basic beliefs and mitzvot is required initially. But if this procedure were not
followed, and the non-Jew was converted ritually (circumcision and ritual immersion) without such information, the conversion is valid notwithstanding (*Yoreh De'ah* 268:2, 12).

Rabbi Uziel concludes that it is permissible—and even a
mitzvah—to accept such converts, even when it is expected
that they would not observe all the mitzvot. Our hope is that
they will come to observe the mitzvot at some future point in
time. We are obligated to give them this opportunity. If they
fail to observe the mitzvot, the iniquity is on their own shoulders, not ours. Rabbi Uziel rejects the argument that since a
vast majority of converts do not observe the mitzvot, we should
not accept converts at all. On the contrary, he argues that it is a
mitzvah to accept these converts. We are obligated not only to
do these conversions to prevent intermarriage, but we have a
special responsibility to the children who will be born of these
marriages. Since they are of Jewish stock, even if only one parent is Jewish, they should be reclaimed for our people. Rabbi
Uziel writes:

> And I fear that if we push them [the children] away com-
> pletely by not accepting their parents for conversion, we
> shall be brought to judgement and they shall say to us: "You
> did not bring back those who were driven away, and those
> who were lost you did not seek" (Yehezkel 34:4).[4]

Whereas Rabbi Kook saw the acceptance of mitzvot as the
sine qua non of entering the Jewish fold, Rabbi Uziel thought it
was not an absolute requirement at all. Whereas Rabbi Kook
believed that the mitzvot are the defining feature of the Jewish
people, Rabbi Uziel stressed the importance of maintaining
the wholeness of the Jewish people, even when the observance
of mitzvot was deficient. The halakhic difference between
them can be apprehended on a deeper level if we consider
their difference in hashkafah.

The act of conversion, according to Rabbi Kook, requires the convert to join the soul of *Kenesset Yisra'el* (a metaphysical representation of the "congregation of Israel"). This can be accomplished only via total acceptance of the mitzvot, which are the essence of the Jewish soul. Rabbi Kook sees *Kenesset Yisra'el* as the highest spiritual manifestation of human existence. He propounds a notion found in kabbalah that there is an essential difference between Jews and non-Jews. Rabbi Kook writes:

> The difference between the Jewish soul, its self, its inner desires, aspirations, character and status, and that of all nations, at all their levels, is greater and deeper than the difference between the human soul and the animal soul; between the latter there is merely a quantitative distinction, but between the former an essential qualitative distinction pertains.[5]

Each Jew is connected spiritually to *Kenesset Yisra'el* through the fulfillment of mitzvot and the ethical demands of Torah. The choice nourishment of the Jewish soul "is the study of Torah in all its aspects, which also includes historical study in its fullness, and the observance of the commandments with deep faith illuminated by the light of knowledge and clear awareness."[6]

In stressing the distinctiveness of the Jewish people and its essential difference from all other nations, Rabbi Kook appears to downplay the ethical universalism implicit in the classic Jewish teaching that human beings were created in the image of God. Instead of focusing on the universal spiritual dignity of all people, Rabbi Kook asserts a radical distinction between Israel and the nations.

On the other hand, Rabbi Kook did recognize the existence of select individuals among the nations who can reach great spiritual heights. Whereas the supreme holiness specific to Israel is not shared by the nations, it is possible for individual non-Jews to imbue themselves with the holiness of Torah and to join the people of Israel.[7]

Rabbi Kook's hashkafah, thus, plays itself out in the halakhic issue of conversion. For him, a non-Jew needs to undergo a transformation of his soul in order to become part of *Kenesset Yisra'el*. Conversion is not just a matter of following a set of prescribed rules and guidelines; rather, it is an all-encompassing spiritual transformation, possible only for a select few spiritually gifted individuals.

Rabbi Kook's hashkafah is imbued with mystical elements. Given his understanding of the nature of the Jewish soul, it follows that he takes an elitist position vis-à-vis accepting converts. Only those who are truly qualified spiritually may enter the fold of Israel. To accept converts who are not absolutely committed to mitzvah observance is, for Rabbi Kook, a travesty.

Rabbi Uziel, too, stressed the distinctiveness of the people of Israel. Indeed, his hashkafah is close to Rabbi Kook's in that he also saw the people of Israel as the ideal model of humanity, embodying the highest form of harmony and spiritual unity.[8]

Although Rabbi Uziel recognized the distinctiveness of the people of Israel, he did not make the same sharp distinction between Jews and non-Jews as did Rabbi Kook. Rather, Rabbi Uziel stressed the connection between Jews and non-Jews, and the responsibility of Jews to set a good example from which the non-Jewish world can learn.

Rabbi Uziel was critical of those Jews who taught that one's Jewishness should be a private matter observed in the home, and who said that one should be a "human being" when in public. He rejected such a notion as being absurd, "since Judaism and humanity are connected and attached to each other like a flame and its coal." The goal of Judaism is to have all Jews be the finest possible human beings so that they could influence humanity for the better. Judaism was not a private matter, but was for application in the world at large.[9]

Rabbi Uziel also rejects the position of those who claimed that Judaism was merely a faith. Clearly, the people of Israel constitute a nation with a distinctive national character. Neither the Torah nor our sages ever divorced Jewish faith from Jewish peoplehood.[10]

Rabbi Uziel rejects the notion that Judaism could survive only if Jews isolated themselves from the rest of society. Those who limited Jewish life to synagogues and study halls thereby were constricting the real message of Judaism. Rabbi Uziel argues that the Torah was quite capable of confronting all cultures and all peoples, without needing to surrender or hide. A living culture has no fear of borrowing and integrating concepts from other cultures, and it can do so without losing its own identity. Jews can learn from the non-Jewish world and still remain faithful to their own distinctive mission of holiness and righteousness. Moreover, as a living culture, Judaism has a message to teach others as well. To constrict Judaism into a spiritual and intellectual ghetto is not true to the mission of Israel. The Torah contains within it a full world-view on the individual and the nation; therefore it is our obligation to recognize and teach our spiritual ideal, and to try to increase our spiritual influence on humanity as a whole.[11]

For Rabbi Uziel, then, the distinctiveness of the Jewish people is not seen as a mystical concept which separates Jews ontologically from non-Jews. Rather, the Jewish people have a positive responsibility of reaching out to the non-Jewish world, to bring them closer to the religious ideals of Judaism.

This hashkafah manifests itself in a greater tolerance and openness when it comes to the halakhic question of conversion. Certainly, it would be best if all Jews and all converts to Judaism observed the mitzvot in full. But since we do not live in an ideal world, we need to strive to attain the best results possible. Our first concern has to be to maintain the integrity of the Jewish people, Jewish families. Non-Jews who wish to become part of the Jewish people are thereby testifying that they wish to come closer to our teachings and traditions. Since Jews and non-Jews are all created in the image of God, the conversion process does not entail an absolute spiritual transformation of the convert's soul, but rather a pragmatic deci-

sion to join the Jewish people and to come closer to the ideals
and teachings of the Torah. This hashkafah gives greater lee-
way to the rabbis who must make specific decisions regarding
conversion, based on the particular situation of each case. Universalism and pragmatism on behalf of the Jewish people,
rather than mystical and metaphysical considerations, should
guide the conversion process.

AUTOPSIES

The hashkafic difference between Rabbi Kook and Rabbi Uziel
concerning the nature of Jewishness also may be demonstrated in another halakhic area: autopsies. In 1931, Rabbi
Kook was asked whether it was permissible to perform autopsies as part of the training of doctors in medical schools. With
the expanding Jewish settlement in the land of Israel, there
certainly was a need to train Jewish doctors. Medical training
entailed autopsies.

Rabbi Kook ruled that disgracing a dead body (*nivul ha-met*)
is a prohibition unique to the Jewish people, since the
Almighty commanded us to maintain the holiness of the body.
He then went on to say that there is a sharp difference
between Jews and non-Jews with regard to their bodies. Non-
Jews consider their bodies *only* as biological structures. They
eat whatever they wish, without restriction. They have no reason to be concerned with the issue of disgracing the dead
body, so long as the autopsy was done for a reasonable purpose such as medical study. Rabbi Kook, therefore, recommended that the medical programs purchase non-Jewish
bodies for the purpose of scientific research. He then stated
that the whole category of disgrace of the dead body stems
from the fact that humans were created in the image of God.
But this image of God is manifested particularly in Jews due to
the holiness of the Torah.[12] The Jewish attachment to Torah
and mitzvot, thus, not only characterizes the Jewish soul, but
also imparts holiness to the Jewish body.

Rabbi Uziel wrote a lengthy responsum on the subject of autopsies, although he specified that his responsum was theoretical rather than a formal legal ruling (la-halakhah ve-lo le-ma'aseh). In reviewing the halakhic literature on nivul ha-met, Rabbi Uziel concluded that this category applies only when a dead body is treated disrespectfully. Autopsies performed in a respectful manner for the sake of medical knowledge do not constitute, according to Rabbi Uziel, nivul ha-met. He points out that there have been many rabbinical sages throughout Jewish history who were also medical doctors. They could not have learned their profession without having performed autopsies. Rabbi Uziel states that "in a situation of great benefit to everyone, where there is an issue of saving lives, we have not found any reason to prohibit [autopsies], and on the contrary, there are proofs to permit [them]."

Rabbi Uziel considers the question of whether it would be preferable to obtain non-Jewish bodies for the purpose of autopsies. His response is sharp and unequivocal:

> Certainly this should not even be said and more certainly should not be written, since the prohibition of nivul stems from the humiliation caused to all humans. That is to say, it is a humiliation to cause the body of a human—created in the image of God and graced with knowledge and understanding to master and rule over all creation—to be left disgraced and rotting in public.

There is no difference between Jews and non-Jews, in the sense that all are created in the image of God. The Jew has no claim to higher status in this regard. If one were to prohibit autopsies, then no autopsies could be performed on anybody—Jewish or non-Jewish. The result would be that no doctors could be trained, with a consequent result of an increase in illness, suffering and death.[13]

It is clear, then, that Rabbi Kook understood the nature of Jewishness in kabbalistic, metaphysical terms. For him, there is a definite and almost unbridgeable gap between the people of Israel and the non-Jewish nations. This hashkafah influenced his halakhic decisions in the areas of conversion and autopsy. On the other hand, Rabbi Uziel stressed the human quality of the Jewish people, the essential Godliness of all people. His generally universalistic outlook recognized the distinctiveness of the Jewish people. But the distinctiveness of Israel is manifested not by separating Jews absolutely from everyone else; rather, it is shown when Jews serve as models to draw others closer to the ideals of the Torah. This hashkafah pervades his discussions of conversion and autopsy.

It has not been our purpose to determine who is right or who is wrong or if both are right—*ellu ve-ellu divrei E-lokim hayyim* ("both positions are acceptable in the eyes of God"). Rather, it has been our purpose to illustrate the interrelationship of hashkafah and halakhah. The philosophy and worldview of a *posek* are not only reflected in his halakhic decisions: they help shape those halakhic decisions.

NOTES

1. *Da'at Kohen*, Jerusalem, 5745, no. 154.

2. *Ibid.*, no. 155.

3. *Mishpetei Uziel*, Jerusalem, 5724, no. 18.

4. *Ibid.*, no. 20. For a discussion of Rabbi Uziel's rulings on conversion, see my article, "Another Halakhic Approach to Conversions," *Tradition*, 12 (Winter–Spring 1972), 107–113. [Included in this volume, below, p. 124.]

5. *Orot*, Jerusalem, 5745, p. 156. See the article by Rabbi Yoel Ben-Nun, "Nationalism, Humanity and Kenesset Yisrael," in *The World of Rav Kook's Thought*, published by the Avi Chai Foundation, 1991, pp. 210 f.

6. *Orot*, p. 145; Rabbi Yoel Ben-Nun's article, p. 224.

7. Rabbi Yoel Ben-Nun's article, p. 227.

8. A series of articles by Nissim Yosha, under the title "Yahid ve-Umah," appeared in the journal *ba-Ma'arakhah*, nos. 300–306, dealing with Rabbi Uziel's understanding of Jewish peoplehood. See also my book, *Voices in Exile*, Ktav, 1991, pp. 202 f.

9. *Hegyonei Uziel*, vol. 2, Jerusalem, 5714, p. 122.

10. *Ibid.*

11. *Ibid.*, p. 125.
12. *Da'at Kohen*, no. 199.
13. *Piskei Uziel*, Jerusalem 5737, no. 32, especially pp. 178–179.

11

ANOTHER HALAKHIC APPROACH TO CONVERSIONS

*I*n considering issues relating to the conversion of non-Jews to Judaism, Orthodox Jews tend to defend a strict policy which we term *the* halakhic approach. Conversion for the sole purpose of marriage is highly discouraged. Conversion when the non-Jew does not intend to observe halakhah in full generally is considered to be no conversion at all. Rabbi Melech Schachter, in a fine article on conversion, states what most Orthodox Jews believe:

> Needless to say, conversion to Judaism without commitment to observance has no validity whatever, and the spuriously converted person remains in the eyes of halakhah a non-Jew as before.[1]

The purpose of this article is to present another Orthodox viewpoint on conversion. The traditional stringency is not the only halakhically valid approach available to us; on the contrary, this may be the proper time to rely on other halakhic opinions. No one will argue that conversion to Judaism for other than spiritual reasons is ideal. Certainly it should be discouraged. However, in terms of practical reality, we may have to be more tolerant of such conversions.

Raphael Hayyim Saban, then the Chief Rabbi of Istanbul, wrote to Rabbi Bentzion Meir Hai Uziel, the Rishon le-Tzion,

Originally published in *Tradition*, Winter–Spring 1972.

in 1943, asking if conversion for the sake of marriage is valid.[2] In his response, Rabbi Uziel opens with a quotation from the Shulhan Arukh (*Yoreh De'ah* 268:12) which states that we must examine a potential convert to determine if his motives for accepting Judaism are sincere. Certainly, the ideal is not to convert those who are insincere. Rabbi Uziel adds that since in our generation intermarriage is common in civil courts, we often are forced to convert the non-Jewish partner in order to free the couple from the prohibition of intermarriage. We also must do so in order to spare their children who otherwise would be lost from the Jewish fold.[3] If we are faced with a *de facto* mixed marriage we are permitted to convert the non-Jewish spouse and the children, when applicable. If this is true when the couple is already married, it is obviously true before they have begun a forbidden marriage relationship. The conversion could offset future transgressions and religious difficulties.

Rabbi Uziel bases his opinion on a responsum of Rambam.[4] The case before Rambam deals with a Jewish man who had a non-Jewish maid-servant. The man was suspected of having conducted himself immorally with his servant. Should the *bet din* have her removed from his house? In his answer, Rambam states categorically that according to the law the maid should be dismissed. After it learned of his wrongs, the *bet din* was obligated to exert all its power either to have the maid sent out or to have the Jewish master free her and then marry her. But there is a law stating that if one is suspected of having had immoral relations with his maid and then he freed her he may not marry her.[5] Rambam says that in spite of this ruling, he has judged in such cases that the man should set his maid free and then marry her. He justifies his decision by stating that it is necessary to make things easier for repentants (*takkanat ha-shavim*). He relies on the famous statement of our rabbis (Berakhot 9:5), "It is time to serve the Lord, go against your Torah" (Tehillim 119:126). Rambam closes this responsum with a significant, profoundly religious comment, "and the Lord in His mercy will forgive our transgressions."[6]

Rambam recognized that his decision was in violation of the ideal halakhah. However, he allowed his human insight to cope with the problem realistically, and he invoked other principles to justify himself. As a man of true reason and faith, he dealt with the situation sensibly while relying on God's mercy. God will understand the motivations for this halakhic decision and will either approve or forgive. In any case, what must be done will be done.

In support of Rambam's approach, Rabbi Uziel cites several talmudic sources which reflect the same attitude.[7] It is better to choose the lesser of two evils, even when the choice is not ideal. It is better to stop adding fuel to evil now, rather than to risk an increase of transgression.

Based on this attitude, Rabbi Uziel says that when an intermarried couple comes to a *bet din* seeking the conversion of the non-Jewish partner, we must allow such a conversion. We may not take the haughty position that these are wicked people who deserve to suffer the fate of transgressors.[8] On the contrary, by coming to halakhic authorities, the couple displays a desire to avoid transgression. They do not want to reject the Torah; they want to be included in the Jewish community.

As was stated earlier, if we are permitted to convert one who already is married to a Jewish mate, we certainly may convert one who wishes to marry a Jewish partner in the future. Even if we know that the main reason for the conversion is marriage, when all is said and done such a conversion is still halakhically valid.[9]

But Rabbi Uziel considers such conversions not only to be permissible, but actually morally required. Not only are rabbis allowed to convert a non-Jew for purposes of marriage, but they are urged not to step away from the positive responsibility to do so. In support of this idea, Rabbi Uziel refers to the strict chastisements of the prophet Malakhi against those who married out of the faith.

Yehudah has dealt treacherously, and an abomination is
committed in Israel and in Jerusalem; for Yehudah has pro-
faned the holiness of the Lord which He loves and has married the daughter of a strange god. May the Lord cut off to
the man that does this (Malakhi 2:11–12).

In view of the stringent prohibition of marrying a *bat el
nehar* (Gentile woman), Rabbi Uziel argues that it is better to
convert the non-Jewish partner so that the Jewish partner
could be spared from this severe transgression. Such conversion also is better for the children who would be born to the
couple, since they now would be considered as fully legal Jews.
Considering the alternatives of conversion or intermarriage,
Rabbi Uziel ruled in favor of conversion.

Rabbi Uziel, however, qualifies his opinion by stating that the
judges should do everything they can to break off the projected marriage and should resort to conversion only when it
is clear that the couple definitely will not be dissuaded. The
judges should direct their hearts to God when they perform
the conversion, and "the merciful God will forgive."

In 1951, Rabbi Uziel received a question from Yehudah
Leon Calfon, a rabbi in Tetuan. The problem involved was:
may we convert the non-Jewish wife and children of a Jewish
man when he is not observant and does not intend to have his
family be observant? If a Jew observes the mitzvot like the
average Jew of his time (*ki-stam Yehudim ba-zeman ha-zeh*) then
there would be no problem, since we could rely upon the
responsum of Rambam. But what about the Jew who does not
observe Shabbat, Yom Tov, kashrut, etc.? Shall we prohibit the
conversions or shall we say that since the Jew still wants to be
included in the Torah community—albeit to a limited extent—
we may convert his non-Jewish wife and children?[10]

Following a preliminary discussion, Rabbi Uziel comes to
grips with this serious problem. He refers to our standard procedure when a non-Jew comes to convert. We teach him the
principles of Judaism—the unity of God, the prohibition of
idol worship. We inform him of some of the easy and difficult

mitzvot, as well as some of the rewards and punishments. We
do *not* teach him everything. The Shakh comments that we do
not tell the would-be convert all the technicalities and stringencies because we might scare him away. If he is really sincere
about his wish to convert, it would be wrong to frighten him
out of his desire.[11]

From this standard procedure, we see that there is no
requirement to ask the non-Jew to observe the mitzvot. We do
not require his assurances that he will be an observant Jew. If
we did, we never could have any converts, because no *bet din*
can guarantee absolutely that the convert will keep all the
mitzvot. The reason we tell the non-Jew some of the mitzvot is
to give him an idea of what is involved in becoming an observant Jew. That way, he may have the option to change his
mind about conversion. If, however, he converts and does not
observe, he is considered as a Jew who transgresses.

Moreover, the procedure of informing the non-Jew about
basic beliefs and mitzvot is required initially. However, if we
did not follow the procedure and we converted the non-Jew
anyway (with circumcision and ritual immersion), the conversion is valid notwithstanding.[12]

Rabbi Uziel remarks that if a non-Jew gives us no indication
that he expects to observe the mitzvot, we still may convert
him even initially.[13] Not only is it permitted to accept converts
on this basis, but it is also a mitzvah upon us to do so. We, of
course, hope that they will observe and we should encourage
them to keep the mitzvot. But if they do not, they still are considered halakhically to be Jews.[14]

There is an argument that since the vast majority of converts
today do not observe the mitzvot even for a short time, we
should not accept converts at all. To this, Rabbi Uziel replies
that it is a mitzvah to accept converts.[15] Furthermore, it is dangerous to forbid conversion, since it will force the Jewish partners of inter-faith marriages either to convert to the other
religion or to maintain the improper relationship. Historically,
those who have been rejected from the people of Israel have

been our worst enemies. Finally, we also have an obligation to the children of these marriages. After all, they are of Jewish stock (*mi-zera Yisra'el*) even if their mother is not Jewish. They are lost sheep whom we must reclaim for our people.

In an emotional passage, Rabbi Uziel writes:

> And I fear that if we push them [the children] away completely by not accepting their parents for conversion, we shall be brought to judgment and they shall say to us: "You did not bring back those who were driven away, and those who were lost you did not seek" (Yehezkel 34:4).

This chastisement is far more severe than the chastisement of accepting converts who in all likelihood will not be observant Jews.[16]

From these responsa, it is clear that Rabbi Uziel offers a halakhic perspective which reflects a profoundly sympathetic and understanding spirit. Recognizing the practical realities of our world, it is essential that halakhic authorities courageously respond to the needs. Ours must not be a haughty and elite attitude towards would-be converts. We have a moral obligation to convert those who seek conversion, not only for their sake, but for the sakes of their children. Of course, we must make every effort to teach them the Torah and to encourage their adherence to the mitzvot. But in the final analysis, we must put our faith in human reason and compassion, and, certainly, we must put our faith in God (*ve-Hu Rahum yekhapper...*).

NOTES

1. *Jewish Life*, May–June, 1965, p. 7. See also p. 11, under the heading, "Commitment to Total Observance."

2. *Mishpetei Uziel*, Jerusalem, 1964, no. 18.

3. See Rabbi Schachter, *op. cit.*, p. 13.

4. *Pe'er ha-Dor*, Amsterdam, 1765, no. 132. See also *Mishpetei Uziel, op. cit.*, no. 21, where Rabbi Uziel also relies on this responsum of Rambam.

5. Yevamot 24b: If a man is suspected of [intercourse] . . . with a

heathen who subsequently became a proselyte, he must not marry
her. (If, however, he did marry her *they need not be separated*.)

6. "We have decided this way because of the desire to assist those
who wish to repent. . . . We have relied on the dictum of our sages
that there are (urgent) times when one must serve the Lord by
(seemingly) breaking the rules of the Torah. He may marry her. God
in His mercy will forgive our iniquities."

7. See Kiddushin 21b, Shabbat 31b.

8. Rabbi Uziel says that the concept of letting the wicked person
suffer the consequences of his deeds (Bava Kamma 69a) does not
apply here.

9. Yevamot 24b. The question is: is a person who converts for
ulterior motives a real convert? The conclusion is that he is. This ruling is cited in the codes. See, for example, Rambam, *Hilkhot Isurei
Bi'ah* 13:17; and the *Tur, Yoreh De'ah* 268.

10. *Mishpetei Uziel, op. cit.*, no. 20.

11. *Yoreh De'ah* 268, *se'if katan 5*.

12. See the Shakh, *se'if katan 3*.

13. "From all that has been stated, we have learned that the condition to keep the mitzvot is not a *sine qua non* for conversion, even initially." See the *Shulhan Arukh, Yoreh De'ah* 268:2, 12.

14. "From all that has been stated and discussed, the ruling follows
that it is permissible and a commandment to accept male and female
converts even if it is known to us that they will not observe all the
mitzvot, because in the end, they will come to fulfill them. We are
commanded to make this kind of opening for them; and if they do
not fulfill the mitzvot they will bear their own iniquities, and we are
innocent."

15. Yevamot 109b, Tosafot, s.v. "*ra'ah*."

16. For other of Rabbi Uziel's responsa on conversion, see *Mishpetei
Uziel, op. cit.*, no. 22; *Mishpetei Uziel*, vol. 1, *Yoreh De'ah*, no. 14; *Mishpetei Uziel*, vol. 2, *Even ha-Ezer*, no. 25.

12

A FRESH LOOK AT CONVERSION

Gerut, conversion to Judaism, is one of the most controversial issues confronting us. Judaism always has welcomed sincere converts who wished to become part of the Jewish people and religion and who willingly accepted the responsibility of observing the commandments. However, in our times, many (perhaps most) candidates for conversion are not motivated by an objective love and commitment to Judaism. Rather, they are non-Jews who wish to marry a Jewish partner, or who are already married to a Jew and now wish to convert for the sake of their children. All too often, the candidates for conversion are not seriously interested in accepting the observance of all mitzvot, and may even so indicate. Sometimes it is clear to the rabbis involved that the would-be convert will not be an observant Jew in the immediate future. The question arises: May a halakhically valid conversion be performed when the motivation is sociological rather than theological, when there is doubt whether the convert will observe the mitzvot?

Rabbinic opinion has varied widely concerning such conversions. Rabbi Avraham Yitzhak Kook insisted that only converts who will be fully observant of the mitzvot should be accepted. If we see that a convert does not observe our religious laws and that the conversion was undertaken for ulterior motives, the conversion is not really proper (*en zo gerut gemurah*). Moreover, those individuals who accept such a convert are blame-

Originally published in *Midstream*, October 1983.

worthy. In one case, Rabbi Kook ruled that a non-Jewish woman who converts to Judaism for the sake of marriage and clearly has no religious dedication to Judaism remains a non-Jew. The conversion ritual was meaningless. "And happy is the one who stands in the breach to guard the purity of Israel, may a good blessing come to him."

On the other hand, Rabbi Bentzion Uziel argued that not only may we accept such converts, but indeed it is a mitzvah to accept them if we believe that this would help create a Jewish home. Even if we know that the convert will not be fully observant, we should perform the conversion in order to prevent intermarriage or loss of children from the Jewish fold.

Between these two positions, there is a wide variety of intermediate opinion, some tending one way, some the other. Since this topic is concerned with the very definition of Jewishness, it has evoked deep emotional reactions. This is not a debate on an abstract point of Jewish law; it touches the source of Jewish identity and existence.

In contemporary Jewish life, the term *giyyur ka-halakhah*, conversion according to Jewish law, has become something of a battle cry. From an Orthodox point of view, any conversion which is not done in accordance with traditional Jewish law is an attack on the integrity of the Jewish people. Conversions performed by non-Orthodox rabbis, or even by Orthodox rabbis who are not experts in *gerut*, generally are regarded as being invalid. On the other hand, non-Orthodox spokesmen claim that the Orthodox should have no monopoly in determining who is really a Jew, who is an "acceptable" convert. They believe there is more than one way to apply the halakhah or that traditional halakhic guidelines are no longer applicable.

Debates on this topic have frightening implications. On a practical level, many conversions are being performed not in accordance with traditional halakhah, and these converts marry Jews and have children. Yet in the eyes of halakhah they are not Jews at all. Thus, we find that a growing number of people who identify as Jews are not considered halakhically to be Jews. There is great confusion concerning which convert is "really" Jewish and which is not; we are in the process of dividing the Jewish people into two (at least) different peoples, and marriage between members of the two groups might be halakhically difficult or even impossible. The Jewish people cannot tolerate this situation. On a theoretical level, there are sharp differences of opinion concerning what makes a person Jewish. It is a sad thing when Jews cannot agree even on so fundamental a definition.

What is needed now is a fresh look at the primary sources dealing with conversion. Perhaps if we can understand the sources, we will gain a new perspective on *gerut* and find an answer to the practical and theoretical problems raised above. We must begin at the beginning—with a definition of what makes a person Jewish.

The peoplehood of Israel is tied inextricably to the religion of Israel. Our distinctiveness derives from our Divinely revealed tradition. If it were not for the Torah and commandments, we would have no *raison d'etre*, no hope for ultimate messianic redemption. One cannot read the Bible without recognizing the centrality of religion in our life as a people. This article should be read with this observation in mind.

Going back to the Bible, we find no specific mention of a formal procedure for conversion. Various non-Israelites had attached themselves to the people of Israel, e.g. the mixed multitude who joined the Exodus from Egypt. Many laws are stated in the Torah on behalf of the *ger*, the non-Israelite stranger who lived among the Israelites in the land of the Israelites, but the biblical term *ger* does not seem to mean a full-fledged convert in the modern sense. In II Melakhim 17:32–33 and in Esther 8:17 we find additional references to groups who in some way attached themselves to the people of Israel, but no clear statement describing a conversion procedure.

134   Seeking Good, Speaking Peace

The classic biblical example of a "righteous convert" is Ruth. She tells her Jewish mother-in-law: "Wherever you go, I shall go; and where you lodge I shall lodge. Your people will be my people and your God will be my God" (Ruth 1:17). Ruth has served as a prototype of the ideal convert, one who accepts the Jewish people and religion sincerely and completely. Yet there is no description of Ruth preparing for conversion through study, or telling a *bet din* that she will observe the mitzvot, or immersing in a mikvah. The details of the conversion process are omitted from the text.

Yehezkel Kaufmann has described biblical conversion as *giyyur ha-artzi ha-tarbuti*, a non-Israelite's acculturation in the dominant Israelite culture. Non-Israelites living in Israel would become absorbed by the national culture, accepting various social and religious mores in the course of time. Essentially, this was an "ethnic" conversion, in which religion played a part. Kaufmann's observation seems fair. Even going back to the case of Ruth, we note that she first identified with the Israelite people and only then with the Israelite God.

Who was an Israelite in biblical times? Anyone who was born into an Israelite family, or anyone who attached himself to the people of Israel and became naturalized. The main factor was *am Yisra'el*, the nation or people of Israel. The strictly religious dimension of conversion did not yet exist.

Kaufmann asserts that after the Israelites were expelled from their land and lost their national center, a new type of *gerut* came into being—*giyyur ha-berit*, a conversion based exclusively on religion. A non-Jew now had to convert to Judaism, not to the culture and people of Israel. In biblical times, the stranger in the land of Israel gradually adopted Israelite patterns of life; in post-exile times, the stranger could retain his own language and live in his own land and still convert to Judaism. Religion replaced land and nationality as the definition of an Israelite.

Yet, I believe that if we consider the talmudic sources dealing with conversion, we shall find that Kaufmann errs. The religion of Israel never replaced the people of Israel as the main element of self-definition. Even in talmudic times, conversion was seen primarily as an act of joining the Jewish people, becoming part of the Jewish national destiny. A procedure was delineated for the conversion process, and the religious dimension was stressed; but in the final analysis, peoplehood was more critical than religion alone.

There are two major talmudic sources on this subject which bear examination.

I. Yevamot 47a–b

Our Rabbis taught: If at the present time a person desires to become a proselyte, he is to be addressed as follows: "Why do you come to become a proselyte? Do you not know that Israel at the present time is persecuted and oppressed, despised, harassed, and overcome by afflictions?" If he replies, "I know and yet am unworthy," he is accepted forthwith, and is given instruction in some of the minor and some of the major commandments. . . . He is also told of the punishment for transgression of the commandments. . . . And as he is informed of the punishment for the transgression of the commandments, so is he informed of the reward granted for their fulfillment. . . . He is not however to be persuaded or dissuaded too much. If he accepted, he is circumcised forthwith. . . . As soon as he is healed, arrangements are made for his immediate ablution. . . . When he comes up after his ablution he is deemed to be an Israelite in all respects.

In the case of a woman proselyte, women make her sit in the water up to her neck, while two [three] learned men stand outside and give her instruction in some of the minor commandments and some of the major ones.

This passage is noteworthy for several reasons. First, we see that our initial comments to a would-be convert relate to the difficulties of being a member of the Jewish people. We must ascertain that he is willing to share the burdens of our people, to share sincerely in our destiny. Only after we are satisfied on this score do we instruct him "in some of the minor and some of the major commandments." Even when we do give this instruction, it is far from comprehensive, i.e. it does not include all the mitzvot, only some of them.

Moreover, we are not supposed to persuade or dissuade too much; rather, we should point out the good and the bad aspects and let the prospective convert judge for himself if conversion is the right choice for him. If he accepts the responsibilities, then he follows the conversion procedure and is accepted as a complete Israelite.

In considering this source, Rabbi Uziel concludes that it is apparent that we do not ask the candidate for conversion to fulfill the mitzvot, and that it is not even necessary for the *bet din* to know that he will fulfill them. The reason for informing him of some of the commandments is simply to give him a chance to change his mind before it is too late. As long as the candidate has a general awareness of our mitzvot, the decision to convert is his.

This source indicates, then, that we are concerned about the convert's becoming a member of our people. One might argue that if a non-Jew agreed to observe all our religious commandments but refused to identify as a member of our people, we would reject his conversion. Accepting Judaism is not identical with becoming Jewish.

We can analyze this point from a different perspective. A person born of a Jewish mother is regarded halakhically as a Jew. He may be completely unobservant of our commandments, or an atheist; yet Jewish law always regards him as Jewish. If we think of being Jewish solely in terms of adhering to Judaism, this law is absurd; something else is involved, namely, peoplehood. A person born of a Jewish mother is biologically part of our people, regardless of his personal feelings or behavior. By being born Jewish, one is linked to our people by destiny and never may be written off completely. (A parent who disowns a child, or vice versa, does not sever the biological relationship. The relationship is fixed and eternal.) Being

Jewish means being part of the Jewish people. Judaism is the religion of our people; it is not the definition of our Jewishness.

II. Yevamot 24b

Mishnah: If a man is suspected of [intercourse] . . . with a heathen who subsequently became a proselyte, he must not marry her. If, however, he did marry her they need not be separated.

Gemara: This implies that she may become a proper proselyte. But against this a contradiction is raised. Both a man who became a proselyte for the sake of a woman and a woman who became a proselyte for the sake of a man . . . are no proper proselytes. These are the words of R. Nehemiah, for R. Nehemiah used to say: Neither lion-proselytes nor dream proselytes nor the proselytes of Mordekhai and Esther are proper proselytes unless they become converted as at the present time. . . . Surely concerning this it was stated that R. Yitzhak b. Shemuel b. Martha said in the name of Rav: the halakhah is in accordance with the opinion of him who maintained that they are all proper proselytes.

Here, the Talmud is concerned with people who convert for ulterior motives—marriage, fear, dreams, etc. Rabbi Nehemiah argues that such conversions are not valid. But his opinion is rejected. The conclusion and the accepted law is that such conversions are indeed valid.

What is the basis of this discussion? Rabbi Nehemiah thinks that individuals who do not convert for idealistic, theological, and philosophical reasons are to be rejected. This opinion makes good sense if we view the conversion process as one in which the non-Jew's primary decision is to accept Judaism. If he wants to be Jewish for practical considerations, but does not genuinely have a belief in and commitment to Judaism, then the conversion process is a sham, an empty ceremonial.

But Rabbi Nehemiah's opinion is rejected. One who converts with ulterior motives *is* a valid convert. The law can be understood only if we assume that conversion means becoming part of the Jewish people, and that if a non-Jew chooses to join our ranks he may do so—even if he is not accepting Judaism from theological convictions. A non-Jew who wants to marry someone Jewish and to raise Jewish children has opted to become part of our people, even though the commitment to our religion may be less than perfect.

Another talmudic passage points in the same direction. Rav and Shemuel (Shabbat 68a) speak of a proselyte who became converted among the Gentiles and who did not even know fundamental laws of Shabbat. Rabbi Moshe Feinstein noted that such a conversion is valid even if the convert still is far removed from observing the mitzvot. This proselyte identified with the Jewish people, although his knowledge of Judaism was quite deficient.

In fact, there is no talmudic legal source that would indicate unequivocally that acceptance of all commandments is a prerequisite for conversion.[1] The central concern of talmudic as well as biblical times is the proselyte's commitment to the Jewish people.

What does it mean to become part of the Jewish people? How can we measure the commitment of a would-be convert to our people? If a non-Jew donates money to the UJA or in some other way demonstrates a tie to us, is this adequate to make the person Jewish?

Obviously, more than a token or casual commitment to our people is required. To think otherwise is to degrade our people and our history. It is not possible to codify exact guidelines as to what does or does not constitute a genuine commitment to the people of Israel. The final decision in this matter is really left to the rabbis who are involved in each case. Each candidate for conversion has his or her own dynamics, and must be evaluated individually.

Some cases, though, clearly seem to be acceptable. A non-Jewish spouse of a Russian Jew who sacrificed much to migrate to Israel and to join our people is one example. A non-Jewish partner in marriage who wishes to convert in order to raise his or her children with a Jewish identity is another. Where it can be determined that the non-Jew is sincerely dedicated to sharing our destiny, carrying our burdens, and participating in our communal life, there is a good basis for conversion. Certainly, we must make every effort to inform candidates for conversion of the beliefs and principles of Judaism, of our mitzvot and customs. These are basic factors in the lives of our people.

In returning to our classic sources in Bible and Talmud, we have arrived at an old but novel understanding of Jewishness. By stressing this view, we can hope to deal more successfully with the contemporary disputes about *gerut*. Certainly, much rabbinic literature has been generated since talmudic times, and the earlier concept of conversion has been blurred in the process. It is all the more important, then, to go back to our primary sources and to look at them objectively.

We can defuse the *giyyur ka-halakhah* issue. The fact is that the talmudic halakhic sources are far more open to receiving proselytes to the Jewish people than some who argue strenuously in the name of halakhah may want to admit. There certainly is ample support to perform conversions for the sake of marriage if the convert has a genuine commitment to the Jewish people—identifying as a Jew, raising children as Jews, settling in Israel, etc. It would be desirable for rabbis of all the movements to agree to the establishment of halakhically valid religious courts to deal with conversions.

It will not be easy for the Orthodox and the non-Orthodox to come to an agreement on this issue. There is a great deal of pride at stake. But if we do not come to an agreement we will cause the Jewish people to be divided. This is a prospect which should terrify all of us. It can be avoided. After examining the original sources which define what makes a Jew, we must conclude that Jewishness is more than the Jewish religion alone. All who sincerely want to join us should be welcome. All who want to divide us will have to answer to God.

NOTES

1. The often-quoted passage in Bekhorot 30b does *not* indicate that a convert who rejects a single commandment is no convert. Seen in context, the passage might mean that we may not approve of such a convert, but he is a convert notwithstanding. Likewise, a priest or Levite might be disqualified from service, but not be deprived of his status as a priest or Levite. For a fuller discussion of this text see my article, "Understanding and Misunderstanding Talmudic Sources," *Judaism* (Fall, 1977), 441–42.

Or, it may mean that if the would-be convert specifically *rejects* a mitzvah, then the conversion cannot be performed. But if the candidate for conversion does not deny a mitzvah—even if he may not intend to observe it—then the conversion may be performed.

13

THE RCA HEALTH CARE PROXY: PROVIDING RESPONSIBLE HALAKHIC LEADERSHIP TO OUR COMMUNITY

WHAT IS A HEALTH CARE PROXY?

A person, Heaven forbid, may become critically ill and be physically or mentally incapable of responding to doctors' questions concerning continued treatment. Who then will have the right to make these life and death decisions? If an individual has prepared a health care proxy form, the person named in that form as his proxy would be empowered to make these decisions. If an individual has not designated a proxy, the medical staff will decide.

Obviously, a Jew who wishes such decisions to be made in consonance with halakhah should appoint a trusted person to be his or her health care proxy and should prepare the necessary health care proxy form. Federal law now requires health care providers to inform patients of their right to a health care proxy.

Religious Jews should utilize this right to assure that their treatment will conform to halakhic standards.

The Rabbinical Council of America has issued a health care proxy form, prepared by Rabbi Dr. Moshe Tendler, Chairman of the RCA's Medical Ethics Commission. Members of the RCA have received a copy of the health care proxy, as well as mate-

Originally published in *Jewish Action* 52, no. 2 (Spring 1992).

rial relating to the medical and halakhic issues involved. A Yom Iyyun was held on November 21, 1991, which included presentations by Rabbi Tendler and two world-renowned medical experts—Dr. Dominick Purpura, Dean of the Albert Einstein Medical College of Yeshiva University and Professor of Neurology; and Dr. Fred Plum, head of the Department of Neurology of the New York Hospital and Cornell University Medical College. (A videotape of the conference is available from the RCA office.) The RCA has taken the responsible position of responding to a pressing communal need, providing vital information to the rabbis of the RCA so that they might guide their congregants wisely.

THE BRAIN-STEM DEATH ISSUE

A significant feature of the RCA health care proxy form is that it accepts brain-stem death as the definition of death.

This definition allows for the possibility of transplants of vital organs. Organs may, with the proper permission and safeguards, be taken from brain-stem dead individuals and transplanted to save the lives of others.

When the brain-stem dies, a fact that can be determined with absolute certainty by means of various tests, a person no longer can breathe independently—the brain-stem controls respiration, as well as other vital life processes. Brain-stem death includes respiration death and is irreversible.

At the RCA Yom Iyyun, Dr. Purpura and Dr. Plum both indicated that the brain-stem death definition today is accepted universally in the medical world. It is policy in all fifty states of the United States. It is defined specifically and can be determined with complete accuracy.

Dr. Purpura, in his lecture to the RCA, pointed out the historical background relating to brain-stem death. Ancient teachers thought that life was centered in the heart and that the brain was useless. By the mid-seventeenth century, researchers discovered that the brain controlled various aspects of the body. During the past several centuries, it has become clear that the brain is the center of life, that it controls all aspects of the living organism. Modern research has demonstrated how each part of the brain controls specific functions, with the brain-stem controlling respiration and other vital functions.

The brain simply cannot be equated with other vital organs. It is unique. Our brain defines who we are.

WHAT BRAIN-STEM DEATH IS NOT

Much of the confusion surrounding the brain-stem definition of death derives from the popular, unscientific use of the phrase "brain death." If a person is in a deep coma, if his upper brain is not functioning, if he is in a persistent vegetative state—he is *not* brain dead. Death occurs only with the death of the brain-stem, not with the non-functioning of the upper brain.

THE HALAKHIC BASIS

The brain-stem definition of death was accepted by the Chief Rabbinate in Israel after thorough discussions with halakhic and medical authorities. The text of the Chief Rabbinate's decision was published in *Tehumin* in 5746 (1986) and in English translation in *Tradition*, Summer, 1989. Based on this decision of the Chief Rabbis, organ transplants do take place in Israel under halakhic supervision. Rabbi Shaul Yisraeli, in evaluating the issues involved, concluded that the decision of the Chief Rabbinate was sound and that the arguments of opponents were halakhically unfounded (*Barkai*, Spring 5747, pp. 32–41).

Rabbi Moshe Feinstein already had accepted the brain-stem definition of death in a responsum dated 5736 (1976). He ruled that when a patient showed no signs of life—e.g. no movement or response to stimuli—then the total cessation of independent respiration is an absolute proof that death has occurred (*Iggerot Moshe, Yoreh De'ah*, 3:132). If a person cannot breathe any longer due to brain-stem death, then a respirator attached to the person is merely pumping air into a dead body. Even if the heart continues to beat, the person is deemed to be dead. Indeed, after death, it is possible for individual organs to move spasmodically. Rambam, in his commentary on Mishnah Aholot 1:6, discusses the case of decapitation, and notes that *pirkhus*, movement of limbs after death, is not to be construed as a sign of life. Rabbi Moshe Tendler has referred to brain-stem death as "physiological decapitation." With the death of the brain-stem, the control center of breathing and other vital functions has been cut off totally and irreversibly.

In a letter dated May 24, 1976, Rabbi Moshe Feinstein wrote to Assemblyman Herbert J. Miller, Chairman of the New York State Assembly Committee on Health. Rabbi Feinstein stated clearly, "The sole criterion of death is the total cessation of spontaneous respiration . . . the total cessation of independent respiration is an absolute proof that death has occurred."

Opponents of the brain-stem death definition have attempted to confuse the public as to Rabbi Feinstein's position. Although they are free to disagree with Rabbi Feinstein's *pesak*, it is unconscionable that they should try to misrepresent his clear and consistent view, i.e. that brain-stem death is the true definition of death. Rabbi Mordechai Halperin (*Assia*, December 1989) researched the issue carefully and concluded that the evidence was clear that Rabbi Feinstein definitely accepted the brain-stem death definition. This position was confirmed by Dr. Ira Greifer of the Albert Einstein Medical College, who had spent several days discussing the issue in great detail with Rabbi Feinstein. Rabbi Feinstein's acceptance of the brain-stem death definition also was confirmed by others who had discussed the question with him. In short, the RCA health care proxy is corroborated by the authoritative decisions of Rabbi Moshe Feinstein and the Chief Rabbinate of Israel. It is based on the very best scientific knowledge available.

SOME IMPLICATIONS

Those who reject the brain-stem death definition consider it murder to remove vital organs from a person who is brain-stem dead, but whose heart is still beating. The implication of this position is that organ transplantation is forbidden. A doctor would not be allowed to remove vital organs from the brain-stem dead body; nor would it be ethical for a patient to benefit from an organ which had been the result of "murder." I asked a rabbi of my acquaintance who opposes the brain-stem definition of death what he would rule if a Jewish doctor asked him whether he could remove the heart of a brain-stem dead body to save the life of another person. The rabbi answered: "Let the doctor rely on Rabbi Tendler!" When I pressed the matter, insisting that he give the *pesak* and not defer to others, he refused to do so. In other words, he publicly went on record opposing the RCA position; and yet, privately, if confronted with a life and death situation he would rely on the RCA position.

Rabbi Mordekhai Eliyahu, in a recent discussion with the RCA, told us that a number of rabbis who publicly oppose the Chief Rabbinate's ruling, nevertheless send their friends and relatives to receive organ transplants—organs which can be taken only from a brain-stem dead body. Several leading rabbis from Israel recently issued a brief statement opposing the brain-stem death definition. We have politely requested a responsum, fully argued and reasoned, so that we might study the basis of their *pesak*. No reply has been forthcoming to date.

Unfortunately, the brain-stem death issue has become a matter of public controversy and confusion. Since life and death decisions hinge on this matter, it is imperative that the public have lucid and accurate information. People may choose to follow the RCA's decision—based on the finest halakhic and scientific authority—or they may choose to reject it. There are serious arguments in opposition to the RCA's position, but everyone should understand what the case for the RCA is and should not misrepresent its position.

People should not intellectualize and abstract the issue; rather, they should see it in personal terms. If a loved one, Heaven forbid, needed an organ transplant in order to live, would you rely on the RCA decision to allow transplants from brain-stem dead bodies? Or would you let the loved one die? Or would you choose the morally repugnant position of allowing the transplant even though you believed that halakhically it entailed murder?

The RCA position is not only well-founded on halakhic and scientific authority. It also is humane, responsible and compassionate. It is a demonstration of responsible halakhic and moral leadership to our community.

14

RELIGIOUS ZIONISM
AND THE NON-ORTHODOX

*O*rthodoxy views itself as the embodiment of the authentic Jewish tradition. Orthodoxy maintains the historic faith in the divinity of the Written and Oral Torah. It governs itself by its commitment to halakhah. The chain of religious tradition begun by Moshe Rabbenu has continued from generation to generation, unbroken, to our own time. It has withstood many pressures from within and without the Jewish people—and Orthodoxy has always maintained itself with strength and courage.

Indeed, it is only the Orthodox who live strictly according to halakhah as reflected in the Talmud, codes of Jewish law, and responsa. An Orthodox Jew can study the vast halakhic literature spanning centuries and emerging from many different parts of the world—and yet feel completely at home in this literature. The basic beliefs, concerns and observances of the pre-modern Jewish world reflect the universal Orthodox faith in the Divine origin of the Torah and halakhah. Non-observant and non-believing Jews were peripheral to the religious heart and soul of the Jewish people.

With the rise of enlightenment and emancipation in Europe, however, the classic Jewish organic connection with Torah and halakhah began to erode. Not only did individual Jews turn

Originally published in *Religious Zionism after 40 Years of Statehood*, ed. Shubert Spero and Yitzchak Pessin (Jerusalem, 1989).

away from tradition, but new "movements" were founded to give modern Jews alternatives to classic Jewish belief and practice. The Orthodox continued to view themselves as heir to the tradition begun by Moshe Rabbenu. The non-Orthodox, however, denied the Divine origin of the Torah and rejected or greatly modified accepted halakhah. The organic connection of the Jewish people with Moshe Rabbenu was in fact being broken, with only the Orthodox maintaining faithful allegiance.

As difficult and painful as was this rift within the body and soul of the Jewish people, Jews still felt that they shared a common peoplehood. All Jews, observant or not, could claim descent from Avraham Avinu. By viewing Avraham as "our father," Jews recognized that they were part of the same family. Even when family members disagree with each other, they do not sever their biological relationship. A Jew, even if he transgresses, is still a Jew. Because of the general perception that all Jews relate back to Avraham Avinu, even Jews with differing religious beliefs and observances had the possibility of a shared language.

A problem which has arisen in recent years is that the Reform movement is now undermining its relationship to Avraham Avinu. The decision on patrilineal descent as well as the performance of large numbers of non-halakhic conversions are resulting in the creation of many people who think they are Jewish, but who are not halakhically part of the family of Avraham Avinu. By assaulting the classic understanding of Jewish peoplehood, they are in the process of breaking their links with Avraham Avinu, after having already broken their links with Moshe Rabbenu. This is a troubling and ominous development, one which seriously wounds the Jewish organism.

Non-Orthodox movements have, until fairly recently, been a development within Diaspora communities. With the growing pressure to import these movements into Israel, it is necessary for religious Zionism to contemplate seriously its relationships with the non-Orthodox Jewish community.

THE GENERAL HALAKHIC STATUS OF THE NON-OBSERVANT

It is a well-known axiom that "a Jew, even if he sins, remains a Jew." But it is also a well-known principle that a Jew who practices idolatry or something analogous (i.e. desecration of Shabbat in public), is subject to the law of *moridin ve-en ma'alin*. (See Rambam, *Hilkhot Teshuvah* 3:8; *Shehitah* 4:14; *Rotze'ah* 4:10; *Avodat Kokhavim* 2:2. See also *Shulhan Arukh, Yoreh De'ah* 158:2). The *Shulhan Arukh* (*Hoshen Mishpat* 34:22) rules that informers, heretics and apostates are considered to be of lesser status than outright idolaters.

A Jew who practices idolatry, or who willfully rejects even one mitzvah, or who desecrates Shabbat in public—such a person has subjected himself to serious halakhic consequences. He is disqualified as a witness; he may not serve as a *shohet*; his wine may not be drunk; he may not be counted in a *minyan*. The *Peri Megadim* (328:47:6) rules that one may not violate Shabbat in order to save the life of such a Jew. The *Mishnah Berurah* (329:9) states that it is not permissible to break Shabbat to save the life of a person who spitefully violates a mitzvah (*mumar le-hakhis*).

The strict adherence to these restrictive and punitive measures might have been practicable in communities where almost everyone was observant of halakhah. In such communities, one who willfully and scornfully deviated from communal norms was subject to communal sanctions. He had willingly and knowingly forfeited his status within the halakhic Jewish community.

Yet, in modern times, a sizeable majority of Jews are not observant. It is the halakhic community which is a distinct minority. Many *posekim* have found halakhic basis for distinguishing between the *apikorsim* and *resha'im* of previous times, and the non-observant Jews of their own days. In the case of one who violates Shabbat in public, for example, distinctions can be made between one who does so spitefully (*le-hakhis*) or who does it for convenience (*le-te'avon*). The latter may be treated more leniently. (See, for example, the responsa of Maharam Shik O.H. 140; and *Tzitz Eliezer* vol. 8, 15:5.) A number of *posekim* have ruled that violators of Shabbat today may fall into the category of *tinok she-nishbah*, since they never learned or truly understood the sanctity of Shabbat. (*Aseh Lekha Rav*, 5:1; *Melammed le-Ho'il*, 1:29; *Binyan Tzion ha-Hadashot*, no. 23.) Rabbi Eliezer Waldenberg suggests that in our generation, many individuals who in the past might have fitted into the category of *koferim* (heretics) no longer should be so designated. Since they are used to their beliefs and practices, and since so many others are like them, their hearts deceive them into thinking that they are behaving properly. Thus, they are not willful violators of Torah; they commit transgressions through error (*Tzitz Eliezer* vol. 9, 41:15).

Rambam (*Hilkhot Mamrim* 3:3) long ago had codified the classic halakhic response to Jews who rejected halakhah. Although those who violated Jewish belief and practice were to suffer the halakhic consequences of their behavior, the children and grandchildren of such individuals were not to be held culpable in the same sense. In speaking of the Karaites, Rambam writes:

> But the children of these erring ones, and their grandchildren, whose parents pushed them into their beliefs, since they were born and raised among the Karaites according to their beliefs—such children are as captive babies among them. They are not anxious to follow the way of the mitzvot since they are "compelled." Even if afterwards one learned of his Jewishness and saw Jews observing their religion, he nevertheless is considered to have been compelled, since he was raised according to their error. . . . Therefore it is fitting to bring them back in repentance and to draw them closer with words of peace until they return to the bastion of the Torah.

According to this position, even though the Karaites know-ingly transgress the halakhah, they are not considered to be sinning willfully—since they do not realize that they are sin-ning at all. This principle applies not only to Karaites, but to all Jews who have been raised outside the halakhic tradition and who do not realize that they are violating halakhah (see Rabbi Avraham Sherman, *Tehumin*, vol. 2, pp. 267–271).

The Hazon Ish (*Yoreh De'ah*, 13:16) argued that the law of *moridin* does not apply to our generation, but only to genera-tions which were blessed with miracles, voices from Heaven, and whose righteous leaders were recognized to have special Divine Providence. But in our time, the law of *moridin*, if it were applied, would do more harm than good. It is our obliga-tion to do our best to bring back the transgressors to Torah—with an attitude of love.

It is clear, then, that there is substantial halakhic authority and guidance which fosters tolerance towards non-observant and non-believing Jews in our time. The spirit of *Ahavat Yis-ra'el* as epitomized by such spiritual giants as Rabbi Avraham Yitzhak Kook and Rabbi Bentzion Uziel, should be the domi-nating element in the attitude of religious Zionism towards the non-observant. Our posture should not be confrontational nor hostile nor condescending.

NON-ORTHODOX MOVEMENTS

The above discussion relates to non-observant and non-believ-ing Jews as individuals. Many of them do not follow halakhah because they were not raised or educated properly, or because they have erred in their judgement. The obligation of the halakhic community, therefore, is to bring such people closer to Torah and halakhah. This relates to the overwhelming majority of Jews in Israel who are not observant of halakhah in the Orthodox sense.

The problem may be different, though, regarding non-Orthodox movements. Whereas individuals may deviate from halakhah through ignorance or carelessness, non-Orthodox movements formally and officially—and willfully—have rejected basic beliefs and procedures of halakhah. Non-Orthodox movements have denied *Torah min ha-Shamayim;* they have rejected the binding authority of halakhah; they have instituted practices which are contrary to halakhah. Whereas we can be lenient with individuals who have strayed from halakhah, can we be equally lenient towards Jews who have institutionalized their rejection of halakhah?

Rabbi Eliezer Waldenberg (*Tzitz Eliezer,* 5:1) has argued that the Reform movement is much more dangerous to Orthodoxy than is the existence of individual deviationists. Since Reformers have made formal organizations and call their leaders "rabbis," they have presented themselves as a legitimate alternative to halakhic Judaism. Rabbi Waldenberg indicated that the Reform movement leads people away from authentic study and observance by claiming that it itself represents the true Judaism.

Many halakhic authorities responded strongly and violently against the Reform movement. Hatam Sofer (6:89) wrote that if he had the power, he would separate Reform Jews from the halakhic Jewish community. He would not allow intermarriages with them. He wished they could be isolated as other heretical sects were isolated in the past. (See also the responsa of Maharam Shik, O.H. 304, 305, 306, 309.) Rabbi Moshe Feinstein is highly critical of the Reform and Conservative movements, and considers them to be antithetical to Torah Judaism. (See, for example, *Iggerot Moshe* Y.D. 1:139, 149, 160, 174; Y.D. 2:100; O.H. 2:40, 46, 50; E.H. 3:3, 23; O.H. 3:30.) Rabbi Waldenberg concludes that the Reform movement has no connection with our religion and our faith, and is based on the egocentric needs of people. He calls for an all-out spiritual battle against Reform.

At the Israel conference of the Rabbinical Council of America (July, 1987), the Chief Rabbis of Israel and of Jerusalem issued battle cries against the introduction of the Reform movement in particular, and non-Orthodox movements in general, into Israeli society. Dealing with individual Jews who are not observant is one thing; dealing with non-Orthodox movements which give official legitimacy to deviation from halakhah is quite another thing.

Rabbi Walter Wurzburger (*Tradition*, Summer, 1986, pp. 33–40) discusses the arguments for and against cooperation with non-Orthodox Jews and movements. He points out that

> the advocates of continued membership in these umbrella organizations (which include representatives of non-Orthodox movements) claim that cooperation on matters of common concern has nothing to do with legitimation of the non-halakhic ideologies. In a pluralistic society, we must build coalitions with all kinds of groups espousing all types of belief in order to obtain various objectives of common interest.

He writes further that "the risk that participation in interdenominational groups may be misconstrued as legitimation of non-halakhic Judaism is negligible when compared with the dire consequences of a move that would entail the loss of many opportunities to expose American Jewry to Torah perspectives." Rabbi Wurzburger, however, is describing the situation in the United States, where the overwhelming majority of Jews are not Orthodox, and where the non-Orthodox movements are well-established and well-organized. Would this same logic apply to the situation in the State of Israel, where non-Orthodox movements are still relatively small? The "official" Orthodox attitude, as reflected in the words of the Chief Rabbis, is to oppose the spread of non-Orthodox movements, to use political means to limit them as much as possible, to eschew official contact with their representatives.

Another possible Orthodox approach would be to deal with representatives of non-Orthodox movements the same way we would deal with individual non-Orthodox Jews. Such relationships could be characterized by tolerance, love, and a genuine desire to bring the non-Orthodox individuals into a closer relationship with Torah Judaism. A strong and confident religious Zionism need not fear individuals identified with non-Orthodox movements; on the contrary, there should be a real sense of challenge and opportunity to win people back to traditional Torah belief and observance. This possibility is far more real in Israel than in the Diaspora. Indeed, the *ba'al teshuvah* phenomenon in Israel should provide Orthodoxy with a greater sense of confidence and security. This brings us to a basic problem: the problem within Orthodoxy itself.

ORTHODOXY: CONFIDENT OR FRIGHTENED?

In *Shir ha-Shirim* (2:15), we read: "Take us the foxes, the little foxes, that spoil the vineyards; for our vineyards are in blossom." Rabbi Moshe Almosnino, a leading rabbi in Salonika in the generation following the expulsion of Jews from Spain, comments on this verse in his book, *Yedei Moshe*. He suggests that the foxes represent wicked Jews who prevent other Jews from following the ways of repentance. They destroy the vineyard of the Lord, i.e., Israel. These little foxes are able to be successful because Israel itself is spiritually weak. The vineyard of Israel is blossoming, but not fully developed. Since Israel is vulnerable, the foxes can cause great damage. But if Israel were spiritually strong and confident, these little foxes would pose no threat.

The fact is that when the religious organism of Israel is strong and confident, it can withstand problems generated by individuals who have broken from the traditional ways. Such individuals might be viewed as nuisances, but not as dangers to the religious integrity of Israel. On the other hand, when Israel is weak spiritually, even little foxes are extremely dangerous and can ruin the vineyard.

The general spiritual condition of the Jewish people, from the Orthodox point of view, is certainly very weak at the present time. Large numbers of Jews are not observant of halakhah, and do not lead their lives according to Torah. The

"vineyard" of halakhic Jewry is threatened, and the non-observant Jews, especially when participating in non-Orthodox
movements, are a clear threat to the halakhic way of life. Non-
halakhic individuals and movements influence Jews away from
halakhah; they attempt to give legitimacy to Jewish life outside
the halakhic framework. When Orthodoxy feels itself strong
and dominant, it can see the non-Orthodox as people who are
our brothers and sisters, who need to be brought back with
love to the Torah fold. They do not frighten us, but distress us;
they are not our enemies, but are fellow children of Avraham,
Yitzhak, and Yaakov. But when Orthodoxy feels threatened,
then the non-Orthodox appear to be spiritual enemies against
whom we must protect ourselves, and even battle when necessary. The greater the degree of fear, the more Orthodoxy will
build walls between itself and the non-Orthodox; the greater
the degree of confidence, the more open Orthodoxy will be to
the non-Orthodox.

The Haredim, whose voices are heard so clearly in the political and religious life in Israel (and in the *golah*), reflect the
attitude of fearing the non-Orthodox. Their public demonstrations, their desire to isolate themselves within their own
neighborhoods, their vehement opposition to the non-Orthodox movements—all indicate their feeling of being at war.
Sometimes, they feel that they are under siege. At other times,
when they feel they can fight back successfully, they wage battle with their "enemies." They have little patience with those
who call for tolerance, dialogue, or a serious consideration of
the concerns of the non-Orthodox.

Indeed, even fully Orthodox individuals who appear more
conciliatory and tolerant are rebuffed by the extremist element within Orthodoxy. One of the truly great rabbis and
sages in Israel, an outspoken *posek* whose decisions have
appeared too "liberal" to the Haredim, told me privately that
he has been prevented from speaking at many yeshivot in
Israel. Other public forums have also been denied him. "Have
you heard of the Mafia? Well, we have a religious and spiritual

Mafia in power today." He told me this with a deep sense of sadness, and without any real hope that the situation would change in the near future.

Netziv (*Meshiv Davar*, 1:44) discusses how extremism can stifle thought, and how it can lead to great inner turmoil for the Jewish people. He points out that during the days of the second Temple, the Jews were divided between Pharisees and Sadducees. The situation was so bad, that if a Jew did even the slightest thing differently from the dominant Pharisee practice, he was called a Sadducee, was ostracized, and was subject to the law of *moridin*. Netziv writes that

> it is not difficult to imagine reaching this situation in our time, Heaven forbid, that if one of the faithful thinks that a certain person does not follow his way in the service of God, then he will judge him as a heretic. He will distance himself from him. People will pursue one another with seeming justification (*be-heter dimyon*), Heaven forbid, and the people of God will be destroyed, Heaven forfend.

Netziv's words are as applicable in our time as they were when he first stated them. Orthodox extremism has led to attacks and ostracism against those fully Orthodox people who have not adhered strictly to the extremists' position. The voice of moderate Orthodoxy is being stifled by extremists.

It is no secret that the image of Orthodoxy in Israel and the *golah* is being molded inordinately by the Haredim, rather than by moderate religious Zionists. Orthodoxy is viewed as being coercive; extreme; medieval. The preachments and actions of Orthodox extremists—which dominate news coverage of the Orthodox in Israel—do not portray the way of the Torah as *darkhei no'am* ("paths of pleasantness"). When Rabbi Elazar said in the name of Rabbi Haninah that *talmidei hakhamim* increase peace in the world, one wonders how to apply that statement to the contemporary situation. The "secular" backlash is an indication of the hostility which has been generated against Torah—by exactly those people who claim to represent it.

A major challenge to religious Zionism is to reestablish the image of Torah in the spirit of *derakheha darkhei no'am;* to highlight the teachings of such Torah luminaries as Rabbi Kook and Rabbi Uziel; to support those Torah scholars and sages within Israeli society whose views reflect the beauty, dignity and *hesed* of Torah. Orthodoxy has the ability to deal with non-Orthodox individuals and movements with confidence, courage, and *ahavat Yisra'el.*

ISRAEL AND THE *GOLAH*: DIFFERENT REALITIES

The emergence and development of non-Orthodox movements is a phenomenon of the *golah.* In particular, it reflects a crisis in Jewish religious life during the last century in Europe, and later in North America. If it were not for cultural, social and intellectual pressures of the non-Jewish world, it is unlikely that Jews would have developed non-Orthodox ideologies and movements. The need was felt among some Jews to modernize and Westernize Judaism in order to make it more compatible with the non-Jewish European and American societies. Although we cannot agree with their decisions, we can sympathize with their dilemma. They wanted to be accepted within the non-Jewish society, and they were attracted to that society; they were ashamed of elements within traditional Judaism which appeared to be old-fashioned and unenlightened.

That these non-Orthodox movements flourished in the European and American Diaspora is a fact of history. But these movements are not indigenous, organic developments from within Judaism. Rather, they began as reactions to the non-Jewish society.

In contrast to the European and American experience, the Sephardic communities in Muslim lands did not develop non-Orthodox movements. Indeed, attempts to divide Sephardic communities on ideological lines are antithetical to the Sephardic religious sensibility. There were, to be sure, individ-

ual Sephardim who were not fully observant of halakhah and/
or had their doubts about the premises of traditional faith.
Nevertheless, Sephardic communities maintained reverence
for tradition. Even when the societies in which they lived
began to Westernize, and more Sephardim moved away from
traditional observance—even then there was no attempt to
organize non-Orthodox movements or to establish non-Orthodox synagogues.

Whereas denominationalism within Judaism is a creation of
European Jewry, the majority of the Jewish population in
Israel is composed of Jews of African and Asian backgrounds.
With the advent of the State of Israel, Jewish communities in
Muslim lands migrated to Eretz Yisrael in great numbers.
Instead of being accepted and appreciated for what they were,
these Jews—for reasons beyond the scope of this article—were
seen and treated as a Jewish underclass in Israeli society. The
non-religious Zionist movements in Israel sought to "modernize" them by stripping them of their religious traditions and by
discrediting the authority of their religious and family leaders.
On the other extreme, Ashkenazic religious zealots sought to
turn these Asian and African Jews into European-style Hasidim and Haredim. Each political and religious movement saw
in the newly arrived Sephardim potential members for their
own causes. Instead of trying to understand and accept them,
these groups practiced a form of cultural colonialism.

How ironic it is to see in Israel rabbis of Moroccan,
Yemenite, Turkish, Iraqi, etc., backgrounds dressed in long
black coats and black hats, in the style of East European rabbis.
I have asked a number of Sephardic rabbis why they dress like
Ashkenazim, and they all have replied to the effect that if they
did not dress in that style, they would not be accepted as real
talmidei hakhamim. The rabbinic, yeshivah world is cast in an
Ashkenazic mold, and most Sephardim have been made to feel
that they must conform to the Ashkenazic guidelines. Historically, Sephardim have been moderate, tolerant and non-
extremist; if we now find Sephardim in Israel who do not fit

this description, it is largely because of the influence of the non-Sephardic religious society.

Now, some people want to introduce non-Orthodox movements into Israeli life. No doubt, they will attempt to attract Jews of African and Asian backgrounds to these movements, just as all the other European-oriented movements have tried to win them over. Yet, is it not morally irresponsible and reprehensible to try to draw people away from their own religious traditions?

The importation of non-Orthodox movements into Israel, therefore, is something which should be resented and repudiated by the vast majority of Israelis who are either Sephardic and/or Orthodox. These movements represent the fears and insecurities of Jews in the Diaspora communities in Europe and America.

THE SEPHARDIC COMPONENT

Religious Zionism in Israel would do well to foster Sephardic religious self-awakening. Sephardim should be encouraged to return to their own modes of religious learning and practice. Sephardic rabbis should be made to feel proud *not* to dress as though they are Ashkenazic rabbis. Sephardic yeshivot should be encouraged *not* to be clones of Ashkenazic yeshivot. Jews of African and Asian backgrounds should not only deepen their pride in their ethnic backgrounds; more importantly, they must deepen their connections with Sephardic intellectual, halakhic and spiritual tradition.

There is a tendency to refer to the groups of Israeli society as "religious" and "secular." Yet, the overwhelming number of Sephardim (who constitute the majority of the Jewish population of Israel) cannot properly be termed "secular." Even non-observant Sephardim often have a deep reverence and respect for tradition. It is among this group of Israeli Jews that religious Zionism should find kindred spirits.

Religious Zionism must remind Israelis in general, and Sephardic Israelis in particular, that non-Orthodox *golah* movements are alien to them. Whether individual Israelis are observant of halakhah or not, they should resent the introduction of ideological movements which preach and teach against halakhah and *Torah min ha-Shamayim*. Why does Israel need to import the divisive movements of the *golah*?

CONCLUSIONS

Religious Zionism in our time must deal sympathetically and intelligently with non-halakhic Jews. Great halakhic authorities have ruled that we should reach out to them with love. They are not our enemies, but our brothers and sisters.

In Israel, non-Orthodox movements are not presently a major factor in the religious life of the people. To the extent that they are established, religious Zionism need not fear them. Indeed, even in the confrontation with non-Orthodox movements in Israel, it would be desirable if the moderate Orthodox voice prevailed. The violent language and public demonstrations of the Haredim create negative backlash against Orthodoxy, and are of real benefit to the forces of the non-Orthodox movements. Whether there should be formal contacts between Orthodox groups and the non-Orthodox movements in Israel is a policy decision which must be left to the good judgement of the groups involved. If the non-Orthodox movements are small and weak, there may be no particular advantage in official associations with them. If they indeed grow to be a powerful force in Israeli life, then it would be foolish to ignore that reality.

Religious Zionists should reach out to Israeli society, stressing the *hesed* and gracefulness of Torah. It would be desirable for religious Zionism to dissociate itself from the actions and words of extremists which are, in fact, detrimental to engendering respect for Torah. The moderate and reasonable Orthodox Jews of Israel should in no way allow the Haredim the privilege of representing Orthodoxy to Israeli society and to the news media abroad.

It is possible to combat the spread of non-Orthodox movements in Israel not by head to head confrontation with them, but by making a case to Israeli society that it is not desirable to import Diaspora ideologies which developed due to Jewish weakness vis-à-vis the non-Jewish European and American societies. In particular, a special case must be made before the Sephardim of Israel, urging them to participate in the renaissance of their own traditions. It is a historical anomaly for a Sephardic Jew to be a Lubavitcher Hasid and it is also a historical anomaly for him to be identified with a non-Orthodox movement. Sephardim have their own traditions which are rich and vital, and which can provide for a strong and vibrant religious spiritual and emotional life.

Finally, our ultimate goal is to bring all Jews closer to Torah and halakhah. Ultimately, this goal must be achieved by winning their hearts and their minds, not by coercing them. Political and social coercion may seem successful in the short term; but in the long term, they generate frustration and resentment. We want people to observe the Torah because they want to observe the Torah. This may seem like a great dream: but religious Zionism has based itself on great dreams.

III
Sephardic History and Culture

15

ASPECTS OF THE SEPHARDIC SPIRIT

After centuries of material and spiritual flowering, the Jews of Spain and Portugal were driven into exile. The process began in 1391, when widespread anti-Jewish riots in Spain led to the death, forced conversion, or flight of thousands of Jews. It ended in 1492, when the Jews were expelled from Spain. In 1496–97, all manifestations of Jewish life were outlawed in Portugal as well. The expulsion of the Jews from the Iberian peninsula resulted in the growth of a far-flung, variegated Sephardic diaspora.

Large numbers of Sephardim found haven in the domains of the Ottoman empire. Others settled in Eretz Yisrael and elsewhere in the Middle East. North Africa also received an influx of Sephardic refugees. Thus, initially, the bulk of Sephardim came to live under Muslim rule.

Some Sephardic exiles sought safety in Western European cities, especially in Italy, but conditions for Jews in Christian countries generally were not as good as they were in Muslim lands.

By the end of the sixteenth century, however, Amsterdam had become a center for ex-*conversos* who now wished to return to the Jewish fold. Greater tolerance toward Jews became manifest in Western Europe, resulting in the emergence of Sephardic communities in such cities as Bordeaux,

Originally published in *The Sephardic Journey, 1492–1992* (New York: Yeshiva University Museum, 5752/1992).

Bayonne, Paris, Hamburg, and London. During the seventeenth century, some Western Sephardim came to the New World and settled in the European colonies of the Americas.

Thus scattered throughout the world, Sephardim were subjected to many diverse cultural, intellectual, linguistic, and political influences. Over the centuries, the various Sephardic communities developed their own particular characteristics. The rich diversity among the Sephardim is well known to students of Sephardic history. But despite all this diversity, certain common threads can be seen in the tapestry of the Sephardic diaspora—or at least through large segments of Sephardic Jewry.

HALAKHAH

Traditionally, Sephardic communities were governed by the halakhah. The generations following the expulsions from Spain and Portugal witnessed a veritable explosion of halakhic creativity in the Sephardic diaspora. This was the era of Rabbi Yosef Karo (1488–1575), compiler of the *Shulhan Arukh,* the standard Code of Jewish Law. It also produced responsa masters such as Radbaz (1479–1573), a native of Spain who became the official head of Egyptian Jewry, and Rabbi Shemuel ben Moshe de Medina of Salonika (1506–1589). Furthermore, this period saw the rise of authors and teachers such as Rabbi Yaakov Berav of Safed (ca. 1474–1541), who was born in Toledo and who later assumed roles of leadership in the Jewish communities of Eretz Yisrael, Egypt and Syria; Rabbi Levi ben Haviv (ca. 1483–1545), a native of Zamora, Spain, who came to Jerusalem by way of Portugal and Salonika; and Rabbi Yosef Taitatzak of Salonika (ca. 1487/88–1545) the son of exiles from Spain.

Professor H. J. Zimmels has commented that it was "amazing that soon after the expulsion in the year 1492, the contributions to the responsa literature by the rabbis who had come from Spain and settled in Turkey reached a height never witnessed before."[1]

Sephardic yeshivot followed the pattern of study developed in Spain, emphasizing practical halakhah. The goal was to arrive at proper halakhic conclusions rather than to engage in abstract intellectual discussions of the texts.[2]

Halakhic creativity has continued to manifest itself throughout the Sephardic world to this day. Thousands of manuscripts and published works, covering every aspect of halakhic literature, amply demonstrate commitment to Torah scholarship on the highest level.

Rabbi Hayyim Yosef David Azulai (Hida; 1724–1806), one of the great figures of eighteenth-century Jewish life, noted that in matters of halakhah, Sephardim inclined to the quality of *hesed,* compassion; they tended to be lenient, as opposed to Ashkenazim, who stressed *gevurah,* strength, and who therefore tended to greater strictness in the interpretation of the Law.[3] Regardless of whether this view corresponds to objective fact, it does reflect the self-image of many Sephardic sages; consequently, it has influenced their approach to halakhah.

In describing the religious life of the Jews of North Africa, the historian André Chouraqui noted that "the Judaism of the most conservative of the Maghreb's Jews was marked by a flexibility, a hospitality, a tolerance," a "touching generosity of spirit and a profound respect for meditation."[4] Rabbi Michael Molho, in his study of the Jews of Salonika, remarked that the members of that community generally eschewed extremism and were characterized by optimism, tolerance, graciousness and hospitality.[5] While both of these descriptions may be somewhat romanticized, they do reflect the general sense of religious life among Sephardim.

A word should be said about the role of the rabbinate among Sephardim. Since halakhah was so central to Sephardim, rabbinical scholars were of paramount importance as teachers of halakhah. However, they were expected not only to be experts on halakhah but also to be saintly human beings. They were

168   Seeking Good, Speaking Peace

prized and revered not only for their intellectual acumen but
also for their spiritual qualities.[6] The members of the community looked to the rabbi not only for halakhic rulings but also
for personal guidance and counseling.

It was the practice of many Sephardic communities to
appoint a chief rabbi. His responsibilities included serving as
the ultimate halakhic authority for the community, teaching
Torah to advanced students as well as to the community at
large, initiating or approving communal ordinances, and acting as head of the rabbinical court (bet din). Sometimes, the
chief rabbi served as the Jewish community's spokesman
before the government.

KABBALAH

The expulsion of the Jews from the Iberian peninsula was followed by a remarkable flowering of kabbalah. Sixteenth-cen-
tury Safed became the hub of the kabbalist world. It was home
to such figures as Rabbi Yosef Karo, Rabbi Yitzhak Luria (Ari;
1534–1572), Rabbi Moshe Alshekh (1507–ca. 1600), Rabbi
Moshe Cordovero (1522–1570) and Rabbi Shelomo Alkabetz
(ca. 1505–1584). The teachings of these personages and of
other kabbalists inspired Jewish spiritual life for generations to
come.

Rabbi Yosef Garson, writing in Salonika shortly after the
expulsion, articulated the position that both the Talmud and
the kabbalah were basic elements in Jewish education.[7] Garson, who himself had studied at yeshivot in Castile, apparently
was reflecting an attitude widely held in the Sephardic world.
Most rabbinic scholars among the Sephardim were well-versed
in kabbalist lore. The Sephardic masses also valued kabbalist
ideas and texts.

Rabbi Hayyim Yosef David Azulai strongly encouraged the
reading of the Zohar, the basic work of kabbalah, even for people who did not understand the sublime implications of the
text. He wrote: "The study of the Zohar is above any other

study, even if one does not understand what it says, and even if he errs in his reading. It is a great corrective for the soul."[8] Even a reader who intellectually cannot grasp the Zohar's teachings will find himself engaged emotionally in a profound religious experience.

The stress on kabbalah was, in a certain sense, a counterpoise to halakhic erudition. Total devotion of intellectual energies to the details of the Law might produce narrow legalists. The study of kabbalah was a means of expanding one's intellectual horizon, of developing the poetic, mystical and spiritual aspects of one's personality.

Professor Joseph Dan has observed that the study of kabbalah and halakhah led to the emergence of "kabbalistic ethics." He noted that ethics in Lurianic kabbalah was not an attempt at achieving personal perfection alone. Rather, it was a set of instructions directing the individual to participate in the common struggle of the Jewish people.[9] Kabbalah infused halakhah with special meaning; it created new rituals and enhanced old ones. By observing halakhah with the proper kabbalist *kavvanah* (intention), one helped to purify the world and make it holy. The performance of mitzvot was not merely a personal obligation; every Jew was duty bound to help other Jews observe the mitzvot themselves. Each Jew was spiritually responsible for every other Jew.

SEPHARDIC PIETISTS

A number of kabbalists composed lists of pious practices to which a person should accustom himself.[10] Thus, the disciples of Rabbi Yitzhak Luria compiled a book of practices observed by their illustrious master. Among the influential books of kabbalist ethics were *Sefer Haredim* (1601) by Rabbi Eleazar Azikri of Safed (1533–1600), and *Reshit Hokhmah* (1575) by Rabbi Eliyahu de Vidas.

Sephardic Jewry produced outstanding individuals who were steeped in both halakhah and kabbalah. If the sixteenth century was a golden age for *musar* (works of moral guidance), so was the eighteenth century. Among the profound spiritual teachers in Morocco were Rabbi Hayyim Ben Attar (1696–1743), who later settled in Eretz Yisrael, and Rabbi Rephael Berdugo (1747–1821). From Eretz Yisrael came Rabbi Hayyim Yosef David Azulai and Rabbi Moshe Hagiz (1672–ca. 1751), the latter a noted opponent of the Shabbetai Tzevi movement. In Turkey, Rabbi Eliyahu Hakohen Ittamari wrote the classic *Shevet Musar* (1712). In Italy, Rabbi Moshe Hayyim Luzzatto (1707–1746) produced a number of *musar* works, including *Mesillat Yesharim*, probably the most influential *musar* volume of the past two centuries. Rabbi Eliezer Papo of Sarajevo, whose activity spanned the first quarter of the nineteenth century, also produced highly important ethical works, the most significant being his *Pele Yo'etz*.[11]

The *musar* writers stressed the need for the individual to serve God selflessly and to deal compassionately and honestly with others. They emphasized that this world was only a temporary dwelling place; the World to Come was of far greater significance. One had to live righteously in this world in order to be blessed in the World to Come. *Musar* teachers also provided advice on ways in which a person could improve himself. Some of these suggestions include keeping a spiritual diary and regularly reviewing one's thoughts and actions; spending time alone in quiet meditation; discussing one's thoughts and deeds with trusted friends who could offer criticism and advice for correction. In short, the *musar* teachers sought to inspire their readers and disciples to strive constantly for self-perfection.

OTHER LITERARY GENRES

The Sephardic world was blessed with gifted individuals who expressed themselves in various literary genres. During the generation following the expulsion, philosophy still enjoyed popularity among some individuals. Rabbi Yehudah Abar-

banel (ca. 1460–after 1523) wrote *Dialoghi di Amore*, a significant neo-Platonic work. Another physician-philosopher, Rabbi
Abraham Ibn Migash of Turkey, wrote: "One must know that
the ultimate human achievement is attained in the most honorable human power—the power of reason."[12] He was an avid
proponent of philosophical inquiry.

True, within one generation, kabbalah had eclipsed philosophy in most of the Sephardic world. But following the Shabbetai Tzevi debacle in the latter part of the seventeenth century,
Western Sephardim tended to turn away from kabbalah and
became increasingly interested in philosophy once more.

RELIGIOUS TEXTS AND APOLOGETICS

Conversos who returned to Judaism during the sixteenth and
seventeenth centuries needed religious instruction. A number
of books were published in the vernacular to explain the prin-
cipal teachings and practices of Judaism. Rabbi Menasseh ben
Israel of Amsterdam played a leading role in the writing and
publication of such works. Among the major works written to
convince the former converts of the Divine origin of the Oral
Law were *Nomologia* by Rabbi Immanuel Aboab of Venice (ca.
1555–1628) and *Matteh Dan* by Hakham David Nieto (1654–
1728).

Professor Yosef Hayim Yerushalmi has noted that it was the
ex-*conversos* who wrote books refuting Christian arguments
against Judaism. A classic example of this genre was *Las Exce-
lencias y Calumnias de los Hebreos* (1679) by the physician, scientist and philosopher Yitzhak Cardoso (1604–1681), in which
the author discusses ten virtues of the Jews and refutes ten
common anti-Jewish calumnies.[13] Jewish apologetic literature
was important not only as a defense against Christian antago-
nists, but also as a means of strengthening the Jewish faith
among the *conversos* who were returning to Judaism. Since
they had been raised and educated as Christians, *conversos* had

to be taught the Jewish answers to Christian arguments against the Jewish religion.

A word should be said about the continued creativity of Sephardim in poetry, both in Hebrew and in the vernacular. Sephardic authors composed a considerable body of *piyyutim*, liturgical poems for various religious occasions.

During the nineteenth and twentieth centuries, various Sephardic authors confronted the challenges of modernity. In Italy, Rabbi Eliyahu Benamozegh (1822–1900) wrote books demonstrating the ethical greatness of Judaism and its universal message to mankind. In London, Grace Aguilar (1816–1847) produced several works interpreting the teachings of Judaism for enlightened Jews. She was particularly anxious that suitable Jewish publications should be available for Jewish youth, especially girls and young women. Rabbi Yehudah Alkalai of Sarajevo (1798–1878), a prolific author and lecturer, called on the Jewish people to return to the Land of Israel; the messianic redemption, he asserted, must be preceded by the resettlement of the Jews in their homeland. Alkalai was a forerunner of modern Zionism; his writings reflect a spirit of Jewish activism and nationalism far ahead of his time.

THE JUDEO-SPANISH TRADITION

Judeo-Spanish was the mother tongue of most of the Sephardim living in Turkey, the Balkan countries, Eretz Yisrael and northern Morocco. Much of the earlier literature in Ladino (the literary form of Judeo-Spanish) consisted of translations of Jewish classics from the Hebrew. However, original works also were produced in Ladino for the benefit of the Jewish masses who were not well-versed in Hebrew.

The major work in Ladino unquestionably was *Me'am Lo'ez*, an encyclopedic project originated by Rabbi Yaakov Huli (ca. 1689–1732). *Me'am Lo'ez* was presented in the form of a commentary on the Bible; however, it also included halakhah, Midrash and ethical guidance, and teachings from many rabbinic sources. The author wrote in a lucid style, with stories and parables, so much so that he became concerned lest people would read *Me'am Lo'ez* purely for enjoyment rather than for uplift.

The first volume of the series appeared in Istanbul in 1730. Rabbi Huli completed the section on Bereshit and much of Shemot. After his untimely death, other authors continued the work along the lines of his approach. Ultimately, volumes were published on each of the five books of the Torah, some of the Prophets, and on the Book of Esther. *Me'am Lo'ez* was received enthusiastically and was printed in many editions.[14]

Among the recurrent themes in *Me'am Lo'ez* are respect for the common man, humility and other virtues, the value of Torah study, and the need for sincere, genuine piety. The work reflects a blend of intellectual acumen and folk wisdom and had a significant impact on the religious lives of many thousands of Sephardim.

During the nineteenth century the Sephardic world witnessed the emergence of a dynamic, modern Judeo-Spanish literature that was primarily secular. From the middle of the nineteenth century, over 300 Judeo-Spanish newspapers were published throughout the Sephardic diaspora. These publications not only provided news but also featured editorials, opinion essays, poetry, satire, and humor. They were an important communications medium among the Sephardic communities and attracted contributions from leading intellectuals.

During that same period there was a burgeoning interest in Judeo-Spanish drama. Hundreds of plays were written and produced in that language, while many others were translated into Judeo-Spanish from other languages, mainly French. This era also saw the creation of novels and short stories in Judeo-Spanish.[15]

Along with this remarkable burst of creativity in Judeo-Spanish, there was also a renewed interest in collecting traditional Judeo-Spanish folklore—proverbs, ballads and stories. Scholars such as Abraham Galante (1873–1961) and Mair José

Benardete (ca. 1895–1990) should be mentioned in this connection.

The Judeo-Spanish folk traditions were rich in references to love and other human emotions. Sephardim tended to view life in a "holistic" fashion, not drawing a sharp demarcation between religion and other aspects of life. Sephardic folk tradition reflects a generally optimistic spirit.

CUSTOMS AND VALUES

A brief outline of some Sephardic customs will reveal ideals and values typical of Sephardim.[16]

A fairly widespread custom has been to name children after grandparents. The normal pattern is for the first son and daughter to be named after the father's father and mother, and the second son and daughter to be given the names of the mother's parents. Subsequent children are named for other relatives, alternating from the father's to the mother's side of the family. The observance of this custom reflects a number of significant concepts. First, it stresses the respect that children owe their parents. It reinforces the sense of family solidarity, of the living ties that unite the generations. It allows grandparents the joy of seeing themselves and their traditions projected into the next generation—and at the same time gives the grandchildren living role models in the people after whom they are named.

Some of these values are manifested also in other Sephardic customs. When a man is called to the Torah, his younger relatives all rise in respect and remain standing until their elder's Torah portion has been read and he has recited the closing blessing. This practice underscores the value placed upon respect for the elders of one's family. It ties the whole family together in a bond of unity. When one man is given an *aliyah*, it is not just an honor for himself; his entire family shares in the distinction.

Sephardic synagogue customs reflect attitudes toward public worship. For example, most of the synagogue service is chanted aloud by the *hazzan* as the congregation chants along. Though the *hazzan* is expected to have a pleasant voice, he is not supposed to be a "performer." His responsibility is to lead the community in prayer; rarely does he have an opportunity to sing an "aria" on his own. Both the *hazzan* and the rabbi are expected to be expert readers of the Torah.

In general, Sephardim placed a high value on esthetics. They enjoyed beautiful things—tapestries, needlework and jewelry. Even the simplest and poorest Sephardic homes were not without objects of beauty. Sephardic cooking was characterized not just by tasty foods but by the manner in which these foods were served. Sephardic women were concerned that the foods they prepared tasted good and looked appealing. They were sensitive to shapes, colors and fragrances.

Sephardic society had its own customs which demonstrated concern for grace, good manners and consideration for others. Women would meet from time to time for *visitas,* or social gatherings. The hostess would prepare special baked goods herself and serve them on her best china. The guests would dress as though they were going to meet a very important person. It was considered an honor to invite guests and just as great an honor to be invited. Thus, even a relatively simple event such as a get-together for coffee and cake assumed great social significance.

Another important custom was the home observance of the anniversary of the death of a loved one. Known as *meldado* ("reading"), this observance normally took place at the home of a close relative of the deceased. Family members and friends would gather for prayer services in the evening. The rabbi would give a brief learned discourse. Those in attendance would read sections from the Mishnah that began with the letters of the name of the person whose death anniversary was being commemorated.

Following the prayers and studying, the guests would be served a light collation prepared by the hostess. Generally, this would include hard-boiled eggs, Greek olives, raisins, fried fish, home-baked sweet rolls and other baked goods. Raki and whiskey also would be offered. The evening thus became a social gathering, an occasion for family and friends to come together to remember the past and to renew family ties.

Five hundred years after their expulsion from the Iberian peninsula, Sephardim still constitute a vital, creative part of the Jewish people. The largest concentration of Sephardim is now in the State of Israel, with other important communities in France, the United States, Canada, England, South America, and elsewhere. Traditional patterns of Sephardic life are undergoing transformations. Yet, there is little doubt that the Sephardic spirit will continue to have a profound influence on Jewish life for generations to come.

NOTES

1. Hirsch Jacob Zimmels, "The Contributions of the Sephardim to the Responsa Literature Till the beginning of the 16th Century," *The Sephardi Heritage*, ed., Richard Barnett, New York, 1971, p. 394.

2. Yitzhak Confanton, *Darkhei ha-Talmud*, Jerusalem, 5741. See also Hayyim Bentov, "Shitat Limud ha-Talmud bi-Yeshivot Saloniki ve-Turkiyah." *Sefunot*, 13, 5731, pp. 5–102.

3. Meir Benayahu, *Rabbi H. Y. D. Azulai* (Hebrew), Jerusalem, 1959, p. 165.

4. André Chouraqui, *Between East and West*, Philadelphia, 1968, p. 63.

5. Michael Molho, *Usos y Costumbres de los Sephardies de Salonica*, Madrid, 1950, p. 155.

6. Marc D. Angel, *The Rhythms of Jewish Living: A Sephardic Approach*, New York, 1986, pp. 79–85.

7. Yosef Hacker, "Li-Demutam ha-Ruhanit shel Yehudei Sefarad be-Sof ha-Me'ah he-Hamesh Esreh," *Sefunot*, 17, 5743, pp. 47 f.

8. Hayyim Yosef David Azulai, *Avodat ha-Kodesh*, Warsaw, 1879, p. 6.

9. Joseph Dan, *Jewish Mysticism and Jewish Ethics*, Seattle, 1986, pp.

100–01.

10. See Solomon Schechter, "Safed in the 16th Century," *Studies in Judaism*, Second Series, Philadelphia, 1908, pp. 292 f.

11. See Marc D. Angel, *Voices in Exile: A Study in Sephardic Intellectual History*, Hoboken, 1991, chapter 8.

12. Avraham ibn Migash, *Kevod E-lokim*, Jerusalem, 5737, p. 51b.

13. For a biography of Cardoso see Yosef Hayim Yerushalmi, *From Spanish Court to Italian Ghetto: Isaac Cardoso, a Study in Seventeenth Century Marranism and Jewish Apologetics*, New York and London, 1971.

14. This work has been translated into English in part by the late Aryeh Kaplan, under the title, *The Torah Anthology: Me'am Lo'ez* (New York and Jerusalem, 1977). See also Marc D. Angel, *Voices in Exile*, chapter 7.

15. *Ibid.*, chapter 11.

16. For a listing of customs of various Sephardic groups, see Herbert C. Dobrinsky, *A Treasury of Sephardic Laws and Customs*, Hoboken, 1988.

16

SEPHARDIC CULTURE IN AMERICA

When the first Sephardic Jews to settle in Seattle, Washington, arrived there in the early 1900's, the local Ashkenazim had difficulty accepting them as Jews. The Sephardim spoke Judeo-Spanish rather than Yiddish. Their names—Alhadeff, Calvo, Policar, etc.—did not sound "Jewish." Even when the newcomers showed their *tefillin*, the Ashkenazim were not absolutely convinced of their Jewishness.

This episode is indicative of the cultural gap that divides Sephardim and Ashkenazim. Products of different historical forces, it is not surprising to find the two groups varying in their attitudes and life-styles. Indeed, the Jewishness of the two groups, though ultimately based on the same beliefs and religious sources, manifests itself in quite different ways. Thus, it is possible for members of one group to misunderstand the Jewishness of the other group.

Certainly, many Ashkenazic Jews have little or no understanding of Sephardic Jews. They either know nothing of Sephardic existence, or they foster false ideas based on incomplete knowledge. The result of this phenomenon is that the Sephardim have not been fully integrated into the American Jewish community, and therefore have not been able to make the cultural contributions of which they are capable.

Since the Ashkenazim form the vast majority of American Jews, their brand of Jewishness has been accepted by the gen-

Originally published in *Jewish Life*, March–April 1971.

eral public as the standard. Jewish stereotypes are inevitably
drawn from Ashkenazic prototypes. When national women's
magazines give recipes for "Jewish" cooking, they describe
Ashkenazic foods like gefilte fish and tzimmes. When politicians want to attract Jewish voters, they drop Yiddish phrases
into their campaign speeches—even when their audiences are
Sephardic. What effect has the equating of Jewishness with
Ashkenazic standards had on Sephardim? How can a legitimate minority within Jewry maintain its identity when its very
existence is misunderstood or ignored?

Before we can answer that question, we first must give a general definition of who the Sephardim in America are and what
their culture is. The old American Sephardic families are, of
course, the most widely known. Their association with the
Spanish and Portuguese congregations of New York, Philadelphia, and Newport has been the subject of many works. Most
recently, Steven Birmingham has written a book about them
significantly entitled *The Grandees: America's Sephardic Elite.* But
these old families represent a minute percentage of the American Sephardim. The largest component of the current American Sephardic community came to the United States during
the twentieth century, mostly from Turkey, the Balkan countries, and the Middle East. Concerning these Sephardim, little
has been written. It is precisely their identity crisis that is most
crucial.

The Sephardic immigrants, descendants of the Jews
expelled from Spain in 1492, had several major obstacles to
overcome in order to adapt to American society. They were
separated from the non-Jews not only by religion, but by language and culture. The last two factors also separated them
from their Ashkenazic coreligionists. Notwithstanding these
problems, the Sephardim made a significant adjustment to
their new environment, and achieved economic security. They
established large communities in New York, Los Angeles, and
Seattle, and smaller ones in such places as Atlanta, Cincinnati,
Indianapolis, Miami Beach, Montgomery (Alabama), High-

land Park (New Jersey), and Portland (Oregon). All of these communities have become quite Americanized within several generations.

The culture of the Sephardim has been profoundly influenced by its Spanish sources. The Sephardic mother tongue, until recently, has been Judeo-Spanish. At all family and communal gatherings, Sephardim would sing Judeo-Spanish ballads and folk songs, developing in the course of centuries a rich folklore. Sephardic culture has been able to blend religion and life into a harmony; thus, Sephardic folklore contains sensitive poems of nature and passionate love songs as well as religiously oriented poems. The religious-secular clash that so much bothers Orthodox Ashkenazim is irrelevant to the Sephardic mind.

Another characteristic of Sephardic culture is its *joie de vivre*. Religion is not austere for the Sephardim. Rather, it is the spirit that subtly pervades their daily activities and celebrations. The Sephardim are optimistic. Their positive view of life manifests itself in their many parties and gatherings, in their love for music, in their enthusiastic communal synagogue singing.

Sephardic culture also imbues the individual with a strong sense of personal pride. Sephardim do not look at themselves as lowly, humiliated people, but as worthy and dignified. They face man and God with self-respect. Rich and poor, learned and ignorant, all have a feeling of self-worth and dignity.

Aside from the features already mentioned, other components which make up Sephardic culture include: liturgy, customs, and cuisine. All of these factors, differing from Ashkenazic modes in so many ways, go into the making of Sephardic Jewishness.

Due to the initial lack of communication between the Sephardic and Ashkenazic groups, the Sephardim were compelled to maintain their culture in isolation. This was feasible in the first generation because the Sephardim were saturated with their Sephardic character. They spoke Spanish to one another, they lived in the same neighborhoods, they enjoyed a closely knit community. These factors served to help them preserve their Sephardic identity. However, the second and third generation Sephardim do not have the same forces working for them. No longer are they tied to their heritage by the Spanish language or the Sephardic neighborhood—hence the identity crisis of the young Sephardic Jew. He may try to delve into his own history and culture, renewing himself as a Sephardi. He may assimilate into the Ashkenazic community. He may, tragically, find no tie to Judaism at all, seeing that his notions of Judaism are tied inextricably to his Sephardic roots and that these roots have become weakened.

The forces of Americanization have nearly destroyed Judeo-Spanish among the new generations. Therefore, the language which bound Sephardim together as Jews for nearly five centuries no longer unites young American Sephardim. With the language, much of the folklore has fallen into obscurity. Celebrations and religious observances have tended to assume an American air. The secularism of American civilization has lessened general religious observance among Sephardim. Americanization and secularization, though, are problems all Jews must face. The particular difficulty the Sephardim have in preserving their culture, however, stems from the fact that Jewishness in America is set by an Ashkenazic standard. The Sephardi's customs and attitudes, his history and people, are ignored. Sephardim are expected to be Ashkenazim if they want to be recognized as Jews, especially as Orthodox Jews. Several years ago, Dr. Alan Corre delivered a paper for the American Society of Sephardic Studies called "The Importance of Being Ashkenazi." Dr. Corre argued that Sephardic culture in America cannot survive on its own, but will assimilate into the Ashkenazic mainstream. He suggested areas where Sephardim might influence the Ashkenazim. Even when addressing Sephardic scholars, Dr. Corre contended that Sephardim must, in effect, become Ashkenazim.

The Ashkenazication process is clearly evident, for example, in the day schools and yeshivot. Sephardic students quickly learn to use Yiddish words, to dress and to think like the other students. Sephardic history and culture are seldom if ever taught. Most Sephardic students, let alone Ashkenazic students, know practically nothing of post-1492 Sephardic history. The yeshivot hardly ever mention the names and works of the great Sephardic rabbis of recent centuries. Thus, Sephardic students who want advanced Jewish education in America run the risk of losing their own culture in the process.

Another example of the Ashkenazication of Sephardim may be drawn from some Ashkenazic rabbis who occupy pulpits of Sephardic synagogues. Although several such rabbis have made sincere attempts at fostering Sephardic culture, others have not. They lead congregations without knowing their congregants' heritage. They casually introduce Ashkenazic melodies into the Sephardic synagogue service. They teach their congregants to call the synagogue "*shul*" instead of "*kahal.*" They preach sermons and give lectures without ever drawing on the classic works of the post-expulsion Sephardim. They do not realize that Sephardim are not Ashkenazim.

The main problem in the preservation of Sephardic culture, though, is the Sephardim themselves. Not having built enough day schools and yeshivot of their own, they have necessitated their children's attendance at Ashkenazic schools. Not having trained enough of their own rabbis, they have been required to turn to non-Sephardim for leadership. Moreover, the inability of the older generations to transmit the Sephardic heritage to their children has been detrimental. They showed their children the external features of Sephardic culture, but did not convey the history and philosophy of Sephardim well enough. Thus, dissatisfied with seemingly superficial culture, many educated young Sephardim have become disenchanted with Judaism and have drifted away. Whatever ties they have with Judaism, though, are linked inextricably with their Sephardic backgrounds. To increase their involvement with Orthodox Judaism, we first must teach them their Sephardic roots. We must explain Judaism to them in terms of their own Sephardic heritage. It is an error to try to attract them to Orthodoxy by asking them to follow Ashkenazic patterns.

People are the products of their culture. In each individual's mind are the latent voices, dreams, and visions of generations of his ancestors. Sometimes when he least expects it, a voice from his past will emerge. He may see something, or hear something, or do something that will give him a profound sense of nostalgia, that will let him penetrate into his past. Without this dimension in human experience, he is deprived of something sacred. To ignore or to suppress Sephardic culture is to deracinate the Sephardim. As their Sephardic roots are weakened, so ultimately will their Jewish roots wither.

The challenge to American Orthodoxy is significant. The Sephardim, whose rich heritage goes back to the Golden Age of Spanish Jewry, historically have been traditional in their Jewish practices. If we seize the day, we may stimulate a renewed interest in Sephardic culture and a consequent return to Orthodox Judaism. The key to the solution rests in the acknowledgement that Sephardim have a right to exist as Sephardim. They have a right to have a Sephardic Jewishness.

Day schools and yeshivot could promote Sephardic studies. Teachers could help their students to appreciate the Sephardic heritage. Ashkenazic rabbis and leaders could make serious attempts at understanding the Sephardim and their past. The Ashkenazic laity could encourage the existence and development of Sephardic culture and not doubt Sephardic Jewishness because Sephardim do not necessarily eat gefilte fish, wear kippot in public, or have the same liturgy as do the Ashkenazim.

The main hope is, of course, that the Sephardim themselves will be able to impart their own culture. There are indications that they are beginning to do just that. The time is ripe for an upsurge in Sephardic culture.

It is not easy for a Sephardic Jew to maintain his identity. Being a Jew, he is a minority among Americans. Being a Sephardi, he is a minority among Jews. But the Sephardic Jew must maintain his Sephardic identity—or ultimately lose his Jewish identity.

17

A CHANCE TO LEARN

*I*n the summer of 1903 the Spanish Senator Angel Pulido was on a voyage traveling aboard a ship from Belgrade. He happened to meet several Sephardic Jews who were conversing in Judeo-Spanish. This meeting changed his life.

The Senator was amazed to discover from his new acquaintances that hundreds of thousands of Jews—scattered throughout Turkey, the Balkans and North Africa—had maintained a Hispanic language, culture and character for centuries. They sang medieval Spanish songs, used medieval Spanish proverbs, spoke in archaic pronunciations, and used archaic Spanish words. In short, here was a group of people— whose ancestors had been expelled from Spain in 1492—who continued to live as Spanish Jews. Pulido wrote a book in which he referred to the Sephardim as *"españoles sin patria,"* Spaniards without a country.

Pulido began extensive correspondence with Sephardic intellectuals throughout the diaspora and helped spur interest in Sephardim among his fellow Spaniards. He wanted Spain to reclaim its exiled children. Spanish scholars turned their attention to the study of the Sephardic experience.

To a certain extent, the Spanish attitude toward Sephardim was characterized by a nationalistic romanticism. Sephardim were seen as long-lost kinsfolk who had been faithful to the land that had cast them out. Feeding this romanticism were

Originally published in *Hadassah Magazine*, January 1992.

some Sephardim who were pleased to have been rediscovered by Spain; they told stories of how Sephardim have shed tears of longing and of love for Spain throughout the generations. Spaniards and Sephardim waxed nostalgic about the Golden Age of Jews in medieval Spain.

During the period when Pulido and his countrymen were enthusiastically reclaiming Sephardim for Spain, my grandparents were migrating from Turkey and Rhodes to Seattle, Washington. My maternal grandfather told stories about how he and several other Sephardim had gone to an Ashkenazic synagogue in Seattle to connect with the existing Jewish community. Instead of being welcomed, though, these young men had their Jewishness questioned. After all, their names did not seem Jewish: Angel, Romey, Alhadeff, Policar. They did not speak Yiddish, nor had they ever heard of gefilte fish. Even when the Sephardim showed their prayer shawls and *tefillin*, the doubts were not eliminated. It took a while for Ashkenazim to recognize their Judeo-Spanish-speaking neighbors as coreligionists.

In the eyes of Spaniards, the Sephardim were a wonderful people, the remnant of the great Jewish community of medieval Spain. In the eyes of many Ashkenazim who came into contact with them for the first time, the Sephardim were strange, exotic, not Jewish in the same ways that Ashkenazim were. Indeed, sometimes they were thought to be Turks, Greeks, Italians, or Arabs.

Both groups did not understand Sephardim for who they really were. The Spaniards romanticized them into a living repository of medieval Spanish culture. The Ashkenazim exoticized them. Both tendencies have persisted in various forms to this day.

When thinking of Sephardim, some people tend to imagine idealized elegant aristocrats in the tradition of R. Yehudah Halevi, Rambam, R. Yitzhak Abarbanel. They see Sephardim as noble heirs of medieval Spanish Jewry. On the other hand, some think of them as Eastern Jews, as exotic types; some Ash-

kenazim may even have disdain or cultural bias against
Sephardim, since the latter group lived in "backward" Muslim
lands.

One can understand the confusion. Five hundred years after
the expulsion from Spain, Sephardim do have Spanish cultural characteristics. At the same time, since they have lived for
centuries in the Ottoman Empire, the Middle East and North
Africa, they also have cultural characteristics developed in
those lands. In short, Sephardim are heirs to medieval Spanish Jewry and they are Turkish and Moroccan Jews as well. To
understand them requires an acceptance of both aspects.

The various observances in 1992 reflect the complexity of
the Sephardic experience. Understandably, Spain is eager to
emphasize the romanticized image of the great age of Jews in
pre-expulsion Spain. Sepharad '92 is sponsoring and coordi-
nating worldwide events and exhibitions highlighting the
achievements and glories of Spanish Jewry. The Quincenten-
nial Foundation of Istanbul is doing the same in its highlighting Sephardic life in the Ottoman Empire—after all, it
welcomed a large number of exiles in 1492 and maintained its
hospitality to Sephardim for the past 500 years. All this goes
on alongside the many other Jewish organizations devoting
programming to learning about Sephardim—there are special
conferences, tours, teaching curricula as well as a myriad
exhibits.

This is exciting. Perhaps there is now a chance that many
will take the trouble to learn more about the Sephardic experience, to overcome stereotypes and cliches. Most people have
little or no real understanding of Sephardic history and culture; now they will have the stimulus to learn more. They will
be able to understand the nature of Jewish life in Muslim lands
on a higher level; the approaches of Sephardic thinkers to
modernity; the Sephardic blend of respect for tradition and
individual autonomy. Instead of thinking of Sephardim
merely as repositories of folklore, they will come to appreciate
their contributions to Jewish spiritual life, philosophy, litera-

ture and modern society. Every mass culture explosion has advantages and disadvantages. Public awareness is growing; this is to the good.

But it always must be remembered that 1492 was a tragic year for the Jewish people. After five centuries, the scars from the catastrophe of the expulsion from Spain are still evident. This somber anniversary is certainly no occasion for celebration. While Spain might prefer to focus on the discoveries of Columbus or on the Golden Age of Sephardic Jewry, the Jewish people should not flinch from calling the world's attention to the horrors that befell our ancestors in 1492.

Five hundred years ago, my ancestors were victims of cruel fanaticism. R. Yitzhak Abarbanel, the leading Jewish figure of the period, described his people:

> From the rising of the sun to its setting, from north to south, there was never such a chosen people [as the Jews of Spain] in beauty and pleasantness; and afterward, there will never be another such people. God was with them, the children of Judea and Jerusalem, many and strong. [They were] a quiet and trusting people, a people filled with the blessing of God with no end to its treasures; a pure and upright people, revering the Lord. I have seen this people in its glory, in its beauty, in its pleasantness.

The expulsion radically altered the history of Sephardim—and the rest of the Jewish people. Many were lost by death or by forced conversion to Catholicism. The Jews who did leave Spain struggled valiantly and heroically to reestablish their communities in the various lands which received them. The past five centuries have witnessed major transformations in Sephardic life—but through it all the Sephardim are still here to tell their story.

In this commemorative year, it is impossible to forget the unmitigated horrors to which our people were subjected by their oppressors. But it is equally impossible to forget the dramatic courage and deep faith of the exiles who kept their traditions alive and flourishing during these past five centuries. A few months ago the peace conference between Israel and its Arab enemies was called to order—in Spain. It is a fitting twist of history that the anniversary of the expulsion is witness to Spain hosting this conference; it is poetic justice that the once persecutor of our people can become an instrument for bringing real peace to the Jewish state.

As Americans spend this year exploring Columbus's voyage to the Western Hemisphere and its consequences, Jews also are embarking on a voyage. They will be discovering through lectures, tours, exhibits, videos, books, and music neither a quaint cultural anomaly nor an exotic Jewish species—but the singular historical, literary and philosophical contributions of the Sephardic diaspora.

18

THOUGHTS ABOUT EARLY AMERICAN JEWRY

*T*he historian, Fernand Braudel, noted that in spite of the Jews' ability to adapt to many societies and situations, they have maintained their "basic personality." The Jewish people have threaded through history and—against enormous odds—have not lost themselves in the process.

> The one thing of which we can be certain is that the destiny of Israel, its strength, its survival and its misfortunes are all the consequence of its remaining irreducible, refusing to be diluted, that is, of being a civilization faithful to itself.[1]

The widespread celebration of America's Bicentennial should be an occasion to give special attention to the mystery of Jewish survival on this continent. Although we know that many Jews have assimilated into their surrounding cultures over the centuries, the wonder is that a remnant has survived at all. Our existence today manifests not only the courage and tenacity of our ancestors but also the providence of God.

Jewish community life began here in 1654 with the arrival of twenty-three Jews in New Amsterdam. They founded Congregation Shearith Israel which to this day maintains itself as a traditional Orthodox synagogue.[2] During the Colonial period, other Jewish congregations were established in Newport, Philadelphia, Charleston, and Savannah. In the 1760's, a congregation was founded in Montreal, Canada. All of these early

---

Originally published in *Tradition*, Fall 1976.

synagogues were Spanish and Portuguese—that is, they followed the liturgy and customs of Western Sephardim.[3]

One of the popular myths about the early Jewish settlements is that they were composed mostly of Sephardic Jews. The fact is that many Ashkenazim—on a relative scale—also arrived during the Colonial period and soon outnumbered the Sephardim. We may refer to the first congregations as Spanish and Portuguese because the Sephardic cultural characteristics dominated. The Ashkenazim, for whatever reasons, adopted the Sephardic norms and participated fully in the leadership of the communities. Intermarriage among the members of both groups was common. The often-asserted notion that the Sephardim looked down on the Ashkenazim has been exaggerated far out of proportion; the Jewish communities were so tiny they could not afford the luxury of intra-group hostilities. On the contrary, there is much evidence indicating how well the two groups got along together.[4]

In order to understand the nature of Colonial Jewry, one must be aware of the major cultural characteristics common to the Western Sephardim. This group of Jews, deriving primarily from Amsterdam and other Western European centers, had a tradition of self-esteem, social flexibility and grace. These qualities, for example, distinguished the famous Aaron Lopez of Newport. Rev. Ezra Stiles, President of Yale University and a friend of Lopez, described the Sephardic merchant as follows:

> In honor and aptitude of commerce, there was never a trader in America to equal him. In business he dealt with the highest degree of seriousness and clear-sightedness, showing always an affability in manner, a calm urbanity, an agreeable and sincere courtesy of manners. Without a single enemy, no one is known who was more universally loved.[5]

Nor was Lopez a unique example of "aptitude in commerce" and "calm urbanity." These traits were part of the Sephardic upbringing. Rev. Edward Peterson, in his *History of Rhode Island and Newport,* notes that between the years of 1750–60, "many families of wealth and distinction" came to Newport from Spanish and Portuguese backgrounds. These Sephardim "contributed largely to the intelligence and commercial prosperity of the town."[6]

One of the notable features of this Jewish group was its ability to adapt to the American milieu while maintaining a reverence for its own religious traditions. Western Sephardim in general were receptive to the cultural forces at work in their societies. They did not isolate themselves in spiritual and intellectual ghettos. Gershom Mendes Seixas (1746–1816), minister of Congregation Shearith Israel in New York, was interested in science; he was known to quote from the New Testament. The historian, Jacob Rader Marcus, goes so far as to compare Seixas to a founder of Reform Judaism, due to Seixas' "insistence on Western dress, decorum, dignity, and an increasing use of the vernacular."[7] Yet, these practices were not Reform at all. Indeed, all of these qualities were typical of Western Sephardic religious leaders long before Seixas was born. What Marcus considers to be Reform practices were normative Orthodox qualities among Spanish and Portuguese Jews. This point must be stressed since so many students of Colonial Jewry err in this regard. The Western Sephardic approach to religion and life was neither Reform nor East European Orthodox; it was an independent tradition which must be considered on its own terms.

In their *History of the Jews of Philadelphia,* Wolf and Whiteman comment that the Sephardic contribution to early synagogue life in Philadelphia lay

> in a tradition of organization, of rules and regulations, which dominated Mikveh Israel and produced a form of prayer, a method of government and a system of keeping records.

Synagogue records were kept in professional style, "out of respect for orderliness and the written word."[8] The sense of order and decorum was a significant characteristic of the Western Sephardim. It was a manifestation of the seriousness and respect given to the synagogue and the community.

Orderliness and dignity were ideals of synagogue life. Not only were the prayer services chanted in a decorous style, but the synagogue buildings were constructed and furnished tastefully. The synagogue structures of Colonial America were impressive in their grace and architectural neatness. The Sephardic aesthetic sense required that the synagogue furnishings be properly cleaned and maintained. Although this concern for detail and physical correctness may seem unnecessary to some, it reflects a deeply rooted attitude concerning the purpose of a synagogue. For the Sephardim, a synagogue was a house of the Lord which demanded respect. On entering it, one should feel the sentiment of Yaakov our forefather:

> How full of awe is this place: this is none other than the house of God and this is the gate of Heaven (Bereshit 28:17).

It is not accidental, I believe, that two Spanish and Portuguese synagogues derived their names from this verse: Beth E-lokim of Charleston and Shaar ha-Shamayim of London.

The names chosen for the synagogues in Colonial America may be a reflection of the Sephardic idea of *kahal,* community, for the names were latent with prophetic meanings. They implied a destiny, and they encompassed all the Jews of the city. Shearith Israel (Remnant of Israel) was the name of the *kehillot* in New York and Montreal. Mikveh Israel (Hope of Israel) was chosen as the name of the *kehillot* in Philadelphia and Savannah. Newport's congregation was Yeshuat Israel (Salvation of Israel). The *kehillot* did not see themselves as mere synagogues, serving only segments of Jewry; rather, they viewed themselves as the communal governments of all the Jewish people within their domains. In contrast, a number of the early Ashkenazic congregations selected less "nationalistic" names: Rodeph Shalom, Anshei Hesed and others of the same type. Their responsibility was to their members.

Whether or not it is fair to read so much into the congregational names, it nevertheless is clear that the idea of the *kahal* as a communal government was central among the Sephardim. Each Spanish and Portuguese synagogue invariably refers to itself as *Kahal Kadosh* (holy congregation). The early records of the Colonial American congregations reflect the *kahal's* concern with all phases of life, from birth to death. They also indicate the central authority which was relegated to the *kahal*.

The *kahal* expected that each Jew in its domain would support and be responsible to it. An entry—dated 26 Nisan 5512 (1752)—in the Portuguese-English record book of Congregation Shearith Israel of New York, notes that anyone who during his lifetime absented himself from the synagogue or was in no way a benefactor of the congregation would not be granted burial in the Jewish cemetery unless the family first received permission from the *parnas* who would set the terms. In 1792 Mikveh Israel of Philadelphia passed a resolution that anyone who did not support the congregation was to be deprived of all communal rights and privileges, including burial.[9] The constitution of Beth E-lokim (1820), states that all Jews who have lived in the city for at least one year

> shall be bound to subscribe to the subscription list, and provide themselves and wives (if any) with seats. . . . This law embraces all persons indiscriminately above twenty-one years of age (Rule 12).[10]

The *kehillot* could impose modified forms of the *herem* (excommunication) to enforce their laws.

The *kehillot* attempted to maintain themselves as the corporate voice of the Jewish people. Even in the realm of prayer, it was expected that services be held only under the auspices of the *kahal*. Charleston's Jews were not unusual in considering an unauthorized *minyan* to be "an atrocious offense," punishable by forfeiture of all rights and privileges in the congregation and a fine.[11] Prayer services were not to be allowed to disunite the community; rather, all Jews were required to pray only with the authorization of the *kahal*.

Although the authority lodged in the *kahal* was great, each person's individuality also was respected. A member of a congregation is known among Sephardim as a *yahid*, individual.

The title conveys a sense of pride, honor, self-worth. In the earliest extant constitution and by-laws of Shearith Israel of New York there is a provision that anyone who caused an affront to an individual was to be fined. Respect and courtesy were to be maintained.

From our perspective, it is noteworthy that these small Jewish communities were able to survive for centuries as Jewish institutions. Their ideals and patterns of organization have weathered the storms of history fairly well. That many Jews were lost along the way through assimilation cannot be denied. And yet, it is remarkable that relatively tiny and isolated communities retained their dedication to Judaism and to the Jewish people without the aid of many great rabbis, scholars, and yeshivot. It has been estimated that roughly ten percent of the Jews in the American cities before the end of the eighteenth century had married non-Jews.[12] This figure stands out when compared to modern intermarriage rates. Somehow, America's first Jews were able to lay the foundations for solid and lasting Jewish congregations. They formed a civilization "faithful to itself." Their accomplishments should not be casually dismissed.

Early American Jews were involved in all phases of the general life of the Colonies and, later, the United States. They participated in the general culture and were—at their best—able to retain a deep attachment to Judaism and the Jewish people. Among the early Jews were industrialists and merchants, authors, craftsmen, intellectuals and patriots of the American Revolution.

During and after the 1820's, the Jewish population of the United States began to grow through a significant increase in immigration. Consequently, the *kehillot* could no longer function in their original capacities. New synagogues sprouted up, new customs were introduced. The Jewish communities became divided and complex. The rise of Reform Judaism also tended to lead to tension within the communities.

The ancient congregation in Charleston, for example, split into two synagogues—Beth E-lokim initiating reforms, and Shearith Israel maintaining tradition. It is safe to say that the pressures for reform were felt in all of the well-established congregations.

When suggestions for ritual changes were made in Shearith Israel of New York in 1891, Rev. Dr. Henry Pereira Mendes, the outspoken spiritual leader of the congregation, made an eloquent response.

> I say it is a very solemn thing for this Congregation with its centuries and proud adherence to historic Judaism to approach the subject of change at all. . . . Are those who have enlisted under the banner of change distinguished for a better observance of the Sabbath? Are they in any way improved religiously? Are their homes more Jewish? Are their children more devoted to Judaism and better exponents of its teachings? . . . No new virtues have been created in the heart of the Reform Jew which are not found in the heart of the Orthodox Jew. Nor is the cultured Reformer more respected than is the cultured Orthodox brother.[13]

Dr. Mendes was a founder of the Union of Orthodox Jewish Congregations of America. He and Dr. Sabato Morais of Mikveh Israel in Philadelphia founded the Jewish Theological Seminary, originally intended to train cultured, English-speaking, Orthodox religious leaders. The classic Western Sephardic reverence for tradition and culture found expression in the works of Dr. Mendes.

From the few small Jewish communities of Colonial days, American Jewry has grown into the largest community of Jews in the world with thousands of synagogues and organizations. Observers of contemporary American Jewish life must be confused by the numerous divisions and directions within American Jewry. But in the midst of the confusion and multiplicity, our oldest congregations stand as quiet witnesses to the tenacity of our people, testifying by their very existence that American Jewry has had the power and fortitude to survive centuries. They are living proof that the Guardian of Israel neither slumbers nor sleeps.

NOTES

1. F. Braudel. *The Mediterranean,* vol. 2 (New York, 1973), p. 826.

2. A history of Shearith Israel in honor of its 300th anniversary was written by David and Tamar de Sola Pool, *An Old Faith in the New World* (New York, 1955).

3. See my article, "The Sephardim of the United States: An Exploratory Study," *American Jewish Yearbook* (New York and Philadelphia, 1973), pp. 80 f. See pages 78–80 for a discussion of the general cultural differences separating Western Sephardim from other groups of Sephardim.

4. See my response to Dr. Malcolm Stern in the pamphlet, "New York's Early Jews: Some Myths and Misconceptions," published by the Jewish Historical Society of New York (1976).

5. F. B. Dexter, ed., *The Literary Diary of Ezra Stiles* (New York, 1901), entry on June 8, 1782.

6. Edward Peterson, *History of Rhode Island and Newport* (New York, 1853), p. 181.

7. J. R. Marcus, *Handsome Young Priest in the Black Gown* (Cincinnati, 1970), pp. 43, 49. (Reprinted from H.U.C. Annual, vol. 40–41, 1969–70).

8. E. Wolf and M. Whiteman, *The History of the Jews of Philadelphia* (Philadelphia, 1957), p. 228.

9. *Ibid.,* p. 224.

10. Charles Reznikoff, *The Jews of Charleston* (Philadelphia, 1950), pp. 116–17.

11. *Ibid.,* p. 118.

12. Wolf and Whiteman, *op. cit.,* p. 235.

13. Dr. Mendes' remarks are found in a letter attached to the Trustees Minutes of Congregation Shearith Israel in New York, vol. 7, p. 406. The letter is dated 5 Nisan 5651 (1891).

19

A LECTURE ON SEPHARDIC CULTURE

I recall having read that when a culture is about to die out, it first experiences a resurgence in nostalgia among its members. There is one last burst of creative energy before it gives way to new and different patterns of life. I do not only think this to be true in an abstract way: I feel it to be true deep within my own experience.

When I was a little boy growing up in the Sephardic community of Seattle, I lived within walking distance of nearly every relative I had. (And I had many. My father was one of eight children, my mother was one of seven children, and most of my aunts and uncles were married and had children of their own.) My cousins and we used to go in and out of each other's houses almost as if we had lived there ourselves. When I hear about the extended-family concept in sociology, I merely call to mind my own youth.

I remember my grandparents Romey so well. My grandfather was a barber. He was proud and strong. He once told me that our family stemmed from the tribe of Yehudah, that we were of nobility. He said this even as a poor barber, who hardly ever had enough money to support his children in anything that approached luxury. Whenever we would take my grandparents for an automobile drive along Lake Washington and watch the sailboats tilting in the distance and the fishermen

Given at the Spanish and Portuguese Synagogue of New York City, December 13, 1973.

198

working on the docks, they would be singing some Judeo-Spanish song or other. They would reminisce about their own childhoods along the Sea of Marmara.

I remember our community on Simhat Torah when so many Sephardim would fill the synagogues to enjoy the holiday festivities. There was singing, dancing, eating and drinking. I remember in my mind's eye one of the old men in our congregation who actually used to bring a folding chair up to the *tevah* (reader's desk), stand up on it, and sing out at the top of his lungs the *Hashem Melekh* during the *Hakafot*.

I remember coming home on Friday afternoons after school and finding the kitchen counter filled with all varieties of foods which my mother had prepared for Shabbat. I still can smell the fresh sweet rolls, the *roscas*, the *bolemas* and *borekas*, the *aros con leche*. Everything. I can remember every detail. I remember the crowded houses on nights of *meldados*. I remember the ladies cooking for *berit milahs* and for weddings. I can still see them stretching the thin *fila* dough over tables and tables.

But here I am reminiscing, filled with nostalgia. And the reason is, I think, that I feel myself at the end of the life-span of a certain culture. A resurgence of nostalgia, a burst of creative energy precede the ultimate demise or—better said—transformation of a culture. I very often feel that I stand at a precipice and in the words of Matthew Arnold, "between two worlds, one dead, the other powerless to be born." Sephardic culture as I knew it is today but a rich conglomeration of memories. My generation is the transition generation between a Sephardic life that was really alive and a new generation for which Sephardic culture will necessarily mean something far different than it has meant in the past.

One does not need to be a profound sociologist or philosopher of history to see that Jewish life in the United States has undergone radical changes over the past several generations. One merely needs to open his own eyes and be honest. Ashkenazim and Sephardim alike are not at all what they used to be. It would be unrealistic, unfair, and impossible to expect that Jewish culture be frozen and not allow for development and change. Some ancient Greek philosophers saw history as a rushing stream, and the simile is apt. Life does not stay still.

In the tightly-knit family and the neighborhood structure which was typical for Sephardim in the last generation, the family and community reinforced their values naturally. One did not have to learn Sephardic or Jewish ideals and practices in the abstract. He saw and lived them. The culture was alive and on fire. There were no questions about identity, because everyone knew who he or she was. One does not become preoccupied with the analysis of his culture unless he feels that it is threatened: when he is thrown among people of another culture or when he feels his own heritage slipping out of his hands irretrievably.

My contention is that Sephardic culture as it was known in former generations is at the end of its historical life span. There is nothing that can or should be done to alter this massive reality. Our problem is not to maintain that heritage of the past: we cannot do it. Our task is rather to make that heritage live in a real way in the future.

You have a right to ask: Am I not overstating my case? Shortly, I shall describe the results of a sociological study I conducted under the sponsorship of the Union of Sephardic Congregations. When you hear some of the trends and realities among American-born Sephardim of Judeo-Spanish origin, you will realize that I am not exaggerating. But before I present statistics, I think that you can better appreciate what I am saying if I cite several illustrations of what I mean when I say that Sephardic culture is not alive and on fire. The Shearith Israel League is sponsoring a Sephardic dinner on January 13, and it will feature Sephardic food and music. To be sure, this is going to be a wonderful party and I would not want to miss it for anything. But think for a moment. If the Sephardim of a generation or two ago wanted to have a dinner party, they would have had no need whatsoever to attach the adjective "Sephardic" to it. The dinner naturally and necessarily would be Sephardic because Sephardic was the normal mode of life. For us today, though, Sephardic is an adjective that must be appended to our dinners. We must realize that the adjective represents something we are not, something exotic and extraordinary, akin perhaps to a Chinese dinner, or an Italian dinner. It is very common to hear of Sephardic congregations who sponsor "Sephardic" or "Oriental" parties.

And stop to think a moment. Why was it that there was so little written about the Sephardic heritage and tradition while Sephardic life flourished? Why is it that we suddenly have a wave of recordings of Ladino songs, and a wish to perpetuate liturgies, when for centuries no formal attempt was made to write down the music? The answer is that when a culture is alive and natural, it is irrelevant for it to examine itself in a scholarly, documentary way. One has to be abstracted from the culture to do this. One has to recognize that the culture is declining and perhaps near extinction. These efforts are the last attempts—the last bursts of energy—before the end, the conscious attempts to salvage something from the mass which is slipping away from us.

Now let us turn to the sociological study. In January, 1972 I sent questionnaires to about 950 American-born Sephardim of Judeo-Spanish origin. I received replies from about 260. For the most part, the questionnaire was sent to Sephardim who still are connected with the Sephardic community, either as members of synagogues or of brotherhoods. Thus, I could not gauge the number of Sephardim outside the fold, so to speak. This crucial factor partially accounts for the significance of the findings. If the rates of assimilation and cultural erosion are intense among affiliated Sephardim, one may assume that the rates are even higher among the unsynagogued and communally unconnected Sephardim. The complete results of this survey appear in the 1973 *American Jewish Yearbook*, together with a long historical introduction. Tonight I shall present only a very brief overview.

Let us consider first the rate of natural increase among Sephardim. My study shows that third-generation American Sephardim have an average of 2.32 children per family, slightly above the zero-population-growth level. This is about the same rate that is prevalent among the general Ashkenazic population. The parents of second-generation American Sephardim, in contrast, had an average of 5.75 children per family. What does this mean in precise terms? We have very small families and no longer can expect our communities to grow in numbers through natural increase. The extended-family concept is curtailed, since there is far less of a family than there used to be.

Consider economic life. The Sephardim have made tremendous financial achievements in the United States, so that we must be considered as being a highly affluent group. Job patterns have changed dramatically. Whereas poverty and manual labor were common in my grandfather's generation, a high standard of living is enjoyed by this generation. Among employed Sephardim under age forty the following occupational pattern emerges: professionals, 39 percent; business people, 53 percent; skilled laborers, 3 percent; artists, 5 percent.

Sephardim have been receiving higher educational levels than their parents did. In response to the question: Did, do or will your children attend college? 203 respondents answered yes, while only three answered no. Compare this to the level of education common among the fathers of American-born Sephardim aged forty and over. Of 139 respondents, 120 had received less than a high school education, fifteen had graduated high school, three had attended some college, and only one was a college graduate.

The implication of the above facts is simple: American Sephardim have adopted the common tendencies of the general American middle class. The differences between Sephardim, Ashkenazim and non-Jewish middle class are decreasing dramatically.

Of all the mentioned factors, higher education should be considered in more detail. With college education so prevalent, it is inevitable that young Sephardim are being influenced by the egalitarian spirit of the campus. It is unrealistic, if not impossible, to expect such a small group of people to band together and remain an entity apart from others. As Sephardic students mingle freely with other students regardless of background, they cannot maintain themselves as a particular group. It is hard enough for them simply to identify as Jews, let alone as Sephardic Jews.

Because Sephardim have greater mobility than ever before, it is more likely that they marry non-Sephardim than the Sephardim of their own communities. The horizons for choosing a mate have expanded vastly from the days of the old Sephardic ghettos. In my study, I found the following marriage pattern among third-generation American Sephardim: 13 percent married Sephardim; 74 percent married Ashkenazim; 12 percent married Christians; 1 percent married spouses who do not fit into these three categories.

What does this mean? It means that Sephardim are becoming physically unable to maintain the particular modes of Sephardic culture. Marriage entails compromises on both sides. Often enough, the Sephardic wife or husband follows the Ashkenazic spouse into an Ashkenazic synagogue. The home, which used to be the strongest force in perpetuating Sephardism, no longer can be expected to fill that role, at least not as it could have done in the past. The typical third-generation American Sephardic home today—to the extent that it still is Jewish—is a mixture of Sephardic and Ashkenazic cultures. The major factor in these homes, however, is the adoption of American culture.

Viewing the religious observance and belief of American-born Sephardim further demonstrates their similarities with Ashkenazim and, to a certain extent, with the non-Jewish middle class. Of 219 respondents, 68 percent claimed that their homes were less observant than those of their parents. In terms of kashrut, 80 percent of the immigrant generation kept kasher homes as compared to only 28 percent of their children. Ninety-five percent of the immigrants had observed at least some Shabbat traditions, while only 63 percent of their children claim to do so. Nearly two-thirds of men and women under age forty do not attend synagogues except on holidays or special occasions. Four percent of the men and 14 percent of the women do not attend at all. Seven percent of the under-forty group claim that their religious beliefs are not in harmony with any of the established forms of Judaism. In the area of religious beliefs and affiliation, there is an unmistakable movement away from traditional religious modes.

In terms of Sephardic customs, foods, in terms of Judeo-Spanish language and folklore, there can be no doubt that third- and fourth-generation American Sephardim are not, cannot, and will not preserve them to a very great extent. The evidence is unquestionable. Sephardic *usos y costumbres* (practices and customs) are merely exotic, nostalgic attempts to preserve things which are associated with pleasant memories. These things do not and cannot live naturally. We are at the end of the Sephardic cycle in history as far as these things are concerned.

I could go on and on, but I shall not. You can read the study in full in the *American Jewish Yearbook*. I simply want to ask the following question: if everything I have stated is true, what then should American Sephardim be doing? For one thing, we should face the facts. We should not talk about a Sephardic cultural renaissance when, in the normal way of understanding this term, such a renaissance is not only impossible but is a vulgar exploitation of unsuspecting individuals who still think Sephardic culture can be revived to be what it once was. There can be no practical renaissance, only a theoretical one as I shall explain in a moment. We must face what Professor Benardete once called "the massive reality" that we are an incredibly small minority and that we necessarily will be swept into the majority stream. We simply cannot resist.

What then should we do in a positive way? I am a great believer in the power of ideas. Matthew Arnold was fond of invoking the term *zeitgeist*, or the spirit of the times, as the vast resource of ideas which pervades society and which changes from age to age. I believe the role of Sephardim is in the world of ideas, in effecting change in the Jewish *zeitgeist*. We have a distinctive culture, or one should say, many distinctive Sephardic cultures. All of these are part of the Jewish experience and belong to everyone, just as the Baal Shem Tov, Rabbi Shimshon Rephael Hirsch, and Rabbi A. Y. Kook belong to everyone. Our task is to communicate our experience to the entire Jewish people, to make our ideas part of the general Jewish spirit.

Perhaps I can explain what I mean by referring to our own congregation. We are the Spanish and Portuguese Synagogue. Our original ancestors in Amsterdam were ex-*conversos*. Our customs, attitudes, style of worship, emphases on certain Jewish values over others are all perfectly legitimate parts of Jewish tradition. Here we are part of a congregation with extremely few individuals who even have ex-*converso* blood in them. We are Turkish Jews and Polish Jews and Syrian Jews and Russian Jews, German Jews and North African Jews; yet we are the ones who are giving the world of Jewry an opportunity to experience the ex-*converso* religious quest. We do this, of course, because Shearith Israel is meaningful to us for many reasons. But *de facto* we are doing something so important for Judaism that if we did not exist Jewish life would be impoverished. We provide an option, an alternative, a different and unique approach to Judaism. This is meaningful to us and therefore it lives and flourishes; but it is vital to the whole Jewish community to know that we exist. They need us desperately. They need us so they can see the vastness and power of Judaism. There is more than one Jewish approach to God.

This is the future of Sephardic culture in America. Our communities will not be based on genetic Sephardim, but on people of all backgrounds who want to explore and experience

Sephardic approaches to Judaism. The task before us, I believe, is to research our ancient communities, to find what is distinctive and meaningful within our histories, to write and to publish, to speak widely, to reinvigorate our synagogues, schools and communal institutions with Sephardic ideas and values. What is good from our tradition should be lived in our own lives and shared with as many others as would like to share with us. We will survive not in flesh and blood so much as in ideas. Our task is to discover and articulate our ideas.

20

SEPHARDIM: WHO ARE WE AND WHAT MAKES US UNIQUE?

I recently had an experience which many of you may also have had. Our family was watching old home movies taken in the mid-1950's. On the screen, I saw myself as a little boy. I also saw my parents, grandparents, many uncles and aunts—all singing and dancing, celebrating happy events in their lives. A good many people in the pictures are no longer alive. And those of us who are living are considerably older and different from the images on the screen. There was a particular poignancy in seeing the film of my late parents, who—in the movies—were younger than I am right now.

I had a seemingly surrealistic encounter with my past. I had the odd sense of being in two places and two eras at the very same moment. I was a grown man sitting on the couch and I was the little boy on the movie screen.

This experience, I believe, contains profound significance. It prods us to think about the meaning of the past, the meaning of history. At the same time, it awakens within us the need to see the connection between ourselves and our past.

Dr. Wilder Penfield, a noted neurologist, wrote an important study in the early 1950's on the nature of human memory. He found that there are three aspects to memory. First, we record in our brain every experience which we have. Second, we have

An address at the plenary session of the annual convention of the American Sephardi Federation, New York City, May 31, 1993.

the capacity to retrieve data from our memory bank, sometimes with more efficiency and sometimes with less. If we did not have the power to retrieve this information, we simply would not know who we are. We would be separated from our own past, from our own cohesive identity. Our lives make sense only insofar as our memory keeps our past alive within us.

Dr. Penfield also described a third quality of memory. He found that when people recall certain experiences, they also bring back to life their actual feelings and sensations when those experiences originally occurred. Each of us has had this happen to us. We have smelled freshly baked bread and have imagined ourselves back in our mother's kitchen. We have heard a song, and suddenly we are teenagers at a party. These memories of past experiences trigger within us an outpouring of emotion. We do not simply recall the past events as objective happenings. Rather, we somehow re-enter the past, actually becoming participants in it once again. If only for an instant, we are transported back in time. We can smell the fragrances, hear the voices, hold the hands—we are there.

These insights underscore the Jewish understanding of history. For us, history is *not* simply an intellectual understanding of the past. Instead, our perception of history is: memory, collective memory. By this, I refer to memory on its deepest level, where we experience the past and in some way relive it. When we celebrate Pesah, for example, we do not say only that our ancestors were slaves in Egypt. The Haggadah teaches that we are supposed to feel that we ourselves were slaves in Egypt and were redeemed by the Almighty. We eat the matzah and the bitter herbs; we re-awaken within ourselves the sensations of slavery experienced by our ancestors. Another example: we have just celebrated Shavuot, which commemorates God's revelation at Mount Sinai. We did not view the revelation simply as a historical event that occurred thousands of years ago. Rather, our tradition teaches that each of our souls was there

at Sinai; each one of us received the Torah. The celebration of
Shavuot brings us back to our own original experience.

The more intense one's memory is, the more he is able to
feel connected to the past. On the other hand, the more we see
history as an objective study in which we contemplate what
happened to other people in earlier times, the more alienated
we become from the past.

One of the great rabbis of our generation was Rabbi Joseph
Soloveitchik, of blessed memory; he passed away during Pesah
this year. In a lecture he once gave in memory of his father,
Rabbi Soloveitchik described himself studying the Talmud. As
he sat at his desk with the volume of the Talmud open before
him, it seemed as though the talmudic sages actually appeared
in the room. He argued with them, offered refutations and
proofs; he entered a heated dialogue with them. As the discussion intensified, other luminaries entered the fray: Rashi,
Rambam, Rabbi Soloveitchik's grandfather and father. The
discussion grew into a lively conversation among various
sages, with Rabbi Soloveitchik himself in the midst of the fray.
He, who was ostensibly sitting alone studying a page of Talmud, found himself in a room filled with great sages. For him,
these figures from the past had become his contemporaries.
They were dynamic, ever-present forces in his life. In some
powerful sense, their lives had transcended their deaths.

This description illustrates a vital point in the Jewish understanding of history. We don't leave history behind; we bring it
along with us. We don't relegate our ancestors to the past; we
bring them into the present.

We now come to the topic which I was assigned:
"Sephardim: Who are we and what makes us unique?" The
fact is, each of us has to answer these questions individually. I
will not pretend to speak for everyone. But to answer these
questions, we need to consider several issues.

First, what is our relationship with our Sephardic past? What
role does it play in our lives? Is it merely something ancient
which gives us pride, or is it also something which we feel is

actually contemporary with us, living with us? To what extent
does the past inspire our lives?

There are several ways in which Sephardim relate to the
past.

Nostalgia! Nostalgia is a beautiful sentiment. We remember
the old days, sometimes with tears in our eyes. We remember
parents and grandparents, famous ancestors and cultural
heroes.

We could not live without nostalgia. We all like to ponder
some golden age which we think existed in the past. I certainly
do not underestimate the value of nostalgia, nor do I under-
value its power in our lives. But nostalgia alone cannot give
our lives meaning. Nostalgia is an appetizer, not the main
course. The question is: to what extent do our ancestors actually participate in our lives, to what extent are they our
friends, our contemporaries? A wit once noted that family lin-
eage is like a potato: the best part of it is under the ground.
But if the best part of our civilization is under the ground,
then we are in serious trouble.

Another connection to our past, besides nostalgia but akin to
it, is ethnic pride. We speak with eloquence about our ethnic
achievements: our cuisine, music, folklore, literature. When-
ever we sponsor a Sephardic event, we see to it that we serve
the foods for which our communities are famed. Why are we
so devoted to these foods? I think it is because they tie us to
our past. They are no longer staples in most of our diets; they
are "specialties" reserved for special occasions, Shabbat and
holidays. For our parents and grandparents, Sephardic food
was their normal diet. But when we eat it, it is not only because
it tastes good. More importantly, it links us to our parents and
grandparents, to an earlier era.

When Sephardim want to intensify their ethnic connected-
ness, they sing old Sephardic songs or listen to recordings of
them. When we hear these songs, we may actually be hearing
the voices of our parents and grandparents in our minds.
Pride in our ethnicity, if not exaggerated out of context, is a

positive feature. But if it becomes the main aspect of cultural identification, then—like nostalgia—it is symbolic of cultural decline, even incipient death.

Nostalgia and ethnic pride cannot easily be transmitted to a future generation. We cannot give over our very personal emotions and memories. Each generation must leave behind many of the sentiments of their parents and grandparents.

We live in a period of transition. Many of us had parents who spoke Judeo-Spanish. But for us, this language is no longer our mother tongue. We may understand some words, we may even use some phrases. But it is not our language of communication. Many Sephardim of my generation and the younger generation are married to non-Sephardic spouses, for whom the traditional Sephardic languages are foreign. All such marriages entail compromises and changes. Our children and grandchildren necessarily will have a different connection to the Sephardic past than we have. This is natural, normal, and is nothing to fear. Our generation is not the same as our grandparents' generation; our grandchildren's generation will not be the same as ours. This is an inexorable fact, a massive reality which we cannot change.

What can be transmitted from generation to generation? What are the essential features of Sephardic civilization which we feel must be passed on to future generations? What are our deepest and best insights, teachings, traditions? If all we can transmit to our children and grandchildren are a few family recipes and some love songs—then we are in trouble! This cannot be the vehicle for the long-term transmission of a culture.

Let us now consider a third way of relating to the past. This discussion relates to the first part of this lecture. We must experience our history as something personal, something alive, something which touches us and inspires us. We must consider the past not as a collection of data.

In the case of nostalgia, we attempt to transfer ourselves out of the present and into the past. But in the case of living history, we attempt to take the past out of the past and bring it into the present. These two modes of remembering are ultimately the vital signs which indicate the life or the death of a culture. If we must transfer ourselves into the past in order to experience our culture, then we know that our civilization is on the verge of death. But if we bring the past into our present, if we make it contemporaneous—then we are moving strongly and creatively towards the future.

What are some of the unique aspects of Sephardic culture which we ought to retrieve from the past and incorporate into the present and future? Let me cite several major themes.

One of the distinctive features of classic Sephardic culture has been the ability to attain excellence in Torah wisdom as well as in general knowledge. Why do we idealize Rambam? He was perhaps the greatest halakhic scholar since talmudic times. And he was, at the same time, a philosopher, medical doctor, logician. He is a shining representative of Sephardic civilization at its best. If we consider other spiritual giants of medieval Sephardic Jewry, we will find that they too were well versed in Torah and general culture. Rabbi Shemuel ha-Naggid was a rabbinic authority—and also a statesman and military leader; Rabbi Yehudah Halevi was a poet, philosopher and medical doctor; Ramban was a talmudist, kabbalist, biblical commentator—and a medical doctor; Rabbi Yitzhak Abarbanel was a statesman, financier, advisor to kings—and a classic biblical commentator. These are our great models. But do they live with us? For some of us the answer is yes, and for some of us the answer is no. How many of us (and our children and grandchildren) actually study the teachings of these luminaries? How many of us consider them our friends, associates and teachers? It is simple enough to rattle off their names and take pride in our ancestry. But it is quite difficult to confront these ancestors and bring them into the present with us. That requires serious study, hard work, genuine devotion. There are no shortcuts. If we relate to our Sephardic ancestors as though they were ornamental portraits on the wall, then our connection to them is weak; for future generations, the connection will only grow weaker.

A second basic feature of Sephardic life has been our sense of traditionalism. Sephardic communities throughout the generations have been devoted to Jewish law, kabbalah, ethical teachings. Our customs and traditions have given our lives stability within an idealistic religious context. Sephardim maintained traditional communities; we did not divide into factions and movements. Our people expected that the community would function according to traditional Jewish law. Certainly, there were individuals whose personal lives did not conform to full Torah observance. But even they expected that the community standards would be maintained. Sephardim were insightful enough and traditional enough to know that ideological divisiveness destroys the fabric of Jewish life. If the Sephardic point of view could have prevailed, then all world Jewry would be much better off today.

The Sephardic vision of Jewish communal life is powerful. It provides a means of holding communities together by relying on traditional standards. It also shows tolerance to those who may not live up to those standards in their private lives. If you ask Sephardim what they think is a basic characteristic of Sephardic life, most will answer: tolerance. Indeed, this has been one of our hallmarks. It is regrettable that Sephardim are now being drawn into the ideological battles which have been created by Ashkenazim.

We are heirs to a profound worldview. Do we share this worldview? Does it impact on our lives? Do we articulate our position within the general Jewish community? In other words, to what extent is this an idea of the past to which we give lip service, and to what extent is it a dynamic force in contemporary Sephardic life?

Another key aspect of Sephardic culture is optimism. In spite of the many adversities we have suffered in our history, we have maintained our self-respect, our positive view of life. Sephardim love to celebrate, to enjoy life. Religious observances are marked by a spirit of happiness. The music in our synagogues is uplifting and encouraging.

Let me make one more point. Throughout the centuries, the Sephardic elite and the Sephardic masses have had a profound connection to kabbalah and ethical teachings. Our tradition contains within it a deep sense of spirituality, an appreciation of meditation and quiet thought. Sephardic culture has recognized that human beings have an inner life which must be nourished and sustained. The perception of holiness in the world has been an important element in our collective consciousness.

Historically, Sephardim have had a very pure faith, a very deep love of God. Even the simplest Sephardic Jew sings his prayers with a spirituality which transcends words.

While this spiritual sense has been basic to Sephardic life over the centuries, our question is: is it a basic feature in our lives today? Is God close and vital to us? When we are in synagogue, do we feel that we are in a strange place, where we are only observers of a performance? Or, do we feel we are in our spiritual home? Other questions: do we pray in synagogue regularly? Do we pray in a Sephardic synagogue? Do we view our lives as being connected with the Sephardic wellsprings of spirituality?

We need to think carefully about ourselves and our future. In America, we are accustomed to think that if we press a button we can attain what we want. We imagine that if we spend enough money or use the right techniques, then we will achieve the desired results. But this approach is deceptive. In the work of transmitting a culture, there are no such magic devices or formulae. If we want Sephardic culture to be alive, we have to invest ourselves in it. We have to enter a living dialogue with the past. Our culture must pulsate within us. Do not imagine that there are simple ways which require less effort and commitment. If we want Sephardic life to flourish, the responsibility devolves on us. We must transcend nostalgia and ethnic pride, and enter into a living relationship with our past.

I started this talk by telling you about my experience watching old home movies. The characters on the screen all seem so alive. Yet, the film is only inanimate celluloid. Likewise, what is a book? It is only paper and ink—inanimate, lifeless things. The collected experiences of our ancestors as recorded in books and articles and documents—all these things are frozen, dead. There is only one way to draw life out of these inanimate items. That is through the power of our own minds and emotions, through our own personal involvement.

When we look at the movies, we bring the people on the film back to life in our minds and memories. When we read a book or experience a custom, we transform those things into living realities.

If we all had this living relationship with our past, we would have had no need for this lecture today. There would have been no relevance in asking the questions "who are we and what makes us unique?" If our culture were truly alive and vibrant, we would have no occasion to wonder about it—we would be living it naturally and without self-consciousness. If we take our religion, our culture, our Sephardic way of life seriously, then what is truly important is not talking about it, not bragging about it, not reminiscing about it: but living it. Our challenge—and it is enormous—is to make Sephardic civilization live within us.

We should be optimistic that we can succeed in some measure. After all, Sephardim are a very strong and vibrant people. We have remarkable talent and resilience. We have overcome many challenges and hurdles in the past. We are a great people.

If we do our share, the Almighty will help us to succeed.

IV

Contemporary Issues

21

THE DEMANDS
OF RABBINIC LEADERSHIP

A little over eighty years ago, a Sephardic teenager from Turkey arrived in Seattle, Washington. He and several other Sephardic newcomers had gone to the Ashkenazic Orthodox synagogue in order to connect themselves with the city's Jewish community. But the Ashkenazim had difficulty recognizing the Sephardim as Jews. The newcomers spoke Judeo-Spanish, not Yiddish; they had "strange" names like Alhadeff, Policar, Romey; they read Hebrew in an "incomprehensible" manner. Even when the Sephardim showed their *tallitot* and *tefillin*, the Ashkenazim were not altogether convinced of their Jewishness. Ultimately, a letter was sent from the Spanish and Portuguese Synagogue in New York testifying that those young Sephardim were really Jewish—and that seems to have clarified matters for the most part.

Yet, this was a painful episode in the lives of the young Sephardic Jews from Turkey and Rhodes. The Sephardic teenager I mentioned earlier was my maternal grandfather, Marco Romey, and he never forgot how his Jewishness was questioned. He lamented the fact that historical circumstances had created such a deep rift between Sephardim and Ashkenazim that one group hardly could recognize its kinship with the other.

Acceptance Speech upon election as President of the Rabbinical Council of America, Homowack Hotel, June 1990.

Now, two generations later, the grandson of that Sephardic immigrant in Seattle has been elected President of the Rabbinical Council of America! My grandfather would have been proud to witness this moment. The Jewish people has made great strides in healing the rifts among us.

The story of my grandfather's experience is an example of the sorrows that have befallen our people during our centuries of exile. *Galut* has succeeded in creating divisions among us, has separated us one from the other, has made it difficult for us even to find a common language of discourse. But we are in the process of redemption now; we are coming back together. This process, too, has its pains and struggles, but they are the pains of birth and new life. We look forward to a better day for all the Jewish people, for the land and State of Israel. It has been the Torah and halakhah which have kept the Jewish people as one people. It is through Torah and halakhah that we will be redeemed.

In this redemptive process, we as rabbis play an important role. Rabbi Elazar said in the name of Rabbi Haninah: *talmidei hakhamim marbim shalom ba-olam* (end Berakhot), "rabbinic scholars increase peace in the world." Yet, in what way do rabbis increase peace? (Indeed, it sometimes appears that rabbis are involved in altogether too much feuding and dissension!)

The answer may be found in Maharsha's glosses at the end of Berakhot and Yevamot. Maharsha tells us that *talmidei hakhamim* bring peace between the people of Israel and their Father in Heaven. By teaching Torah, the prayers and blessings, the reverence and love of God—rabbis lead Jews to find peace in their relationship with God. When all is said and done, that is our ultimate responsibility. The Rabbinical Council of America exists in order to help lead our people to find peace between themselves and our Father in Heaven. All of our work, even the most tedious and mundane, must be guided by this clear responsibility. We may not be side-tracked by the *gashmiyut* (mundane) part of our enterprise. All our work is infused with the desire to bring *shalom ben Yisra'el va-Avihem ba-shamayim* ("peace between God and Israel").

Maharsha notes that our sages were sometimes *oker davar min ha-Torah* (deviated from the technical letter of the law) in order to bring peace among the Jewish people. For example, they offered lenient rulings in order to save a woman from being in the plight of an *agunah* (abandoned wife). Thus, *talmidei hakhamim* are guided by what is right in the eyes of God and humans. They try their utmost to generate and maintain harmony in society. They do not aim to be stringent or lenient; they aim at serving God and Israel in truth. Because of this attitude, they increase real peace among people. Rabbis must be known as peacemakers, not as troublemakers. People should see us as agents of harmony, not as agents of discord. (See, for example, Yoma 86a.)

The Rabbinical Council of America is imbued with a religious vision. This is not a political club, nor an organization seeking publicity and power. Our vision far transcends the mundane and parochial. We are striving for peace between Israel and God, for peace among all the people of Israel. We pursue these goals not through coercion and anger, but through persuasion and love. We are committed to achieving authentic shalom.

At the same time, we are committed to truth. We need to see things as they really are, to understand things from a spirit of calm analysis. The Talmud (Pesahim 50a) relates the story of the seeming death of the son of Rabbi Yehoshua ben Levi. The son came back to life. Rabbi Yehoshua asked him: what did you see on the other side? He answered: *olam hafukh ra'iti*. The world there was an inversion of this world; those who are great here, are small there; those who are small here, are great there. Rabbi Yehoshua ben Levi responded: *olam barur ra'ita*. No, my son, the world you saw was not inverted at all, *it* was the real world, the clear reality. In this world, humans often misjudge who actually is great or insignificant, powerful or weak. But these misjudgments are rectified in the next world, the true world.

But then Rabbi Yehoshua asked his son: where were we, the rabbinic scholars, in the next world? And the son responded: we were the same there as we are here. In other words, it is precisely the *talmidei hakhamim* who see things as they really are, in their true clarity. The Torah gives us the ability to keep our eyes on what is real, to see through illusions. We live in a world of noise, confusion, and verbosity. There is so much commotion from so many directions that it becomes difficult to think quietly and clearly. Yet, that is the responsibility and challenge posed to rabbis—to think carefully, quietly, truly. We need to clarify what is important from that which is unimportant. We need to know when to speak and when to remain silent, when to act and when to refrain from action.

During this administration, I am hopeful that the RCA will be devoting much time to quiet and peaceful thinking in an atmosphere of love and respect. We will be having special sessions at every executive board meeting at which we will have the opportunity to explore major issues with which we must deal. We are not afraid of ideas. Let each member state his opinion, share his feelings and insights. Let us come to a consensus and move ahead together. The role of the President is not to dictate policies for the organization, but to help mold a consensus. Rav Ashi, before answering a question on the kashrut of an animal which had been slaughtered, first would call all the *shohetim* in town to give their opinion. His rationale was that they all should share in the responsibility of making a decision. I rely on this advice. I call on all members of the RCA to state their opinions on all issues. All opinions will be factored into the ultimate decisions reached by the organization.

Thus far, I have spoken of *shalom* and *emet*, peace and truth. I now turn to a third key element in religious life: *hesed*, compassion. A *talmid hakham* must be more than just a *tzaddik*. He must not only do what is right and just. A *talmid hakham* must be a *hasid*. It is a fundamental teaching that Jews are supposed to emulate God: just as He is compassionate, so we are to be compassionate; just as He is gracious, so we are to be gracious. This goes beyond simply doing what is just and fair. This entails an overwhelming drive to be genuinely pious, to go beyond what is expected of us by the letter of the law.

I think one should apply this analysis to the verse: *Tzaddik Hashem be-khol derakhav, ve-hasid be-khol ma'asav* (Tehillim 145:17, "The Lord is righteous in all His ways, and gracious in all His works"). When it comes to His approach to things, God is a *Tzaddik*. But when it comes actually to doing things, God is a *Hasid*. By extension, when we think, we must think of what is absolutely right and understand what is absolutely true; but when we act, we must act in the spirit of *hesed*, compassion, human sympathy and understanding. As we balance the pressures of *emet* and *hesed*, we arrive at *shalom*.

Our world is filled with imperfections. Each of us has his own various failings. None of us is perfect in every respect. Yet, in spite of our many weaknesses, we know that God is *Rahum* and *Hanun* (compassionate and gracious); He forgives our sins; He is patient with us. Rabbi Moshe Cordovero, in his *Tomer Devorah*, has taught that just as God is compassionate and patient even with the wicked, we too must be compassionate and patient with everyone. Our attitude towards others must be loving and respectful, not judgmental or harsh. As rabbis, we must speak favorably about all Jews and for the State of Israel. To do otherwise is to betray our responsibility as religious leaders.

I would like to close with an insight which came to me when I was walking alone through the streets of Jerusalem. I was pondering the talmudic statement that the Temple was destroyed due to *sinat hinam* (Yoma 9b). Ordinarily, we translate the phrase to mean baseless or unjustified hatred. Yet, it is very difficult to understand this type of hatred. No one says that he hates someone else for no reason. On the contrary, he can present reasons to justify the hatred. The reasons may be irrational or based on false information—yet the hater almost always believes that his hatred is justified and appropriate.

So, it seems that *sinat hinam* must mean something else. It occurred to me that the word *hinam* is derived from the word *hen*, meaning grace or charm. One of the tragedies of society is that people tend to judge others as objects, to see them as stereotypes. It is easy to hate someone who has been dehumanized, who has been labeled with an odious title. But it is far more difficult to hate someone when you look into his eyes and realize that he, too, has *hen*. He too has human feelings. He loves his family, he has fears and hopes and aspirations, he has virtues and ideals. *Sinat hinam* occurs when people hate to see the *hen* in other people. They deal with others as stereotypes, not allowing themselves to enter a sympathetic human relationship. Thus, it was *sinat hinam* which led to the downfall of the Temple in Jerusalem. Jews broke into groups and vilified those who did not share their views or practices. They came to see each other not as human beings with unique grace and sympathy, but as objects. Labels are part of the process of dehumanization.

We must be open to all Jews and not fear to see their *hen*. Even when we disagree with them, we cannot lose sight of their humanity. Calling people "Haredim" or "right-wing" or "left-wing" or "Reform" does not help us to deal with fellow Jews in a personal and loving way. These labels create barriers, barriers that can be dangerous and actually lead—God forbid—to disdain for others.

This administration will have two mottoes: (1) *talmidei hakhamim marbim shalom ba-olam*; (2) *derakheha darkhei no'am vekhol netivoteha shalom* ("its ways are the ways of pleasantness, and all its paths are of peace"). I pray that we will work together in the spirit of these teachings, so that the Rabbinical Council of America will achieve great progress in bringing peace between the people of Israel and their Father in Heaven, and in bringing peace among our people and between Israel and the nations of the world.

22

A BROAD AGENDA FOR RABBIS

*I*n Pirkei Avot (6:9), we find the fascinating story of Rabbi Yosei ben Kisma. As you recall, he was offered an abundance of gold and precious jewels if he would agree to serve in a certain community. His response was: "If you were to give me all the silver, gold, and precious stones in the world, I would dwell only in a place of Torah."

At first glance, Rabbi Yosei ben Kisma appears to be a selfless person. He was willing to forgo tremendous prosperity in order to dwell among Torah scholars, to engage in Torah learning. He would prefer to retain his simple and pure life of spiritual fulfillment, rather than to travel to another place where he would be a wealthy man, but have a less conducive Torah environment. This indeed appears to be a great sacrifice for the sake of Torah.

On the other hand, Rabbi Yosei ben Kisma's attitude might also be seen as being selfish. His concern was only with his own spiritual well-being. He could not be induced to sacrifice his own peace of mind in order to serve a community which could have benefitted from his spiritual leadership. What would happen if all of us followed the example of Rabbi Yosei? Who would serve the Jewish communities scattered throughout North America? Who would take the challenge to teach Torah

Annual Report by the President of the Rabbinical Council of America, delivered on Tuesday evening, June 11, 1991, at the Annual Convention of the RCA at the Homowack Lodge.

in communities where there is not a strong Torah presence? Doesn't genuine spiritual leadership entail self-sacrifice?

I believe that the next Mishnah should be studied as a response to Rabbi Yosei. The Mishnah tells us that the Almighty has five *kinyanim* (acquisitions) in this world. Torah is one of them. But there are four other categories as well: Heaven and earth, Avraham, Israel, the Bet Mikdash. Heaven and earth remind us that our responsibilities must transcend our own immediate domain. The universe is vast, and it demands our attention. Avraham was a man of "outreach." He preached the unity of God to a pagan society; he made converts; he was interested in the needs of others. Israel is charged with being a holy people, with teaching the word of God to the world. The Bet Mikdash symbolizes not only service to God, but also compassion to fellow human beings. This thought is epitomized in the Midrash which states that the Bet Mikdash was built on the site where two brothers met, each in the process of selflessly trying to help the other. In other words, the Mishnah responds to Rabbi Yosei ben Kisma by saying that the responsibility of a spiritual person transcends studying Torah in a self-contained community. On the contrary, religious leadership must be genuinely selfless, compassionate and outward-looking.

During the first year of this administration, we have maintained a strong commitment to all five *kinyanim*. We have been able to build on the achievements of previous administrations, and we also have been able to break new ground in important areas.

The first *kinyan* is Torah. Without a commitment to Torah, we have no reason to exist. We are first and foremost an organization of rabbis devoted to studying and teaching Torah. Everything else flows from this commitment.

We have instituted the practice of allowing for learning and discussion for at least one hour during each of our Executive Board meetings. We have had lectures, *shi'urim* and symposia on a wide variety of topics. This process has enabled all of us to learn and to share our own insights.

We have been committed to the proper functioning of our Halakhah Commission. We are blessed with a Commission composed of leading rabbinical scholars from within the RCA. They have been dealing with a number of complicated questions, and we are hopeful that several of their *piskei halakhah* will be made public during the coming year. To underscore the importance of the Halakhah Commission, this convention has invited each member of the Commission to deliver a *shi'ur*. We have all been impressed by the erudition and sincerity demonstrated in these *shi'urim*. It should be clear to all of us that the RCA has the ability and the talent to serve as the halakhic authority for our community.

We can take pride in the health care proxy issued under the auspices of our Medical Ethics Commission. This is a clear example of responsible Torah leadership. This health care proxy will provide a vast service to our community.

This administration has devoted much time and effort to strengthening our Bet Din. We have worked closely with the officers and board members of the Bet Din of America. At this convention, the Bet Din will announce the name of our new Rosh Bet Din. I am delighted that we have reached this point, and am confident that the Bet Din will grow in stature during the coming years.

Anyone who has participated in any of the meetings, conferences or in this convention will have sensed that Torah comes first and foremost for the RCA. Our integrity as rabbis depends on our Torah learning and teaching. Our credibility as a rabbinic council is only as strong as our commitment to Torah.

Shamayim va-aretz kinyan ehad. We must be concerned with the grand issues, with the span of heaven and earth. And we are.

Interestingly enough, last week I represented the RCA at a conference of the Joint Appeal in Religion and Science, a group dedicated to environmental and ecological issues. We discussed the problems of *shamayim*—the gap in the ozone layer and global warming trends. And we discussed the needs of the earth—conservation, world hunger, etc. When the Joint Appeal in Religion and Science searched for an Orthodox Jewish participant, they came to the RCA. We are known and respected for our worldly concerns.

The RCA has forcefully expressed itself on a number of moral issues affecting the well-being of society in general. We have called for more public attention to the problems of the homeless. We have stated publicly that we are alarmed by the breakdown in moral values in society. We have deplored the growing acceptability in our society of homosexuality as a valid lifestyle. Through our statements to the press, to government officials, to leaders of various organizations—we have made it clear that the RCA is a force for morality and decency in society at large.

In terms of social action, we have reemphasized the Torah commandment instructing us to contribute ten percent of income for charitable purposes. We have noted with pain that a number of public officials have reported giving extremely small amounts of money to charity. A mayor of a large city reported giving only $125.00 to charity last year, plus a few hundred dollars worth of old clothes to the Salvation Army. This is not proper moral leadership. If we truly believe that we have a responsibility to society, then we all must be prepared to pay our share to make things better. We have called upon our members to make sure that they are setting the example by giving at least a tenth of their income to charity each year (*ma'asser*). Moreover, we have asked our members to preach and teach on the importance of the *ma'asser*. If all members of society would meet this simple responsibility, then much of the pain and suffering of our society could be relieved. We are calling not just for gifts of money; we are calling for an expenditure of time and effort, a new spirit of volunteerism. We must care about others, and we must teach others to care.

Avraham kinyan ehad. Avraham is known for his compassion and outreach to others. We share in our forefather's traditions.

During this administration, we have made many efforts to keep lines of communication open with other groups in our community. On the right, we have had ongoing communication with the Agudath Israel. On the other side, we have had a number of meetings with the leadership of the Central Conference of American Rabbis (Reform) and the Rabbinic Assembly (Conservative). These meetings have been candid, and have not been free of pain. However, we are firmly convinced that honest communication ultimately serves the best interests of the Jewish community.

I would also like to report that under the auspices of Dr. Norman Lamm at Yeshiva University, there is an Orthodox presidents group which meets regularly at Yeshiva. This group is quite creative and progressive, and considers a wide range of issues affecting American Orthodoxy. During this past year, a joint conference was sponsored by Yeshiva University, the Rabbinical Council of America, the Orthodox Union, and Young Israel on the topic of rabbinic-lay relationships. I think this was the first time these four important groups worked together to present a unified program. Additionally, this presidents group has dealt with such issues as Orthodox participation in UJA-Federation, and with the religious absorption of Soviet Jews in Israel. We also have opposed the appointment of an intermarried person to serve in a position of leadership in a Jewish educational project.

We have reestablished the Achdut Commission with the Orthodox Union. This is symbolic of the increasingly warm relationship between our organizations, and of the mutual commitment to strengthen each other, thereby strengthening American Orthodoxy.

The RCA, through our participation in the Synagogue Council of America, also maintains lines of communication with the non-Jewish religious world. Our concern has been broad and deep.

Yisra'el kinyan ehad. In this category, I include commitment to Medinat Yisrael and the people of Israel. The RCA was a fiery and forceful advocate of the needs of Israel throughout the course of this past year, as in past years. As an organization, we have worked with cohesiveness, energy and effectiveness. It was the RCA which spearheaded the Shabbat of Protest this past October, following a United Nations condemnation of Israel in which the United States participated. It was the RCA which called on its membership and the community at large to recite extra Psalms on the Fast of Tevet, protesting the political siege of Jerusalem taking place at the United Nations. These events were widely covered in the press throughout the United States, Canada and beyond. It was the RCA which joined with the Orthodox Union and Young Israel to sponsor a day of learning during the Gulf crisis. These groups issued guidelines, including the recitation of Psalms, during the entire period of the war.

In December, the RCA sent a solidarity mission to Israel at a time when tourism had all but dried up. We were there in good numbers, and we were greeted warmly by the Israeli people, government and media. We held our mid-year conference in Washington, D.C. This was one of the greatest mid-year conferences I have ever attended. We had the opportunity to hear opinion makers in government; more importantly, we had the opportunity to be heard. And we were heard. Our various statements and resolutions made their impact. We have conducted a series of ongoing visits to government officials, and we also have carried on an extensive correspondence to bolster the position of Israel.

Much of what we have done has been reported in the press. We were in the *New York Times*, in stories put out by the Associated Press, and I even had the opportunity to be on CBS National News. We also have been heard on radio stations in various communities throughout the United States.

During this administration, we have revitalized our Ezra Fund. Years ago, the Ezra Fund served to raise money to ship packages to Jews in the Soviet Union. We have shifted our attention now to the spiritual absorption of Soviet Jews in Israel. We have already begun to raise considerable funds to invest in vital projects in Israel to provide religious books, ritual objects, and instruction to Soviet Jews.

Bet ha-Mikdash kinyan ehad. The Bet Mikdash stands for *hesed*, compassion. During this administration, we have made efforts to raise the level of civility, to take the high road. As an example, the first meeting of this administration was at the Yom Iyyun last August, where we discussed issues relating to homosexuality. We had four papers delivered, and there was plenty of room for controversy. We had an excellent attendance, and everyone wanted to state his opinion. We announced the ground rules: everyone would have the opportunity to speak, but must limit his comments to three minutes or less. Virtually everyone complied with this rule. Everyone had a chance to speak, all opinions were heard, everything was done respectfully and with dignity. Indeed, at the end of the day, everyone was congratulating each other on how well things went. That Yom Iyyun was an example of the RCA at its best.

We have established a Shemirat ha-Lashon committee for the purpose of ensuring civil speech within the community. Not only do we want to encourage respectfulness among ourselves, but we want to influence the community at large to conduct themselves with respect and propriety.

We have dealt with a number of stories in the media which have presented distortions of the RCA. These stories have caused pain and concern to all of us. But we have not responded harshly. Even when we were maligned, we responded gently and responsibly.

We have refused to be dragged down to the gutter. And I am proud to say this. As rabbis and teachers, we must remain above the fray, we must keep our sense of propriety and dignity, and we must strive with all our might to create a spirit of conciliation and harmony.

We have attempted to reach out to our colleagues. When-ever I visited communities for lectures, I tried to arrange meetings with RCA colleagues in those cities. I always was pleased by the reception and enthusiasm of those whom I met. We have maintained an ongoing line of telephone communi-cation with many of our members. A number of our commit-tees have functioned outside the New York area. Before many of our Executive meetings, I sent letters to members of the Executive Board throughout the country in order to inform them of the issues on the agenda and to solicit their sugges-tions and guidance.

The RCA also has reached out to our younger members by establishing a committee of young *musmakhim* (ordained rab-bis). Indeed, we are all impressed by the wonderful attendance of younger colleagues at this convention.

In order to increase the level of communication among our membership, we have revised the format of the *RCA Record*. It comes out more frequently and includes more news about the inner workings of the organization. Moreover, it affords the opportunity for each of our members to express his own opin-ion on various matters of concern to the RCA.

I would also like to note the regular meetings of the Future Directions Committee, which focuses on issues of concern to us which will be arising within the next year, two years and beyond. In other words, our concern must be geared not only for our present situation, but for preparing for future chal-lenges as well.

Although we have made much progress during the course of this past year, there still remain a number of problematic areas. Not always have we been able to mobilize ourselves to work as a cohesive group. Strong differences of opinion some-times have prevented our moving ahead in a unified and forceful fashion.

While the RCA is certainly open to a wide range of ideas and opinions, some individuals have not always been happy with our absolute commitment to freedom of expression. It was told of Winston Churchill that during World War I, when he was a leading military figure in England, he was fond of reading the poetry of Siegfried Sassoon, a pacifist. Some people complained to Churchill that he should not be reading the poetry of a pacifist, that it was demoralizing to the troops. Churchill responded: "I am not a bit afraid of Siegfried Sassoon; the man thinks. I am afraid of people who do not think." Likewise, we need not fear people who have ideas different from ours, if their ideas are thought out and reasoned. We need to fear those individuals who simply do not think, who do not want to reason things out.

Another growing problem area relates to the Synagogue Council of America. From my perspective, the groups involved are not entirely satisfied with the organization. There are real problems on a number of levels. At a recent meeting at the Synagogue Council, I raised the following questions: "If there were no Synagogue Council of America, would we gather together today to establish it? Does this organization fill a deeply felt need on the part of all our organizations?" I believe that these are serious questions. Aside from the ideological issue, on a sheer pragmatic level we constantly need to reevaluate our involvement in the Synagogue Council of America. Does this involvement serve a real purpose for us and for the community at large? Are there other ways of achieving our goals? I don't think we can answer these questions at this moment, but I do think they have to be considered very carefully during the coming year.

Finally, I think there has been somewhat of an erosion in our sense of religious leadership. We have been embattled from the right and from the left. We are being attacked constantly for one reason or another by people who have their own agendas and who seek to undermine the Orthodoxy for which we stand. We are a strong group, and we need to build on our strengths. We need a shared vision, a sense of public mission. We need to reaffirm that we are answerable to the Almighty. Our eyes should be in the direction of Heaven, not glancing with fear or anxiety to individuals on the right or on the left of us. Without a clear sense of purpose, and a sense that we have the ability to accomplish our goals, the RCA is weakened.

The final chapter of the Pirkei Avot ends with the statement: "All that the Holy One, blessed be He, created in His world, He created only for His own honor." We don't serve the RCA and the Jewish community for our honor or for the honor of our families. We work solely for the honor of the Holy One, blessed be He. This is an enormous challenge and privilege. I am proud to say that after one year as president of the RCA, I feel that our men are worthy of this challenge and privilege.

23

THE NATURE OF GENUINE PIETY

*R*eligion has two faces. One face is that of saintliness, idealism, holiness, and selflessness. But the other face is one of hatred, cruelty, selfishness, and egotism. Within the world of religion, one can find the most exemplary human beings; and one also can find inquisitors. In his play *The Father*, August Strindberg has one of his characters state: "It is strange that as soon as you begin to talk about God and love, your voice becomes hard and your eyes full of hate." This is a reflection of the second face of religion, when a person cloaks himself in religious garb but actually is filled with hatred and cruelty.

I think all of us can think of examples of religion at its worst as well as examples of religion at its best. Each of us has seen the two faces of religion.

But I think we all would agree that every person who claims to be religious actually thinks himself to reflect the loving and beautiful face of religion. Even those who are cruel and hateful believe themselves to be righteous and good. Perhaps it is a feature of human nature for individuals to delude themselves, to judge themselves in the best possible light.

But what are the standards by which we can measure true piety? How can we know if we are living religion at its best?

President's Report to the Rabbinical Council of America, delivered on Tuesday evening, June 16, 1992, at the Annual Convention of the RCA at the Homowack Lodge.

235

How can we tell if our own faces reflect the saintliness and idealism of religion?

The Talmud (Berakhot 4a) offers us a framework by which we can evaluate genuine piety. In Tehillim 86, King David asks God to guard his soul, *ki hasid ani*, "for I am a saint." The word *hasid* denotes true and selfless piety. It is religion at its best. Several opinions are offered by the Talmud in order to understand exactly why King David referred to himself as a *hasid*.

The first observation is:

> Said David before God: Master of the universe, am I not a *hasid*? All the other kings of the east and west sleep until three hours [of sunlight], but I arise at midnight to thank you.

What was King David saying? All other kings slept late, they were concerned with their own honor and comfort. But King David woke up in the middle of the night in order to praise God. In other words, he did not stand on ceremony, thinking that as a king he was entitled to pamper himself. He demonstrated that his commitment to God was his primary concern. King David was a *hasid* because he was not egocentric—he was theocentric.

It is not always easy for a person to be able to distinguish true piety from false piety. One must be scrupulously self-critical in order to root out egocentrism. Pertaining to this subject, we have the concept of *yuhara*. *Yuhara* refers to behavior which ostensibly is pious, but which actually stems from arrogance and presumptuousness.

Rabbi Eliyahu Israel, an important Sephardic *posek* during the eighteenth century (in Rhodes and Alexandria), dealt with a case of *yuhara* in his book of responsa, *Kol Eliyahu*. As you may know, the general Sephardic custom is to remain seated during the reading of the Ten Commandments. This practice is in contradistinction to the custom of many Ashkenazim, which is to stand during this reading. Rabbi Israel was presented with a case which arose in a Sephardic congregation. When the Ten Commandments were being read, the congregation—appropriately—remained seated. However, several young men arose for the reading. This generated controversy in the congregation. Obviously, those young men who arose thought they were performing an act of piety. After all, they stood in order to show respect to the Ten Commandments. Rabbi Israel ruled that these would-be pietists were wrong. By standing when the rest of the congregation remained seated, they actually were insulting the congregation and its accepted custom. They were trying to show themselves to be more respectful and more pious than everyone else. This constitutes *yuhara*—arrogance in the garb of piety. Rabbi Israel ruled that these individuals desist from this practice in the future. Moreover, if they did stand while the congregation remained seated, they were to be subject to communal censure.

The *Sedei Hemed* (3:28) deals with an even more subtle issue. May a person perform an act of excessive piety when he is alone in his own home, when no one else can possibly see him? The general opinion is that such activity does not constitute *yuhara*, since no one else witnesses it. However, the *Sedei Hemed* cites an opinion which states that even in this case the person is guilty of *yuhara*. How can this be? No one even sees him or is aware of his behavior! The point of this opinion is that *yuhara* is a frame of mind. A person may do acts of great piety in private, and nevertheless fill himself with feelings of self-righteousness and self-importance. Even though no one sees him, he comes to consider himself as being an ultra-pious individual. This feeling is not true religion: it is egocentrism.

It is clear, then, that one needs to be exceedingly careful in evaluating his own motives. Is he acting as a *hasid*, or is he only promoting himself while hiding in the clothing of *hasidut*?

It sometimes happens that people engage in in-fighting, power struggles, defamation of character—all in the name of religion. They spread controversy and dissension, yet they pose as peace-makers and lovers of God and Israel. Such behavior, though, is not a reflection of the true ideals of religion: it is demagoguery, it is false. It needs to be exposed for what it is.

The Talmud offers another explanation of why King David was a *hasid*.

> Said David before God: Master of the universe, am I not a *hasid*? All the other kings of the east and west sit in large groups for their honor, whereas my hands are dirtied with menstrual blood in order to permit a woman to her husband.

There are several issues here. First, this statement shows that King David took personal responsibility. He dealt with difficult halakhic issues, and did not seek to shirk his own duty. Rabbi Hayyim David Halevi (*Aseh Lekha Rav*, 2:61) dealt with a question from a rabbinic judge who came to a certain halakhic decision. But a greater authority disagreed with him. The question was: should the judge follow his own opinion, or should he defer to the greater authority? The question implies that the judge had reviewed the decision of the greater authority, but nevertheless felt that his own decision was correct. Rabbi Halevi ruled:

> Not only does a judge have the right to rule against his rabbis; he also has an obligation to do so [if he believes their decision to be incorrect, and he has strong proofs to support his own position]. If the decision of those greater than he does not seem right to him, and he is not comfortable following it, and yet he follows that decision [in deference to their authority], then it is almost certain that he has rendered a false judgment [*din sheker*].

Rabbi Moshe Feinstein (*Iggerot Moshe*, Y.D. 3:88) dealt with a case of a rabbi in Benei Berak who was not sure if he was allowed to disagree with rulings of the Hazon Ish, who had been the halakhic authority for that community. Rabbi Feinstein ruled that the rabbi had every right to disagree with the Hazon Ish, as long as this was done in a respectful way. Moreover, the Hazon Ish never could have believed that he was infallible and that no one would ever criticize or disagree with some of his teachings.

Thus, one must have the ability to take responsibility, to argue his case. One must not fold under pressure or lose heart due to opposition.

During the past two years, I have learned that not everyone has this quality. Often enough, we have reached decisions after discussions and deliberations. As expected, there were always those who opposed the decisions and launched their attacks. As the criticism and opposition intensified, a number of those involved in the original decision backed away. A handful of individuals were left to fight the battles—many others scurried for the sidelines.

King David's *hasidut* was manifested not only in his courage to take personal responsibility, but also in his concern for basic human situations. He did not say that he was too important or too good to deal with the nitty-gritty of human life. He got his hands dirty. He made his judgments based on first-hand experience, not on theoretical knowledge.

As you all know, there has been considerable controversy surrounding a recent paper issued by the RCA Round Table on the subject of intermarriage. While you may agree or disagree with that particular paper, every rabbi who has spoken to an intermarried couple or who has dealt with actual cases of conversion has had first-hand experience with the issues involved. Such rabbis are not afraid to get their hands dirty. They don't make pronouncements from ivory towers: they base their decisions on what their own eyes see, what their own minds think, what their own hearts feel. I recently had a discussion with a Rosh Yeshiva who was strongly critical of the Round Table paper. He told me that before the paper was issued, we should have consulted with some *gedolim* (sages). I asked him to let me know the names of *gedolim* who actually deal with intermarried couples and who perform conversions. He responded that my point was irrelevant.

Yet, it is not irrelevant at all. When passing judgment on issues which affect family life in so profound a way, one must have personal experience. King David was able to rule as he did precisely because he got his hands dirty. Rabbis also must get their hands dirty. They must deal with complicated and troubling cases. They do not have the luxury of hiding away in safe havens.

I commend the rabbis of the RCA for their heroic, front-line work on behalf of Torah. It is the quality of a *hasid* to face the problems of life forthrightly. People who don't get their hands dirty in performing the sacred work of Torah have no right to pass judgment on those who have the courage and moral integrity to involve themselves in difficult problems.

The Talmud offers a third criterion for being a *hasid*:

> Whatever I do, I first consult Mefiboshet, my teacher, and ask him: "Mefiboshet, my teacher, have I judged correctly? Have I punished fairly? Have I vindicated fairly? Was I correct in my judgments of purity and impurity?" and I was not embarrassed [to consult him].

King David was willing to face criticism and correction. He was interested in finding truth, not in maintaining his own position at any cost. In other words, he was an idealist, seriously devoted to truth: he was not an egotist.

Hatam Sofer (vol. 1, *Orah Hayyim* 208) writes:

> But those who specifically wish that their colleagues will rule for them—with the intent of swaying their [the colleagues'] opinions to their own [opinions], such people are deviating from the path of truth and are going after crooked judgment.

There are those who take a position and then are ashamed to back down—even when they are wrong. They will fabricate every kind of argument to bolster their position, no matter how absurd. While pretending to argue for the glory of God, they actually argue only for their own glory.

During these past several years, we have had more than our share of controversies. There were controversies from within our own ranks and controversies which were imposed on us from outside organizations and individuals. I was extremely saddened by my perception that a high percentage of the discussions were not for the sake of Torah. Rather, the controversies were dressed up as Torah debates, but in fact were power struggles. And this leads to another troubling condition: an environment of intimidation and narrowness.

Earlier in the year I attended the Presidents' Conference meeting in Israel. President Herzog addressed our group, and made special mention of the fact that the Haredi press in Israel is the most vitriolic and vicious. The Haredi newspapers regularly engage in slander and defamation of character. Although we attribute this vice to the "right-wing," we must be honest enough to state that intimidation and coercion also exist on the left. What is the meaning of this name-calling? Simply stated, it is an attempt to discredit opposition. It is an attempt to limit options, to force conformity. If people are intimidated, they will be afraid to offer differing opinions from those in power. When options narrow, thinking narrows: when thinking narrows, religion becomes ugly and hateful. The ugly face of religion holds sway.

The overwhelming pressure to create conformity in thinking is symbolized by the overwhelming conformity in the area of clothing. Yeshiva students are expected to look the same, with their black suits and black hats. Rabbis are expected to fit a certain sartorial pattern. Interestingly, a certain Sephardic rabbi from Israel came to my office some years ago in order to raise funds for his yeshivah. This rabbi has a wonderful Spanish name. Yet, he was dressed as though he had been born and raised in Lithuania. I asked him why he dressed as he did and he answered: "If I don't dress like this, I will not be accepted as a *talmid hakham*. This is the way the rabbis must dress."

There is something frightening about this seemingly harmless response. Why should a Sephardic rabbi of a distinguished Moroccan-Jewish family need to look like a Lithuanian Jew in order to be accepted as a proper rabbi? Why is it necessary for this man—and so many hundreds like him—to be cut off from his own rich and vital traditions in order to conform to only one model of Jewish experience?

In fact, the Orthodox community *needs* to have diverse rabbinic models. Don't forget: the vast majority of Jews are not Orthodox. In order to reach them, we need different approaches within halakhic Judaism. We need Hasidic rabbis and B'nei Akiva rabbis and Sephardic rabbis and Lithuanian rabbis. We need to be able to speak one message with many voices and from many approaches. All attempts at stifling the legitimate diversity within Orthodoxy ultimately weaken the fiber of Torah Judaism.

The loving face of religion is characterized by humility, feelings of inadequacy, love. It is open to the mystery and vastness of human spirituality. But it is a difficult and often lonely path which must be followed by those who want to live religion at its best.

During the sixteenth century, a question came to Rabbi Shemuel de Medina (Rashdam). It concerned a certain rabbi who became fed up with his public responsibilities. He simply wanted to devote himself to Torah study. He took an oath not to become involved in any public matters on behalf of the community or even on behalf of any individual.

In responding to this case, Rashdam obviously sympathized with this rabbi's frustrations. Yet, he stated that such an oath was basically unacceptable and invalid, since it violated a basic Torah teaching that one must be involved in helping other Jews. He asked: "Are you better than our teacher Moshe of blessed memory? How much did he labor and how much did he suffer on behalf of the people of Israel! And in spite of this, they spoke badly of him and even wanted to stone him to death. This is the great reward hidden away for the leaders of Israel, to bend their shoulders to suffer." Each individual member of the RCA must strive to emulate the quality of being a *hasid* as exemplified by King David. In this way, we as individuals and the RCA as an organization will reflect the loving and pious face of religion.

Five hundred years ago, my ancestors were busy packing their bags, preparing to go into exile after having been expelled from the kingdom of Spain. No doubt, they wondered whether they would survive the ordeal, whether the Jewish people would be able to weather this terrible storm. They transplanted themselves in Turkey, and in fact created a vibrant Jewish life which was able to transcend the generations. Perhaps it is more than a historical accident that the President of the RCA five hundred years after the expulsion of Jews from Spain should himself be a descendant of those Jews who had been expelled. This is symbolic of the continuity of the Jewish people, the commitment of all the Jewish generations. May the Almighty bless all of us so that we may serve Him and our people as representatives of religion at its best: with saintliness, idealism, selflessness, and love.

24

BREAKING THE COERCION CYCLE

Several years ago, I was visiting the Technion (Institute of Science in Haifa) with a group of American supporters. At a reception sponsored in honor of the group, I was one of the very few men in the room wearing a kippah. A woman from the Technion spotted me, learned that I was an Orthodox rabbi and began to harangue me on the "evils" of Orthodoxy. She ended with the announcement that she was planning to go to a Bedouin village the following week (this was just before Pesah) to buy pitas to feed her family during Pesah.

The woman annoyed me. I hadn't asked about her religious attitudes; why then did she feel she had the right to abuse me with her anti-religious sentiments? "Can't you get along for seven days without bread?" I asked her. "Yes," she answered angrily. "I don't eat much bread all year long. But on Pesah, I do eat it. And do you know why? Because I don't want the religious Jews to think they can control me."

I responded with a glib comment to the effect that she was, in fact, allowing the religious Jews to coerce her. She had given up her freedom to observe Pesah properly. Because of her desire to spite religious Jews, she was being coerced to buy bread to eat on Pesah. She hesitated for a moment. Her face grew calm, and she admitted I was right. She was in a real bind, she told me. She wanted to live in a traditional Jewish setting; she wanted to observe Pesah as she had done in her

Originally published in the *Jerusalem Post*, November 30, 1990.

childhood. But her anger at Orthodox extremists was more powerful than her desire to observe Pesah according to tradition.

Recently, I read that some Jews in Israel were handing out free ham and cheese sandwiches on the street. This was a protest against the terms granted to Agudath Yisrael in return for their participation in the government coalition. These purveyors of pork were making a similar statement: "We will not be coerced by the religious extremists."

But again, we might ask them: Isn't this reaction, so repugnant to Jews with even a moderate respect for Jewish tradition, an example of being coerced? Would these individuals have passed out ham and cheese sandwiches of their own free will, without any external impetus?

These examples are profoundly saddening. All of us—religious and non-religious—must ask ourselves whether we really want Jewish society to reflect such antagonism. Extremism from the religious leads to extreme reactions by the non-religious (or less religious); insensitivity from the non-religious stimulates extremism among the religious. A vicious cycle feeds on itself, polarizes the people, and fosters extreme positions to which the proponents might never have resorted without external stimulus. Don't all Jews—religious or non-religious—wish to live a life of dignity and freedom, without coercion and harassment?

There is a historical model that can help us break out of this unfortunate dilemma. I call it the Sephardic model.

Through the 19th and early 20th centuries, Sephardic communities generally were able to blend their disparate members into a homogeneous society. Sephardic intellectuals and the Sephardic masses did not break up their communities on religious or ideological grounds. Not everyone observed Judaism in the same way, nor were they equal in their beliefs; yet the communities were characterized by a spirit of tolerance. (Certainly there were exceptions; yet, this mode was clearly dominant throughout the Sephardic world in Muslim lands.)

Sephardim recognized that the communal structure had to remain in consonance with halakhah and with tradition. Certainly all marriages, divorces and conversions were performed according to Jewish religious law. The community maintained halakhic standards for kashrut, mikvah, synagogues, etc., and individuals understood the need to curtail their own individual freedoms somewhat for the sake of communal order.

On the other hand, in their personal lives, Sephardim did exercise freedom. Tolerance was a hallmark of the classic Sephardic community. While rabbis wanted their communities to adhere fully to halakhah, they generally understood that not everyone would. Rather than interfering, the rabbis conceded that it was not their role to force observance onto others. Instead, they gently tried to bring people closer to Judaism by demonstrating its greatness.

When people do not feel threatened and coerced, they can live with a higher degree of personal freedom and happiness. Jewish society would benefit vastly from a revitalization of the classic Sephardic model. Individual Jews, regardless of whether they identify themselves as religious or not, should support universal halakhic standards to maintain the integrity of the community; at the same time, however, they should not coerce others in matters of personal observance. They should depend on the power of persuasion, not coercion.

If a Jew is going to eat bread on Pesah or consume a ham and cheese sandwich, it shouldn't be out of spite against religious Jews. Indeed, religious Jews shouldn't want to do anything which would provoke others to violate the Torah *le-hakhis* (spitefully). On the other hand, non-religious Jews should not undermine the halakhic structure which has governed the Jewish people over the centuries. Halakhic standards should be allowed to prevail, at least on a communal level. Attacking the halakhic structure only provokes extreme and angry responses.

If the religious and non-religious continue to provoke each other, neither group can be happy or free. If they can find a *modus vivendi*, such as in the Sephardic model, antagonism will decline and tolerance will increase. Everyone—except the most contentious—will be happier.

This is a goal worth striving for.

25

ORTHODOXY AND ISOLATION

Gershom Scholem has described a mystic as one who struggles with all his might against a world with which he very much wants to be at peace. The tense inner dialectic, I think, is true not only of a mystic, but of every truly religious person. A religious person devotes his life to ideals, values, and observances which generally are at odds with the society in which he lives. He fights with all his power to resist succumbing to the overwhelming non-religious forces around him. Yet, he does not *want* to live his life as a struggle. He wants to be at peace. He wants to be able to relax his guard, not always to feel under siege.

There are "religious" communities where the tensions of this dialectic are suppressed successfully. Within a tightly knit Hasidic community or in a "right-wing" Orthodox enclave, the positive forces of the community strongly repel the external pressures of the non-religious world. It is easier to create what Henry Feingold has called a "Pavlovian Jewish response" within a vibrant and deeply committed religious colony. Religious observance is the norm; children learn from the earliest age what they should and should not do; outside influences are sealed out as much as possible. In such communities, the individual need not feel the incredible loneliness and pain of struggling by himself against society. His own society reinforces him. His own community—as a community—is rela-

Originally published in *Moment*, September 1980.

tively self-sufficient spiritually, and it is this entire community which withstands the outside world.

But the modern Orthodox Jew feels the intensity of the dialectic struggle to the core of his existence. He is as Orthodox and as Jewishly committed as the Hasidim or as the "right-wing" Orthodox. He does not feel he is less religious because he does not have a beard, does not wear a black hat. No. The Orthodox Jew who is a college graduate, an intellectual, a professional, an open-minded person, can pray to God with a deep spirituality and can dedicate his life to fulfilling the words of God as revealed in the Torah.

Yet, because his eyes are open and because he is receptive to the intellectual and social life of the society around him, the enlightened Orthodox Jew finds it difficult to be at peace. He generally does not live in a community which helps him shut off external influences. He does not have a large reservoir of friends who share the depth of his religious commitment while at the same time sharing his openness to literature, philosophy, or science. He is at war with society, but wants to be at peace with society. Really, he is alone.

In *The Castle*, Kafka describes the predicament of Mr. K, a land surveyor. K comes to a place which is composed of two distinct entities: the Castle and the Village. K spends a good deal of time trying to make his way from the Village to the Castle but—in typical Kafkaesque style—he becomes lost in labyrinthine confusion. At one point, someone tells K: You are not of the Castle, you are not of the Village, you are nobody. K's predicament is especially meaningful to an enlightened Orthodox Jew. He is neither a part of the Village nor the Castle. And often, he wonders if he, too, is nobody.

This is not metaphysics, not philosophy; it is the pragmatic reality for many thousands of devoted Jews in this country.

And in the most confusing situation of all we have the enlightened Orthodox rabbi. Not only is he busy with his own personal struggles, fighting his own wars, but he also is responsible for the struggles and battles of his community.

Sometimes, his congregation may not even realize there is a war. Sometimes, he may appear to be a modern version of Don Quixote. Sometimes, he is perceived as being too religious and idealistic, and sometimes, he is perceived as being crass, materialistic, secularist. For some people he is not modern enough, while for others he is a traitor to tradition.

Imagine for a moment the dilemma of an enlightened Orthodox rabbi. He is religiously educated and committed. He is trained in the humanities and the sciences. The Orthodox community on the "right," which scorns university education, looks upon this rabbi as a fake and imposter. The non-Orthodox community looks upon him as a religious reactionary who is trying to maintain ancient standards of kashrut, Shabbat, mikvah and so many other laws in a society where these commandments seem almost meaningless. The right-wing Orthodox community condemns him for associating with non-Orthodox rabbis and with non-Orthodox Jews. And the non-Orthodox rabbis and non-Orthodox Jews may "respect" him from a distance, but they innately recognize that he is "not one of us."

When Moshe came down from Mount Sinai the second time, the Torah tells us that his face emitted strong beams of light. It was necessary for him to wear a mask so that people could look at him. One can imagine the terror of little children when they looked at the masked Moshe. One also can imagine the profound impact such a mask must have had on all the people of Israel. But we must also stop to think about how Moshe must have felt wearing such a mask, knowing that there was a strong, visible barrier separating him from his people. Who can know? Perhaps Moshe cried in misery and loneliness behind that mask.

While people to the right and people to the left will judge, condemn, patronize, "respect" the enlightened Orthodox rabbi, few people take the time to wonder what is going on behind his "mask." He also has ears, eyes, and senses. He knows what people are saying and thinking. He knows that his

authenticity as a religious figure is challenged from the right
and from the left. He knows that his ideals and visions for his
community are far from realization, perhaps impossibly far.
He knows that his best talents are not enough to bring his people to a promised land.

Imagine the quandary of an Orthodox rabbi who works with
non-Orthodox rabbis in Jewish Federations or Boards of Rabbis. On the one hand, his open-mindedness compels him to be
involved in communal Jewish affairs and to work for the good
of the community with all interested people. Yet, it is possible
that the Reform rabbi sitting next to him has eaten a ham
sandwich for lunch, drives to the synagogue on Saturday, and
has performed marriages which should not have been performed according to halakhah. Is this Reform rabbi—whom
he likes and respects as a human being—his friend and col-
league? Or is this rabbi his arch-enemy, a person dedicated to
teaching Judaism in a way which the Orthodox rabbi considers
mistaken and even dangerous? And as this conflict nags at
him, what is he to do with the voices of the right-wing who
condemn him as a traitor for recognizing or legitimizing non-
halakhic clergy? And what is he to do with the voices of the
non-Orthodox who condemn him for not being flexible and
open enough on religious questions?

Or imagine another case. An enlightened Orthodox rabbi
may recognize a variety of ways which could ameliorate the
position of women in halakhic Judaism. His liberal education
has made him receptive to a host of ideas, many of which can
be implemented within the guidelines of traditional Jewish
law. Yet the "right-wing" Orthodox would condemn such ideas
as basic violations of Jewish law and tradition. And at the same
time, the non-Orthodox are fast to condemn the enlightened
Orthodox rabbi for being too conservative and rigid.

He has the right ideas, but no medium of communication.
He can speak, but he has few who will listen.

And yet another example. An enlightened Orthodox rabbi
may recognize the need for compassion and understanding

when dealing with the issue of conversion to Judaism. He may want to work within the halakhah to encourage would-be converts to accept halakhic Judaism. He may reject the narrow and unnecessary stringencies advocated by colleagues on the right wing. And he will be roundly criticized and condemned by them. On the other hand, because he absolutely believes in Torah and halakhah, he will require converts to undergo a rigorous program of study as well as circumcision and mikvah. Because of his standards, the non-Orthodox community views him as old-fashioned, unenlightened and even insensitive.

With all these tensions and conflicts, with all the voices to the right and to the left, the enlightened Orthodox rabbi tries to serve his God and his people in an honest and authentic way. It is very tempting to give up the battle. The internal pressures are sometimes too much to bear. But he cannot succumb to the temptation; he is the prisoner of his commitments and beliefs.

Moshe, behind his mask, may indeed have been lonely and sad. But he never forgot who he was. In fact, he probably spent more time thinking about his condition when he wore the mask than when he did not. It is difficult to have a barrier between yourself and others. But perhaps a mask helps you to develop the courage and strength to stand alone in the battle against a world with which you want—with all your being—to be at peace.

26

MODERN ORTHODOXY
BEYOND APOLOGETICS

I began my studies at Yeshiva College in the fall of 1963. I was born and raised in Seattle, Washington, and had attended Franklin High School.

I remember finding Yeshiva College to be an intellectually alive place. A central feature of my experience here was my introduction to the worlds of Torah and Madda. One of the popular words in those days was "synthesis."

In those days, we were part of an Orthodoxy which wanted to show the world that we could be sophisticated and intellectually *au courant*, while at the same time being faithful to our traditions as Orthodox Jews. We took pride in the fact that the President of Yeshiva, Dr. Belkin, was a *talmid hakham* and a classicist; that Rabbi Joseph Soloveitchik was not only a world authority in Torah, but also a profound philosopher, deeply steeped in the intellectual life of Western civilization. I studied Talmud from Rabbi Lichtenstein, who earned his Ph.D. from Harvard University in English Literature. I studied biology from Rabbi Tendler; English from Rabbi Maurice Wohlgelernter; history from Rabbi Irving Greenberg. My Latin teacher was Dr. Louis Feldman, who could often be found in the *bet midrash* studying Talmud. In short, we had living models of Torah and Madda, excellence in a holistic view of Judaism.

Remarks on receiving the Bernard Revel Award in Religion and Religious Education—Yeshiva University, on May 14, 1992.

Today, our son Hayyim attends Yeshiva College. While in my generation, I think that our focus was primarily to demonstrate the validity of our position to the outside world, today the focus seems to have shifted. There is now a greater emphasis on the issues of the Orthodox right. As the apologetic in my generation was to show that although we studied Torah we also could be well versed in worldly wisdom, the apologetic today is that although we study secular subjects, we also can be authentic Orthodox Jews who know Torah.

It seems to me that we have reached that stage in American Orthodox life where we should stop offering apologetics in either direction. On the contrary, we should fall back on the vision of Rabbi Dr. Bernard Revel and others like him, who viewed the combination of Torah and Madda not as an apology or compromise, but as the most desirable philosophy of Judaism. If we can be true to this vision, and work towards its implementation with dynamism and creativity, then we will have made a vital contribution to world Jewry. We need to see this philosophy not as a compromise with modernity, but as a fulfillment of the highest ideals of Torah Judaism.

Rabbi Bentzion Uziel, the late Chief Rabbi of Israel, once wrote that those who forsake halakhah, thereby forsake Torah and Jewish tradition; those who maintain Torah, but only in isolation from the world, thereby forsake the glory and universal message of the Torah. Rabbi Uziel cited a passage in Mishlei (4:25–27), which may be used as the proper model for our philosophy of Judaism: "Let your eyes look right on, and let your eyelids look straight before you. Make plain the path of your feet, and let all your ways be established. Turn not to the right nor to the left; remove your foot from evil."

27

TEACHING THE "WHOLENESS" OF THE JEWISH PEOPLE

*O*ur heritage is rich and vast and we claim that we teach it. But do we truly understand the wholeness of the Jewish people, or is our knowledge really limited and fragmented? Do we, can we, inculcate the concept of Jewish unity in our students? If we as educators are unaware or disinterested in Jews who have had different historic experiences than we have had, how can we convey the richness of Judaism? How can we, in fact, demonstrate the sheer wonder of halakhic Jewry without a sense of awe at the halakhic contributions of all our diverse communities throughout the world, throughout the ages?

We may study the Talmud of Babylonia and Israel; the codes of sages in Spain; the commentaries of scholars of France, Germany, Italy; the responsa of rabbis of Turkey, the Middle East and North Africa; the novellae of sages of Eastern Europe; the traditions and customs of Jewish communities throughout the world. We study this diverse and rich literature and realize the phenomenon that all these Jewish sages and their communities operated with the identical assumption—that God gave the Torah to the people of Israel, that halakhah is our way of following God's ways. As we contemplate the vast scope of the halakhic enterprise—and its essential unity—we begin to sense the wholeness of the Jewish people.

Originally published in *Ten Da'at*, Heshvan 5749 (Fall 1988).

If, for example, we were to study only the contributions and history of the Jews of America, we would have a narrow view of Judaism. If we limited our Jewish sources only to a particular century or to a particular geographic location, we would be parochial. We would be experts in a segment of Jewish experience; but we would be ignorant of everything outside our narrow focus.

In order to teach the *shelemut* (wholeness) of the Jewish people, we need to have a broad knowledge and vision of the Jewish people. We cannot limit ourselves to sources only from Europe, just as we cannot limit ourselves to sources only from Asia or Africa. Often enough, however, Jewish education today fails to include in a serious way the Jewish experiences in Asia and Africa. How many educators can name ten great Jewish personalities who lived in Turkey in the seventeenth century; or in Morocco in the eighteenth century; or in Syria in the nineteenth century? How many have studied any works of authors who lived in Muslim lands over the past four to five centuries? And how many have taught this information to their students? And have they learned?

There is a vital need to teach "whole-istic" Judaism, drawing on the great teachings of our people in all the lands and periods of their dispersion. To do this, we ourselves need to study, to think very seriously, to feel genuine excitement in gathering the exiles of our people into our minds and consciousnesses. When we are engaged in this process, we can help our students share the excitement with us. Jews who are "not like us," whose families came from countries other than "ours," should not be viewed as being exotic or quaint. There is more to a Jewish community than a set of interesting customs or folkways. We need to be able to speak of the Jews of Vilna and of Istanbul and of Berlin and of Tangiers with the same degree of naturalness, with no change in the inflection of our voices. We need to see Jews of all these—and all the other—communities as though they are part of "our" community.

Consider the standard *Mikra'ot Gedolot* (a common edition of the Bible). There are commentaries by Rashi (France); Ibn Ezra and Ramban (Spain); R. Hayyim ben Attar, the Ohr ha-Hayyim (Morocco); R. Ovadia Seforno (Italy), and many others. The commentaries of the Talmud, Rambam, *Shulhan Arukh* are also a diverse group, stemming from different places and times. It is important for teachers to make their students aware of the backgrounds of the various commentators. In this relatively simple way, students are introduced to the vastness of the Torah enterprise, and of the value of all communities which have engaged in Torah study. To quote Sephardic *gedolim* together with Ashkenazic *gedolim*, naturally and easily, is to achieve an important goal in the teaching of *shelemut*.

Most teachers teach what they themselves have learned. They tend to draw heavily on the sources which their teachers valued. It is difficult and challenging to try to reach out into new sources, to gain knowledge and inspiration from Jewish communities which one originally had not considered to be one's own.

The majority of Jews living in Israel are of African and Asian backgrounds. Students who gain no knowledge of the history and culture of the Jews of Africa and Asia are being seriously deprived. They will be unable to grasp the cultural context of the majority of Jews in Israel, or they will trivialize it or think it exotic. But if Jews are to be a whole people, then all Jews need to understand, in a deep and serious way, about other Jews. This is not for "enrichment" programs; this is basic Jewish teaching, basic Jewish learning.

I am very saddened by the general narrowness I have seen in some Jewish schools. There is a reluctance to grasp the need for *shelemut* on a serious level. Time is too short. Teachers don't want more responsibilities. But Judaism goes far beyond the sources of Europe and America. Giving lip service to the beauty of Sephardic culture; or singing a Yemenite tune with the school choir; or explaining a custom now and then—these don't represent a genuine openness, a positive education.

Standard textbooks don't teach much about the Jews of Africa and Asia, their vast cultural and spiritual achievements, their contributions to Jewish life and to Torah scholarship. Schools often do not make the effort to incorporate serious study of these topics, and so our children grow up with a fragmented Jewish education.

To raise awareness and sensitivity, teachers should utilize the resources within the community—including students, community members and synagogues representing diverse backgrounds, customs, and history that can enlighten students. Spending Shabbat with diverse communities, within the United States as well as when visiting Israel, can be a moving way of sharing cultures and customs.

To attain *shelemut* in Jewish education entails considerable work on the part of administrators, teachers and students. It may cost time and money. But can we really afford to continue to deprive our children and our people of *shelemut*?

28

COVENANT

JEWISH VIEW

Covenant in religious terms refers to an agreement between God and human beings. The concept that the Almighty and Eternal God would make a covenant with mortals whom He has created is itself a striking theological insight. It supposes that God maintains a relationship with human beings—and He is willing to bind Himself in some way to the terms expressed in covenants.

Covenants between God and human beings are a vital feature of the Jewish Bible. Following the flood, God spoke to Noah and his sons saying: "As for me, behold, I establish my covenant with you and with your seed after you and with every living creature that is with you. . . . And I will establish my covenant with you; neither shall all flesh be cut off anymore by the waters of the flood; neither shall there anymore be a flood to destroy the earth" (Bereshit 9:9–11). And God set the rainbow in the sky as an eternal token of this agreement.

God made a covenant with Abraham, promising the patriarch that he would be the father of a great and numerous nation, and that his people would possess the land of Canaan forever: "I will maintain My covenant between Me and you and your offspring to come as an everlasting covenant

Originally published in *A Dictionary of the Jewish-Christian Dialogue*, ed. Leon Klenicki and Geoffrey Wigoder (New York: Paulist Press, 1984).

throughout the ages, to be God to you and to your offspring to come. I give the land to you to sojourn in, to you and your off-spring to come, all the land of Canaan, as an everlasting possession; and I will be their God" (Bereshit 17:7–8). God re-established this covenant with Isaac and Jacob.

God established a covenant with the entire people of Israel at Mount Sinai. He revealed Himself to the people, gave His commandments, and emphasized the special relationship between the people of Israel and God. The people of Israel accepted the responsibility to observe God's commandments and in return God promised His blessings for the people. If Israel reneges on its responsibilities, God warns of a host of punishments and curses. But God also promises that the covenant He has established with Israel is eternal, that He will never terminate His covenant with the people of Israel. After listing numerous punishments which will befall Israel if they do not fulfill the commandments, God reminds them: "I will remember My covenant with Jacob, and My covenant with Isaac, and also My covenant with Abraham will I remember; and I will remember the land. . . . When they are in the land of their enemies, I will not reject them, neither will I abhor them, to destroy them utterly, and to break My covenant with them; for I am the Lord their God. But I will for their sakes remember the covenant of their ancestors whom I brought forth out of the land of Egypt in the sight of the nations that I might be their God: I am the Lord" (Vayikra 26:42, 44–45).

The eternal nature of God's covenant with Israel and its irreversibility is a fundamental aspect of Judaism. Even when Israel is in exile and is suffering oppression, the Jew may never conclude that God has severed His relationship with Israel. The prophets of the Bible speak of a renewal of God's covenant with Israel and of His ultimate restoration of Israel to its land.

It is especially important that this idea of covenant be understood in the Jewish-Christian dialogue. Any suggestion by Christians that God's covenant with Israel has been transferred to a "new Israel" is obviously offensive to Jewish beliefs. Any statement implying that God's covenant with the Jewish people has been discontinued or has been replaced by a covenant with others is totally unacceptable to Jewish religious belief, and goes against the Bible itself.

The idea of a "covenant of grace" in Christian covenant theology has its own meanings and interpretations, and is based on Christian assumptions. Judaism does not interpret Adam's transgression as a "fall" which required a new covenant of grace. Rather, in the Jewish view, all human beings are confronted with good and evil, right and wrong. Everyone is expected to make the right choices, but everyone—at one time or another—will choose incorrectly, will commit iniquities. He is expected to repent for these transgressions, to improve his ways. Punishment for transgressions may be forthcoming either in this world or in the World to Come. The spiritual struggle of making proper choices and of avoiding iniquity has been part of human nature since Adam and Eve. Each individual has the power to repent, to turn to God and to gain God's forgiveness. Judaism does not teach that one must be "saved" by a special act of God's grace.

The Hebrew word designating covenant is *berit*. Abraham was circumcised as a sign of the covenant between himself and God. To this day, the circumcision ceremony is known among Jews as *berit milah,* the covenant of circumcision. For Jews, then, circumcision is not viewed as a medical procedure; it is a religious act which brings the baby boy into the covenant.

One born of a Jewish mother is by his or her very birth part of the people of Israel. By birth, a Jew is automatically bound to the covenant established between God and the ancient Israelites at Mount Sinai. It is not a matter of free choice. Any Jew who does not fulfill the obligations of the covenant will be held responsible by God. According to Jewish law, even if a Jew renounces the covenant or converts to another religion, he remains Jewish notwithstanding, bound to the covenant in spite of anything he says or does. He shares the covenant by destiny.

A non-Jew may choose to enter Israel's covenant with God by converting. A convert to Judaism is expected to learn and accept the terms of the covenant, i.e., the commandments, the responsibilities, the spiritual benefits. The conversion process is not complete for a male until he has been circumcised, the physical sign of Israel's covenant with God. Both male and female converts are required to be immersed in a ritual bath, symbolic of spiritual rebirth as members of the Jewish people.

Although individuals who are born Jewish are automatically partners in the covenant with God, their upbringing and education should lead them to an intellectual awareness of the rights and responsibilities of the covenant so that they will be knowledgeable and enlightened participants. With proper education and spiritual development, a Jew learns to accept the covenant with God by choice, with free will.

29

RABBIS AND THE PROBLEMS
OF INTERMARRIAGE

Some years ago, I participated in a conference on "outreach to the intermarried" sponsored by a large Jewish organization. The program included an address by a noted sociologist, as well as comments by a Reform and Conservative rabbi. I was the Orthodox rabbinic spokesman.

The sociologist provided much data on the phenomenon of intermarriage. One aspect of his talk which interested me was that the intermarriage rate was significantly higher among Jews who had little Jewish education and who did not observe mitzvot. Although intermarriage occurred among the observant Orthodox, the rate was dramatically less than that among other segments of the Jewish community.

When it was my turn to speak, I commented on this data. I stated that if we were serious about stemming the tide of intermarriage, we ought to encourage Jews to keep kosher homes, to observe the Shabbat, to educate their children in Jewish day schools. Interestingly, this comment evoked a loud spontaneous laughter from the audience, almost all of whom were not Orthodox.

I questioned their laughter. What was so funny? Based on the data before us, the logical conclusion was to combat intermarriage by increasing Jewish commitment to the observance

Originally published in the *Jewish Press*, March 13, 1992.

of mitzvot. The correlation between serious mitzvah observance and a lower intermarriage rate was clear.

Several answers were given to me. Most Jews won't keep the
mitzvot anymore. Most Jews aren't ready to accept an Orthodox lifestyle. Many Jews don't really object to intermarriage all
that much. We can't put the genie back into the bottle.

Many members of the audience apparently wanted quick
and easy answers. They urged fast and undemanding conversions. Some even wanted "rabbis" to officiate at intermarriages. They wanted communities to be warm and accepting to
intermarried people, so as not to make them feel guilty or to
turn them off from Judaism altogether.

I responded that the Orthodox position was to stress pre-
vention of intermarriage, and that this attitude has had some
success worthy of communal attention. When conversion of
the non-Jewish partner is a viable option according to halakhah, Orthodoxy provides a meaningful and acceptable way
for the conversion to take place. Not everyone is willing to
make the commitment to a halakhic way of life. But the Orthodox approach has been to ask potential converts to strive to
attain our standards.

In the years which have passed since that conference, I have
become increasingly convinced of the correctness of the
Orthodox approach which I had advocated then. But in spite
of its ultimate correctness, the intermarriage rate has continued to skyrocket. Most Jews, like members of the audience at
the conference, have not been willing to understand or to follow the Orthodox approach.

Recent studies have shown that the intermarriage rate has
passed the 50 percent mark. Some Orthodox individuals take
this as evidence that only Orthodoxy can survive in the long
run, since most other Jews will be marrying out of the faith.
Orthodoxy takes pride in a number of vibrant and vital Orthodox communities, brimming with youthful enthusiasm and
strength, which seem immune to the problem of intermarriage. Some Orthodox leaders have favored a hard-line posi-

tion against intermarried couples. Family and social sanctions, they reason, can serve as deterrents to others.

But other Orthodox rabbis favor outreach to intermarrieds, in the hope of winning at least some of them back to halakhic Judaism. This position recognizes a responsibility to the thousands of intermarried couples and their children. It also is cognizant of the existence of intermarriage even within the Orthodox community, and even in the most observant of families. Intermarriage is a problem which cannot be wished away. Closing our eyes will not make the problem less real.

The internal discussion within the Orthodox rabbinate was brought to a new level during a series of regional conferences sponsored by the Rabbinical Council of America. Rabbis throughout North America met to discuss the facts, the strategies, the successes and failures of our community vis-à-vis intermarriage. There were some heart-rending stories, some soul searchings. We were struggling to find consensus on issues which go to the very core of Jewish life in America. It is difficult to discuss issues of intermarriage and conversion without intense emotion. Orthodoxy is deeply, absolutely, viscerally opposed to intermarriage, and we struggle with all our strength against it. But what about the intermarrieds, the actual people who have become involved in intermarriage? What is our attitude to them as human beings, as individuals who have been part of the Jewish community all their lives? Do we simply write them and their children off as dead?

There is a growing awareness among some thoughtful Orthodox rabbis that the Orthodox rabbinate has a particularly important role to play in reaching out to the intermarried Jews. It isn't enough to condemn intermarriage. It isn't enough to inveigh against patrilineality and against non-halakhic conversions. It isn't enough to lament the staggering ignorance of most Jews in matters of Jewish law and tradition. Orthodox rabbis must present a positive agenda to the community, an agenda based on thoughtfulness, self-respect and respect for others, integrity. While we offer no short cuts nor compromises, while we maintain our halakhic commitment, we still can demonstrate an openness to the struggles of others and try to be of help and guidance. A number of Orthodox rabbis have taken this position, and others are moving towards it. On the other hand, some Orthodox individuals violently condemn this attitude as a horrendous compromise, as a weakening of defenses against intermarriage.

Interestingly, the Rabbinical Council of America was criticized strongly by some "right-wing" rabbis for even deigning to discuss outreach to intermarrieds at our conferences. One group attacked the RCA without even bothering to ascertain our actual positions; facts just weren't important to them. They were expressing outrage and horror that Orthodox rabbis should face this subject with anything other than blanket rejectionism.

Clearly, a variety of attitudes exists among Orthodox rabbis on what is the proper response to the phenomenon of intermarriage. The best answer is to work to prevent it. Yet, it seems to me that Orthodox rabbis have a responsibility to reach out to those intermarried couples where the non-Jewish spouse would be interested in a halakhic conversion. It does not serve the interests of the Jewish people if we simply avoid confronting a problem which is undermining the well-being of the Jewish community. Most American Jews will not be moved by our protestations and sanctions. This is tragic, but it is nonetheless true.

The Orthodox rabbinate has within it the strength and courage to assume leadership in this troublesome and emotion-filled area. There always will be critics outside of Orthodoxy who say we don't do enough and that we are too demanding; and there will also be critics within Orthodoxy who say we are doing too much and that we are compromising standards.

Our task is not to let the voices of these critics divert us from a proper course of action which includes absolute faithfulness to halakhic standards and sympathetic understanding of the needs of human beings. Ultimately, we are not answerable to our critics: we are answerable to God.

30

"LAND FOR PEACE": SLOGAN FOR WAR

*I*n evaluating prospects for peace in the Middle East, the popular wisdom seems encapsulated in the phrase "land for peace." The implication: if only Israel would return land it captured from Arab countries in the 1967 war, the Arabs would make peace with Israel. The international media preach to Israel, claiming that Israel's security can be ensured not by land, but only by peace treaties with its belligerent neighbors.

Interestingly, advocates of land for peace rarely indicate that Israel captured land in a defensive war, a war forced on it by Arab neighbors who had promised to annihilate Israel. Nor do they apply the slogan to the Arabs themselves. If Syria wants peace, why not ask it to sacrifice land—the Golan Heights—for a peace treaty with Israel?

Nor do very many land-for-peace proponents remind the world that when it made peace with Egypt, Israel returned over 90 percent of the land it captured from the Arabs in the 1967 war. Memories are short, and Israel's monumental sacrifices for peace are ignored almost completely.

As anyone who has looked at a map of the Middle East knows, Israel is a tiny country. Its land mass is less than the size of New Jersey; its total population less than New York City's. It is surrounded by hostile Arab countries commanding vast land masses and huge populations.

Originally published in the *Jerusalem Post*, December 19, 1991.

Nor have the Arab countries and the Palestinians been shy in expressing the destruction of Israel as their clear and unequivocal goal. Hatred of Israel and of Jews is rooted deeply in the Arab world. Even Egypt, which has signed a peace treaty with Israel, hardly has shown warm friendship. Its media continue to demonize Israel and the Jewish people. Egypt has also opposed the effort to rescind the heinous U.N. resolution equating Zionism with racism.

Living in a sea of viciously hostile (and violent) neighbors, Israel has every reason to be cautious in its efforts to achieve real peace. I wonder: How many Americans would react favorably to the suggestion that the U.S. turn over the suburbs of Washington, D.C., to the likes of Hafez Assad, Saddam Hussein, Yasser Arafat or Muammar Qaddafi?

Yet, Israel—vastly smaller and less powerful than the U.S.— is being asked to surrender settlements on the outskirts of Jerusalem to people who historically have been hostile and violent. The "West Bank" isn't some remote territory; it is a relatively small area, exceedingly close to Israel's main population centers.

Pundits suggest that Israel should return the Golan Heights to Syria. Have they ever been to the Golan Heights? Do they know that up till 1967, Syria used the strategic Golan Heights to fire on Israelis living in the valley below? What rational person would want to give a hostile neighbor access to a position from which he could then launch attacks against him and his family? Would a peace treaty with Assad guarantee that the Syrians will not mount forces and missiles on the Golan Heights at some future time? Should Israel be asked to jeopardize its basic security in the name of that catchy slogan, "land for peace"?

Who will guarantee a real peace? And who will pay the price if the peace does not hold? Who will come to Israel's aid if the Syrians use the Golan Heights once again to launch an attack?

Land for peace is a formula which historically has led to war and destruction. One of the world's guiltiest villains in this respect is the U.S. itself. It signed dozens of peace treaties with American Indians throughout the 19th century. The settlements generally followed the principle of "land for peace." If the Indians ceded territory or territorial rights to the U.S., they were promised a lasting and wonderful peace.

But the U.S. broke virtually every treaty. With each Indian concession, the Americans simply made greater demands. One of the great Indian leaders, Chief Red Cloud, emphatically stated the results of the land for peace policy: "They made us many promises, more than I can remember, and never kept but one: they promised to take our land, and they took it."

The American intention was not land for peace. It was to gain land. "Land for peace" was a ploy to attain the real goal. In trusting the U.S., the Indians were decimated, and their lands taken away.

A more recent historical example: Neville Chamberlain signed a treaty with Hitler in 1938, agreeing that Czechoslovakia should cede the Sudetenland to Germany in return for peace. Understandably, the Czechs were opposed to this plan, since it undermined their defense against a hostile Germany. No matter. Chamberlain came back to England after his meeting with Hitler and received a hero's welcome. He declared that he had achieved a lasting and honorable peace. The media called Czechoslovakia obstinate for not agreeing to this "land for peace" solution. Of course, once Germany had control of the Sudetenland, it was an easy matter to vanquish all of Czechoslovakia—which it promptly did, without as much as a whimper from the Western allies.

Land for peace does not work if one side gives land and the other side gives a promise of peace. That promise may be broken too easily. One needs absolute examples of good faith and trust before even entertaining the idea of surrendering territory vital to defense.

Instead of talking about "land for peace," diplomats in the Middle East ought to be talking about "peace for peace."

Let all the countries sign peace treaties. Let Palestinian autonomy be established. Let normal political, commercial and cultural ties begin. After five years of normal relations, there will be a record to examine. It may or may not lead to finding other ways to expand the peace.

If people are really interested in peace, they ought to drop the phrase "land for peace." They ought to concentrate on peace itself.

31

ISRAEL IS NOT JUST ANOTHER JEWISH ORGANIZATION

*T*he hysteria over the so-called "who is a Jew" issue was perplexing. The State of Israel, in a democratic election, gave increased representation to religious parties who wished to promote their causes. Because many American Jews did not care for the positions of the religious parties, they were in a frenzy, and they have spent fortunes in time and money to fight the Israeli religious parties in particular, and Orthodoxy in general. Even the UJA-Federation networks, which are supposed to be apolitical, tried to get one million signatures on petitions to influence the Israeli government not to accept the demands of the religious parties.

The commotion and emotion within American Jewry clouded people's ability to deal with the issue at hand in a calm, reasonable way. The non-Orthodox made strident claims that the "who is a Jew" issue would divide Jewry, that the Orthodox were denying the Jewishness of the non-Orthodox. Non-Orthodox Jews threatened to cut their financial and political support of Israel. The plea was made on many fronts that defining Jewishness according to halakhah would shatter precious unity.

Let us consider this question in a different light. Every non-Orthodox rabbi and leader knows that conversions not performed according to halakhah are not valid according to hala-

Originally published in the *Jerusalem Post*, January 16, 1989.

khah. This is a tautology which should be obvious to anyone. Regardless of what the Israeli government decides on the issue, non-halakhic converts will remain non-Jews in the eyes of halakhah, in Israel and everywhere else. Those who oppose divisiveness and who work so diligently for the unity of our people should be mounting a petition drive against non-Orthodox conversions.

Halakhic Jews follow the pattern of conversion accepted by Jews everywhere for thousands of years. It is the non-Orthodox who have changed the rules; and who now become angry because the faithful have rejected their changes. The blame, though, does not rest with those who maintain halakhah; it rests with those who have deviated from it and have misled thousands of people into thinking their conversions are acceptable.

Those leaders who speak so passionately for Jewish unity ought to have launched a major attack on the decision of Reform Judaism to consider "patrilineal Jews" as Jews. There probably has been nothing more divisive in modern Jewish history than this unilateral decision to change the definition of Jewishness. Thousands of "patrilineal Jews" simply are not Jewish according to halakhah.

And proponents of Jewish unity ought to be exerting all their efforts to ostracize those non-Orthodox "rabbis" who officiate at mixed marriages.

The hysteria over the "who is a Jew" issue, thus, is not an issue of maintaining Jewish unity. Many far more divisive issues pass uncriticized by American Jewry. It is not an issue of responsible American Jewish involvement in Israeli life. Actually, to try to force an opinion on democratically elected officials in Israel is irresponsible.

The real issue is this: American Jewish leadership, most of whom are non-Orthodox, feel jeopardized if the Israeli government doesn't reflect their "values." American Jewish leaders are nervous at the prospect of Israeli leaders having backgrounds and world views entirely different from their own. They worry that they will lose their influence, and that Israel will somehow become something different from what it has been.

American Jewish leadership is all the more nervous now that the religious parties have gained so much power on the Israeli political scene. The religious will become even more powerful. They have large families; they are learning to use their numbers and their energies to promote their ideals and goals. The people of Israel have every right to elect whichever officials they wish; if they one day choose to elect a large percentage of religious Jews, then Israel will indeed change. This perfectly legitimate process frightens non-Orthodox American Jewish leaders (as it frightens "secularists" in Israel).

The non-Orthodox spokesmen of American Jewry will not have control over the religious parties and politicians in Israel. The real issue, then, is not Jewish unity or pluralism; the real issue is power. American Jewish leadership—non-Orthodox, with many intermarried family members—is afraid that Israel will follow its own independent political proclivities and ignore the American community's former power and influence.

Israel is not another Jewish organization. Israel, as an independent country, is obligated to govern itself according to the wishes of its citizens, not according to those Jews who live in the Diaspora. Any Jew who threatens to withhold support from Israel because Israel is not in his image—such a Jew is not a true friend to Israel after all.

The "who is a Jew" question is serious; that is certain. But it must be addressed calmly and wisely by people who are respectful of all its ramifications. Emotionalism, name-calling, threats against the Orthodox and against Israel—these are the wrong ways to deal with the question. We must be wise enough to speak to each other quietly, calmly, without public fanfare. We must be strong enough to love Israel not as a dependent child, but as an independent adult capable of making independent decisions.

32

CRYPTO-JEWS SHOULD MEET HALAKHIC STANDARDS

Stories have appeared recently in the general and Jewish press about the discovery of a group of Catholics in New Mexico who believe they have Jewish ancestors. A number of them are interested in returning to Judaism.

Historians who have studied this community suggest that crypto-Jews of Spanish origin migrated to the American Southwest four to five centuries ago. They lived as Catholics, but maintained vestigial Jewish practices. At least in some cases, there seems to have been a living tradition of Jewish identity that was passed down from generation to generation.

I have publicly expressed my own sense of awe concerning this amazing phenomenon. It is a tribute to the power of the human spirit that a feeling of Jewishness could have survived so long among people who lived as Catholics. I am as happy as anyone that their Jewishness is now surfacing, and that some manifest a sincere desire to embrace Judaism. They certainly should be encouraged and welcomed.

Because their ancestors were of Sephardic origin, I—being a Sephardic rabbi—have a particular sense of kinship with them. My ancestors and their ancestors may have been friends or even relatives.

I want for them what I would want for anyone who wishes to be part of the Jewish community: 100 percent acceptance as

Originally published in the *Jewish Week*, May 24–30, 1991.

Jews. To attain this they should be true to the standards of the Sephardic religious tradition to which they claim to belong. Jewishness is defined by halakhah as being determined by matrilineal descent or, alternatively, by valid halakhic conversion.

If any of these individuals in New Mexico can verify their Jewishness according to halakhah, this is wonderful. But if they cannot, they need to undergo halakhic conversion.

For their own reasons, some Jewish spokesmen have argued that compassion demands that we accept these people as Jews immediately, without requiring any halakhic documentation. They portray the position I have presented as being "hard-line Orthodox."

The media have tended to depict a controversy pinning the hard-hearted Orthodox "bigots" against the compassionate and tolerant non-Orthodox leaders. This is a terrible distortion that has serious ramifications for the Jewish people. The Orthodox are not any less compassionate or sympathetic than the non-Orthodox. But we are concerned with a much larger question, one that others apparently choose to ignore.

Consider the following case. An immigrant from a foreign country comes to the United States. He says that he loves America, that he believes he had ancestors who lived here hundreds of years ago, that he wants to be an American.

He asks you—as a compassionate and sympathetic person— how he can go about becoming an American citizen. Would you tell him: "You don't need to do a thing. I consider you an American citizen right now. After all, you have sacrificed much to come here, you have expressed a genuine love for America, you had ancestors hundreds of years ago who were Americans."

If you would give him this advice, you would be doing him a disservice. When he went to vote, he would be turned away. When he wanted a passport declaring him an American citizen, he would not receive it. The fact is, there is a process of naturalization required in order to become a citizen of the

United States. To tell him that he need not worry about the process does not help him. It creates a false illusion, setting him up for future disappointment.

A truly compassionate friend would tell such an immigrant: Welcome to America—we are glad you have chosen to join us. In order to formalize your citizenship it is necessary to follow a procedure of naturalization. Consult a lawyer, get the necessary papers, meet the requirements—then you will be an American citizen.

By analogy, when Jewish spokesmen tell the people in New Mexico that they are accepted as Jews because they have gone through a lot, because they love Judaism, because they have ancestors who were Jews several hundred years ago—they are misleading these individuals. By following their advice the New Mexican group will not gain legal acceptance within the entire Jewish community. They always will have a cloud over their Jewishness.

On the other hand, a compassionate and wise guide would tell them that he is glad of their interest in embracing Judaism, and that to be accepted as Jews they should follow the necessary procedure: halakhic conversion. In this way these individuals can achieve a genuine and universal acceptance among the Jewish people.

As Jews, we ought to be a self-respecting people, appreciative of our profound and wise tradition. We do have standards for inclusion among our people. These standards have been maintained—and have maintained us—for thousands of years. To glibly eliminate these standards ultimately is to undermine the distinctiveness and the integrity of the Jewish people.

The controversy surrounding the people in New Mexico is not between those with compassion and those who lack compassion. All involved are compassionate. The controversy is about the definition of Jewishness. It is between those who believe in maintaining classic Jewish standards and those who would abandon them.

I believe that respect for the Jewish past and concern for the Jewish future should result in our coming down on the side of maintaining Jewish standards. To espouse this position is not only intellectually sound—it is compassionate in the real sense.

33

IT'S TIME TO FORGE NEW COALITIONS
AND ENTER NEW DIALOGUES

 S ympathy with the oppressed is an age-old Jewish value. Rabbinic tradition refers to Jews as *rahamanim benei rahamanim*, "merciful children of merciful parents." Causes of social justice always have found Jewish support. The Jewish messianic idea has inspired our people to strive to achieve the harmony and peace that the messianic age promises.

In his new book, *Make No Law*, Anthony Lewis describes the civil rights struggles in the South during the early 1960's. He reminds us of black students who risked their lives to attend public school; of blacks relegated to the back of buses; of blacks who had to fight for the simple right to be served at a lunch counter.

We cannot recall the tragic and profound hatred poured out against black people without feeling pangs of empathy. Many of us have spoken out against racism and have worked for the cause of civil rights. All of us have felt revulsion in our hearts when contemplating the horrible injustices to which innocent people were (and are) subjected—only because of the color of their skin.

When I was a child growing up in Seattle, my father had hired a black man to work in his grocery store. This man had come from somewhere down South. He told how he had been

Originally published in *Intermountain Jewish News*, October 11, 1991.

refused lodging in motels, how he was turned away from public eating places. One restaurant owner, feeling some sympathy for him, gave him scraps of food on condition that he would eat out back. He was told that he could drink water from the trough—which was used by animals. Such stories seared our earlier years and implanted within us a deep-rooted commitment to fight racism, oppression, injustice.

A recent issue of the *Smithsonian Magazine* reports on a new memorial to the civil rights movement which was erected in Montgomery, Alabama. The article quotes a Jewish visitor, a survivor of the Holocaust, who stated that he grew up in Poland where he had never seen a black person. Upon coming to the U.S. and learning of the discrimination against blacks, he became involved in the civil rights movement. He recounted that he had been deprived of liberty and dignity in a Nazi concentration camp; he knew from his own experience what it means to be oppressed. Therefore, he wanted to work for the liberation of those who still were suffering oppression. This goes beyond mere sympathy; it is empathy. Jews, who themselves have been victims of irrational hatred and injustice, have understood in their bones the pains and sufferings of blacks.

But now we find ourselves in a kind of dilemma, a serious inner conflict. How are we to respond to the cruel and vicious anti-Jewish actions and words from the black community in Crown Heights? How are we to react to the unabashed anti-Jewish statements of various black leaders, ministers, even a professor at the City University? Have our sympathies and efforts been betrayed?

We hold dear the ideals of justice for all, civil rights for everyone. But at the same time, can we avoid the responsibility of self-preservation, self-defense? Is it realistic to expect Jews to fight for justice for blacks while some blacks spew anti-Jewish propaganda and perpetrate violence against Jews?

When a universal ideal seems to come into conflict with our particularistic interest, what takes precedence? Jews have reacted differently to such dilemmas. To take one extreme example, in 1933 Hitler delivered an oration to inspire the German people. Of course, it included strong anti-Jewish statements. In the *New York Herald Tribune* of May 19, 1933, a columnist praised the speech of the German Chancellor, stating that "we have heard once more, through the fog and din, the authentic voice of a genuinely civilized people." The columnist went on to justify the German persecution of Jews as satisfying the German need to conquer someone. He described the Nazi anti-Semitism as "a kind of lightning rod which protects Europe." The columnist was Walter Lippmann, a Jew. Apparently, he felt that the need for "peace" in Europe was a sufficiently great ideal that it took precedence over the particular concerns of Jews. Jews simply would have to be sacrificed.

In the recent Crown Heights disturbances, some individuals—including Jews—have argued that the blacks turned to violence out of frustration. Since they have been so oppressed, it is only natural and justifiable that they lash out against others. This reflects a social philosophy which attempts to justify acts of violence by blaming the victims of that violence for somehow having deserved it. That there are evils in society, no one will deny. That these evils justify hatred and violence against innocent people is a repugnant and dangerous concept.

On another extreme, some Jewish militants have seen the problem as we—the good guys—against them—the bad guys. They have touched a responsive chord in some Jews who are fed up with black anti-Semitism. It is time to fight back. The civil rights coalitions of the past have evaporated. This position serves to undermine the progress which the Jewish and black communities have achieved. It causes us to abandon our universal ideals and to devote our strength to defending ourselves.

The current crisis, then, demands a blending of universalistic idealism and pragmatic courage. We will not surrender our idealism, our commitment to justice and fairness, our unflinching opposition to racism and oppression. We must work tirelessly and fearlessly for a better society; we must raise our voices against bigotry. To give up this commitment is to give up an essential part of our very being.

On the other hand, we must not tolerate anti-Jewish propaganda, incitements against Jews. Those who preach hatred against us—whatever their race, religion or nationality—must be confronted courageously. But we must direct our struggles against those hate-filled individuals, rather than against all members of their group. We need to help those who need help and to fight those—and only those—who threaten us. This is a good time to forge new coalitions, to enter into new dialogues. This is not the time to let anger or fear create a chasm between Jews and blacks. Creating a just society requires the commitment of all individuals and groups.

Ultimately, we must realize that Jewish self-interest is served best by our being faithful to our universal ideals of justice and compassion. One must be strong and confident in order to be truly just and compassionate.

34

JEWS, BLACKS AND A SHARED DREAM

*T*he injustices perpetrated against American blacks over the centuries must make any sensitive person shudder. Dr. Martin Luther King Jr. summarized these injustices in one word: dehumanization. Blacks were not considered full human beings; they were slaves, inferiors. Even after Emancipation, many white Americans believed blacks should be segregated.

Dr. King described the pathos of the black predicament in a poignant story. His six year old daughter asked him to take her to a children's amusement park that had been advertised on television. After running out of excuses, he had to tell her the truth. The amusement park did not allow blacks. How does one explain to a child that she—and all her people—were rejected, scorned and hated? What scar does such a lesson leave in a child's soul and in a parent's heart?

When Dr. King spearheaded a national movement for civil rights, he saw himself as working for the good of America. He was not raising his voice only for the oppressed blacks: he was calling for a just, compassionate and loving society. He saw the mission of black Americans as helping all Americans create a respectful and honest nation. And he argued that his goal could be achieved only by means of nonviolent demonstrations, by love rather than by hate.

Originally published in *The Westsider*, December 24, 1992, and the *New York Amsterdam News*, January 9, 1993.

He was an American visionary whose message cannot go unheeded if we are, in fact, to achieve a just, compassionate America.

Among Dr. King's earliest and most fervent supporters were American Jews. Jews have a natural empathy for the oppressed, an instinctive idealism, a yearning for a perfect society. Having suffered centuries of oppression, Jews know from personal experience that dehumanization of victims is at the root of human corruption and violence. Dr. King recognized this kinship of spirit between blacks and Jews. Indeed, he would point to the Jewish people as an example of an oppressed group that successfully struggled to maintain its dignity and honor. He admired the Jewish commitment to education and self-help. He respected Jewish idealism, Jewish involvement in humanitarian efforts.

All thoughtful and fair-minded blacks and Jews must recognize their shared ideals and commitments. They must respect each other and see each other as partners in a great enterprise—creating a decent American society that does not dehumanize any group or any individual.

The visionary dream shared by blacks and Jews (and by everyone else of good will) becomes more difficult to achieve when real problems and tensions blur our focus. And there is a long list of complaints. Jews are outraged by viciously anti-Jewish comments and publications by certain black personalities. Jews are troubled by acts of violence against Jews and Jewish property. Blacks express rage, thinking that Jews have all the advantages and that they don't wish to share them with blacks. Blacks see Jews as part of the American society which exploits them. Because blacks and Jews tend to live in big cities, there are plenty of opportunities for them to come into contact and into conflict.

Our problem has been that the focus of black-Jewish relations has shifted to the realm of grievances—real or imagined. Each side makes its case, justifying itself and blaming the other. While it would be foolish to ignore genuine tensions which exist in the community, it is far more foolish to ignore the shared idealism, the shared dream. Jews and blacks know the searing pain that comes with being dehumanized by oppressors. Attempting to dehumanize each other is not only pragmatically unsound; it is also morally repugnant.

There has been too much irresponsible rhetoric on both sides, too much inflammation of emotions and fears. We need to look into each other's eyes and see a human being, not a stereotype, not a heartless enemy. Blacks and Jews (and everyone else) have a right to human dignity. They have a right to live in a just and harmonious society. Hatred and confrontation are not merely threats to our personal well-being; they undermine the fabric of our entire society.

Dr. King had a dream. It is worthwhile for every American to share that dream. It is proper for every American to focus on that dream and not let fears and antagonism win the day. We can achieve this dream by love, not hatred; by learning to trust each other, not by fanning suspicions; by dialogue, not by confrontation.

We must see ourselves as partners in the building of a better society. We must face our problems in the spirit of friendship. We share the same dream.

35

EULOGY AT WOUNDED KNEE

*W*e stand at the mass grave of men, women and children—
Indians who were massacred at Wounded Knee in the bitter
winter of 1890. Pondering the tragedy which occurred at
Wounded Knee fills the heart with crying and with silence.

The great Sioux holy man, Black Elk, was still a child when
he saw the dead bodies of his people strewn throughout this
area. As an old man, he reflected on what he had seen: "I did
not know then how much was ended. When I look back now
from this high hill of my old age, I can still see the butchered
women and children lying heaped and scattered all along the
crooked gulch as plain as when I saw them with eyes still
young. And I can see that something else died there in the
bloody mud and was buried in the blizzard. A people's dream
died there. It was a beautiful dream. For the nation's hoop is
broken and scattered. There is no center any longer, and the
sacred tree is dead."

Indeed, the massacre at Wounded Knee was the culmination
of decades of destruction and transformation for the American
Indian. The decades of suffering somehow are encapsulated
and symbolized by the tragedy at Wounded Knee. Well-armed
American soldiers slaughtered freezing, almost defenseless,
Indians—including women and children. Many of the soldiers
were awarded medals of honor for their heroism, as if there
could be any heroism in wiping out helpless people.

Originally published in *The Westsider,* July 9–15, 1992.

How did this tragedy happen? How was it possible for the soldiers—who no doubt thought of themselves as good men—to participate in a deed of such savagery? How was it possible that the United States Government awarded medals of honor to so many of the soldiers?

The answer is found in one word: dehumanization. For the Americans, the Indians were not people at all, only wild savages. It was no different killing Indians than killing buffaloes or wild dogs. If an American general taught that "the only good Indian is a dead Indian," it means that he did not view Indians as human beings.

When you look a person in the eye and see him as a person, you simply can't kill him or hurt him. Human sympathy and compassion will be aroused. Doesn't he have feelings like you? Doesn't he love, fear, cry, laugh? Doesn't he want to protect his loved ones?

The tragedy of Wounded Knee is a tragedy of the American Indians. But it is also more than that. It is a profound tragedy of humanity. It is the tragedy of dehumanization. It is the tragedy which recurs again and again, and which is still with us today. Isn't our society still riddled with hatred, where groups are hated because of their religion, race, national origin? Don't we still experience the pervasive depersonalization process where people are made into objects, robbed of their essential human dignity?

When Black Elk spoke, he lamented the broken hoop of his nation. The hoop was the symbol of wholeness, togetherness, harmony. Black Elk cried that the hoop of his nation had been broken at Wounded Knee.

But we might also add that the hoop of American life was also broken by the hatred and prejudice exemplified by Wounded Knee. And the hoop of our nation continues to be torn apart by the hatred which festers in our society.

Our task, the task of every American, is to do our share to mend the hoop, to repair the breaches.

The poet Stephen Vincent Benet, in his profound empathy, wrote: "Bury my heart at Wounded Knee." This phrase reflects the pathos of this place and the tragedy of this place.

But if we are to be faithful to Black Elk's vision, we must add: Revitalize our hearts at Wounded Knee. Awaken our hearts to the depths of this human tragedy. Let us devote our revitalized hearts towards mending the hoop of America, the hoop of all humanity. That hoop is made of love; that hoop depends on respect for each other, for human dignity.

We cry at this mass grave at Wounded Knee. We cry for the victims. We cry for the recurrent pattern of hatred and dehumanization which continues to separate people, which continues to foster hatred and violence and murder.

Let us put the hoop of our nation back in order. For the sake of those who have suffered and for the sake of those who are suffering, let us put the hoop of our nation back in order.

36

WHY WOULD THE CATHOLIC CHURCH CONSIDER DECLARING ISABELLA A SAINT?

A civilization expresses its deepest feelings and aspirations through the heroes it chooses. These role models epitomize its highest values; they serve as mirrors to the soul of the culture they represent.

In a profound way, heroes reflect the nature of a civilization more accurately than do official pronouncements or public statements. For example, if a culture speaks of peace but idealizes warriors, then it is actually war-like. If it preaches the virtues of poverty and self-effacement but prizes heroes who are rich, aggressive and arrogant, it is really materialistic.

Traditional Jewish communities have always prized pious Torah scholars. This indicates that the real values of these communities include piety, education, devotion, selflessness. Nazi Germany's dominant hero was Hitler. This indicates that their deepest values included racist nationalism, xenophobia, brutality, merciless oppression. Other civilizations have chosen as their major heroes individuals of different types: philosophers, poets, warriors, athletes, saints, merchant princes and others. In each case, the society's choice(s) revealed its own inner dynamic.

Originally published in *Jewish Advocate*, February 1, 1991.

In recent weeks, there has been considerable discussion about the possibility of the Catholic church following a process leading to declaring Queen Isabella of Spain to be a saint. Jewish groups understandably have been upset by this suggestion. After all, Isabella's Catholic zeal showed itself in the establishment of the Inquisition, which led to the systematic torture and execution of thousands of victims whose beliefs were declared "heretical." Isabella was behind the expurgation of Judaism from Spain.

According to our family tradition, my ancestors were among those many thousands of Jews expelled from Spain by Isabella and Ferdinand in 1492. I cannot think of her or mention her name without feelings of outrage and disgust. She symbolizes the very worst in religious fanaticism; indeed, it is difficult to imagine a person who could be so cold-hearted, vicious, and savage. In the name of her religion, she caused the torture, death and expulsion of innumerable victims. The tears of those victims are an eternal testimony to the wickedness of a very misguided queen.

Catholic historians and religious leaders no doubt know all of this. They do not need Jews to remind them of the frightening and dreadful deeds of Isabella. And yet, the Catholic church still entertains the idea of conferring sainthood on her. The very fact that the suggestion was not dismissed immediately is troubling. That it might actually be accepted is remarkable.

But if the Catholic church declares Isabella to be a saint, this is not at all an insult to Jews; Isabella's cruelty will not be erased. Her fanaticism and bigotry will not be forgotten. She will not cease to be remembered as an evil, demonic tyrant.

The real issue should not be central to non-Catholics. Isabella will never be counted among our heroes. This is a pivotal issue only for the Catholic church. Is Isabella to be declared a hero of faith, a saint? If so, what does this reveal about Catholicism? What values does it foster if it idealizes a woman who promoted the notorious Inquisition, who thought that it was proper to torture, murder and expel those whose beliefs differed from hers? If Catholics will think her a saint, what does this say of their own deepest feelings and attitudes? Wouldn't the Catholic church be indicting itself by declaring Isabella a saint?

King Louis IX of fourteenth-century France called for a crusade. He told crusaders that it was proper and virtuous to murder Jews and plunder their property. He is best known as St. Louis! It is not the Jewish victims who were shamed by this designation of Louis IX; it is the Catholic church alone which bears the shame. In calling him a saint, what do Catholics say about themselves and about their own values?

And in calling Isabella a saint, what will the Catholic church be saying about itself and its own values?

As a descendant of victims of her ruthlessness, I will have no rancor if sainthood is conferred on her. I will be saddened by the thought that after all these centuries, the poison of Isabella has continued in the veins of the Catholic church. And I will imagine that this poison will ultimately kill the faith of good Catholics who will be profoundly ashamed to call Isabella a saint.

37

TIME TO BUILD HOMES

*W*e first opened our synagogue's shelter for homeless men in the winter of 1985. Dozens of congregants and friends volunteered to staff the shelter, serving food, offering pleasant conversation, trying to be helpful to our guests. We all were proud of ourselves—we weren't just talking about a problem of society; we were actually doing something about it. We kept a log, which included comments by the volunteers. Running through the log were two themes:

1. Until we actually spent time with homeless people, we didn't really understand what homelessness was all about;

2. Whatever we are doing is not anywhere near enough.

During the ensuing years, these two themes have continued to surface. Working with homeless people has opened our eyes to a segment of society with which we ordinarily would never have come into such direct human contact. But our volunteers have often stated that our shelter is only a temporary solution for a few people. It keeps them out of the cold at night. But what about their lives? What do they do all day? How do they eat? How do they wash themselves? How will they find jobs, housing, friends? How will they stop being homeless?

Over the years, I have had many conversations with our homeless guests. Here are some of the things they have taught me about being homeless. They have a sense of not belonging, an inability to rest peacefully, a feeling that things are not

Originally published in *The Westsider*, December 19, 1991.

right. Many complained that they felt vulnerable, unsafe; they were suspicious of others; they didn't want to go to city shelters since they feared being robbed or hurt by other homeless people. Some told me that they had lost trust in "the system"; no one really cared about them. Some conveyed the sense of their own unworthiness, their failure. Loneliness, despair, anxiety were there; but somehow, they hardened themselves to these emotions and concentrated on making it from one day to another.

The shelter relieved some of their immediate difficulties. But it did not solve their existential problems, it did not remove their deeply felt fears and anxieties.

The cure for homelessness is not a shelter: it is a home. And that is something our society cannot grasp, or feels it cannot afford to achieve.

Perhaps our inability to create homes for the homeless is a reflection of our own feelings of homelessness. Like the men who stay in our synagogue shelter, so many in our society feel that they don't belong, that things are not right. So many who have houses and apartments, still feel that they lack security. They don't feel safe, they are suspicious of others. And many have lost confidence in "the system." They have come to think that no one does care. Feelings of unworthiness and failure, loneliness and dependence are not exclusively in the province of those labeled "homeless." Deracination and hopelessness afflict many members of our society. Spiritual and emotional homelessness abound.

The cure for homelessness—including spiritual and emotional homelessness—is not a shelter. It is a home. It is sense of belonging, a feeling that life means something; a sense that people can work together in love and harmony, that people can be trusted, that individuals have dignity and worth.

I have found that some of the volunteers in our shelter have themselves found a home in the shelter. They have found a way to transcend themselves, to make a commitment to help others, to do their share in improving the world—if only a little. Through their work with the homeless, they have come to understand not only the nature of physical homelessness, but also the nagging force of emotional and spiritual homelessness.

The problems of the homeless are the problems of our society made more visible and obvious. Providing more shelters, while temporarily helpful, does not address the fundamental issues that homelessness implies. A safe, loving and harmonious society—in which individuals do not feel emotionally and spiritually homeless themselves—will have the compassion and concern to create homes, not just shelters.

Those who foster dissension, hatred, violence and selfishness are keeping all of us in shelters.

It is time for the good people of this city to shake off their own sense of homelessness, to create a good and compassionate society that respects human dignity. It is time to express dissatisfaction with shelters. It is time to be building homes.

BIBLIOGRAPHY OF THE WRITINGS OF RABBI MARC D. ANGEL

I. Hashkafah: Jewish Thought, Philosophy, and Values

"Afterlife" and eleven other essays ("Church and Synagogue," "Covenant," "Creation," "Dogma," "Law—Halakhah," "Messiah," "Pharisees," "Prayer," "Repentance," "Revelation," "Tradition"). In *A Dictionary of the Jewish-Christian Dialogue*, edited by L. Klenicki and G. Wigoder. New York: Paulist Press, 1984.

Aging and Dying as Aspects of Living. Judaica Series, UJA Young Leadership Cabinet. New York: UJA, 1984.

"Authority and Dissent: A Discussion of Boundaries." *Tradition*, vol. 25 (Winter 1990), pp. 18–27.

"Elia Carmona: Judeo-Spanish Author." *Jewish Book Annual*, vol. 44 (New York, 1986), pp. 132–140.

The Essential Pele Yoetz. Condensed and translated by Marc D. Angel. New York: Sepher-Hermon Press, 1991.

The Jewish Orphaned Adult. Palm Springs: Institute for Jewish Hospice, 1992. 18 pages.

"A Jewish Philosophy of Death: A Jewish Philosophy of Life." *Proceedings of the Association of Orthodox Jewish Scientists*, vol. 8–9 (1987), pp. 1–15.

"Judah Abrabanel's Philosophy of Love." *Tradition*, vol. 15 (Fall

295

1975), pp. 81–88.

"Life After Death." In *Body and Soul in Judaism*, edited by J.J. Schacter, pp. 10–13. New York: Orthodox Union, 1991.

"Nahmanides' Approach to Midrash in the Disputation of Barcelona" (with H. P. Salomon). *American Sephardi*, vol. 6 (Winter 1973), pp. 41–51.

"The New Amsterdam Contract and Jewish Traditional Values in the Practices of Self-Help." *Jewish Social Work Quarterly*, . (May 1976), pp. 29-37.

"On the Death of a Parent." In *The Hadassah Magazine Parenting Book*, edited by Roselyn Bell, pp. 83-88. New York and London: Free Press, 1989.

The Orphaned Adult: Confronting the Death of a Parent. New York: Human Sciences Press, 1987.

"Other Thoughts About Jewish Pluralism." *Midstream*, vol. 36 (January 1990), pp. 35-38.

"The Pirkei Abot of Reuben Eliyahu Israel." *Tradition*, vol.11 (Spring 1971), pp. 92–98.

Rabbi David de Sola Pool: Selections from Six Decades of Sermons, Addresses and Writings. Edited by Marc D. Angel. New York: Union of Sephardic Congregations, 1980.

"Reflections on the Death of a Parent." *Jewish Action*, vol. 48 (Rosh Hashanah, 5749/1988), pp. 29–31.

"Religious Understanding of History." Emunah Women's Magazine, vol. 40 (Spring-Summer1992), pp. 4 and 31.

The Rhythms of Jewish Living: A Sephardic Approach. New York: Sepher-Hermon Press/Sephardic House, 1986.

Thoughts About Prayer. New York: Sephardic House, 1983. 8 pages.

"The Thrust of the Time-Spirit." *Jewish Life*, vol. 40 (April

1973), pp. 15–21.

Voices in Exile: A Study in Sephardic Intellectual History. Hoboken, N.J.: Ktav, 1991.

"When a Generation Goes." *Hadassah Magazine*, vol. 69 (October 1989), pp. 40-42.

II. Halakhah: Issues in Jewish Law

"A Fresh Look at Conversion." *Midstream*, vol. 29 (October 1983), pp. 35–38.

"Another Halakhic Approach to Conversions." *Tradition*, vol. 12 (Winter-Spring 1972), pp. 107–113.

"Halacha and Hospice." *Journal of Halacha and Contemporary Society*, no. 12 (Fall 1986), pp. 17–26.

"Modern Orthodoxy and Halakhah: An Inquiry." *Journal of Jewish Thought*, (RCA Jubilee Volume,1985), pp. 102–116.

"The Prohibition of Showing Disdain for Others." In *The Neglected Mitzvot*, edited by J. J. Schacter, pp. 5-10. New York: The Orthodox Union, 1990.

"The RCA Health Care Proxy: Providing Responsible Halachic Leadership to our Community." *Jewish Action*, vol. 52 (Spring 1992), pp. 60, 62.

Religious Zionism and the Non-Orthodox." In *Religious Zionism after Forty Years of Statehood,* edited by Shubert Spero and Y. Pessin, pp. 108-120. Jerusalem, 1989.

"A Sephardic Approach to Halakhah." *Midstream*, vol. 21 (August–September 1975), pp. 66–69.

"A Study of the Halakhic Approaches of Two Modern *Posekim*." *Tradition*, vol. 23 (Spring 1988), pp. 41–52.

"Understanding and Misunderstanding Talmudic Sources." *Judaism*, vol. 26 (Fall 1977), pp. 436–442.

III. Sephardica

"A Sephardi Treasury." *Jewish Life*, vol. 39 (October 1972), pp. 57–59.

A Sephardic Passover Haggadah. Hoboken, N.J.: Ktav, 1988.

"An Approach to Teaching About Sephardic/Oriental Jews. *Pedagogic Reporter*, vol. 37 (January 1987), pp. 1–2.

"Aspects of the Sephardic Spirit." In *The Sephardic Journey (1492–1992)*, pp. 21–29. New York: Yeshiva University Museum, 5752/1992.

"Books: Sephardim on Sephardim." *Present Tense*, vol. 16 (May/June 1989), pp. 58-59.

"Destruction of the Jews of Rhodes." In *Sephardim and the Holocaust*, edited by Solomon Gaon and M. Mitchell Serels, pp. 87–94. New York: Yeshiva University, 1987.

"Israel and the Nations: Sephardic Perspectives." *Emunah Women Magazine*, vol. 38 (November 1990), pp. 17 and 31.

"The Jewish Community of Istanbul." *Jewish Life*, vol. 36 (April 1969), pp. 11–18.

"The Jews of Rhodes: The Challenge of Mediterranean Culture." In *The Sefardim: A Cultural Journey from Spain to the Pacific Coast*, edited by Joshua Stampfer, pp. 74–94. Portland, Oreg.: Institute for Judaic Studies, 1987.

The Jews of Rhodes: The History of a Sephardic Community. New York: Union of Sephardic Congregations/Sepher-Hermon Press, 1978.

"Judeo-Spanish, a Language of the Sephardim." *Keeping Posted*, vol. 17 (December 1971), pp. 21–23.

"Judeo-Spanish Drama: A Study in Sephardic Culture." *Tradition*, vol. 19, no. 2 (Summer 1981), pp. 182–185.

"La Liturjia djudia en ladino." *Aki Yerushalayim*, nos. 28–29

(January–July 1986), pp. 22–24.

"Rabbi Mosheh Israel, Rabbi of Rhodes." *Shevet Va-am*, Second Series, vol. 2 (April 1973), pp. 103–107.

"Rabbi Yaacov Huli." *Jewish Book Annual*, vol. 47 (1981), pp. 162-69.

"Recent Books in English on Sephardim." *Jewish Book Annual*, vol. 49 (1991), pp. 48–52.

"Recent English Works on Sephardic Jewry." *Jewish Book Annual*, vol. 35 (1977), pp. 92–96.

"Seguloth in a Manuscript from the Island of Rhodes." *Estudios Sefardies de Sefarad*, vol. 1 (1978), pp. 83–89.

"Sephardic Approaches to Teaching Siddur." *Pedagogic Reporter*, vol. 33 (December 1981), p. 19.

"Sephardic Culture." *Jewish Spectator*, vol. 37 (December 1972), pp. 23–24.

"Sephardic Customs as Reflections of a Religious World View." *Jewish Education News* (Summer 1990), pp. 21–22.

"Sephardic Shabbat." *Judaism*, vol. 31 (Winter 1982), pp. 21–25.

"The Sephardic Communities of the Eastern Mediterranean Islands." In *The Sephardi Heritage*, vol. 2, edited by R. D. Barnett and W. M. Schwab, pp. 115-143. Grendon: Gibraltar Books, 1989.

Sephardi Voices, 1492–1992: A Study Guide. New York: Hadassah, 1991.

IV. American Sephardim

"The American Experience of a Sephardic Synagogue." In *The American Synagogue: A Sanctuary Transformed*, edited by Jack Wertheimer, pp. 153–169. New York: Cambridge University Press, 1987.

"Congregation Shearith Israel." *Judaica Post*, May–June 1979, pp. 913–921.

"David Barocas, the Man and His Ideas." In *Studies in Sephardic Culture*, edited by Marc D. Angel, pp. 1–14. New York: Sepher-Hermon Press/Sephardic House, 1980.

"David de Sola Pool." In *Jewish-American History and Culture: An Encyclopedia*, edited by Jack Fischel and Sanford Pinsker, p. 512. New York: Garland, 1992.

"Henry Pereira Mendes." In *Jewish-American History and Culture: An Encyclopedia*, edited by Jack Fischel and Sanford Pinsker, pp. 386–387. New York: Garland, 1992.

La America: The Sephardic Experience in the United States. Philadelphia: Jewish Publication Society, 1982.

"The Literary, Social and Cultural Life of the Judeo-Spanish Sephardim During the Immigrant Generation." *Proceedings of Sephardic House Conference, April 5, 1981*, pp. 2–10. New York: Sephardic House, 1981.

New York's Early Jews: Some Myths and Misconceptions. New York: Jewish Historical Society of New York, 1976, pp. 18-27.

"Notes on the Early History of Seattle's Sephardic Community." *Western States Jewish Historical Quarterly*, vol. 7 (October 1974), pp. 22–30.

"*Progress*—Seattle's Sephardic Monthly, 1934–5." *American Sephardi*, vol. 5 (Autumn 1971), pp. 91–95.

"Religious Life of American Sephardim." In *Dimensions of Orthodox Judaism*, edited by Reuven Bulka, pp. 212–218. New York: Ktav, 1983.

"Ruminations About Sephardic Identity." *Midstream*, vol. 18 (March 1972), pp. 64–67.

"Sephardic-Ashkenazic Intramarriage." *Sh'ma*, January 20, 1984, pp. 44–46.

"Sephardic Culture in America." *Jewish Life*, vol. 38 (March–April 1971), pp. 7–11.

"The Sephardic Theatre of Seattle." *American Jewish Archives*, vol. 25 (November 1973), pp. 156–160.

"Sephardim." In *Jewish-American History and Culture: An Encyclopedia*, edited by Jack Fischel and Sanford Pinsker, pp. 569–571. New York: Garland, 1992.

"Sephardim in America." *Present Tense*, vol. 4 (Autumn 1976), pp. 12–14.

Sephardim of North America. New York: Council of Jewish Federations, 1981. 8 pages

"The Sephardim of the United States: An Exploratory Study." In *American Jewish Year Book, 1973*, pp. 77–138. Philadelphia: Jewish Publication Society, 1974.

"Shearith Israel." In *Jewish-American History and Culture*, edited by Jack Fischel and Sanford Pinsker, pp. 572–573. New York: Garland, 1992.

Studies in Sephardic Culture. Edited by Marc D. Angel. New York, Sepher-Hermon Press/Sephardic House, 1980.

"Thoughts About Early American Jewry." *Tradition*, vol. 16 (Fall 1976), pp. 16–23.

V. Reviews, Introductions, Miscellaneous Essays

"A Chance to Learn." *Hadassah Magazine*, vol. 73 (January 1992), pp. 10–11.

"Dialogue Comments: How an Ashkenazi American Jewry Relates to a Sephardi Israel." *Congress Monthly*, vol. 53 (March–April 1986), pp. 13–14, 17.

"Five Translations of the *Aeneid.*" *Classical Journal*, vol. 62 (April 1967). pp. 295-300.

"In Search of Shelemut: Teaching the 'Wholeness' of the Jewish People." *Ten Da'at*, vol. 3 (Fall 1988), pp. 12–13.

Introduction to *Abraham Galante: A Biography*, by Albert Kalderon. New York: Sepher-Hermon Press/Sephardic House, 1983.

Introduction to *The Beauty of Sephardic Life*, by Sam Bension Maimon. Seattle: MaimonIdeas Press, 1993.

Introduction to *Hispanic Culture and Character of the Sephardic Jews*, by M. J. Benardete. New York: Sepher-Hermon Press/Sephardic House, 1982.

Introduction to *The Influences of Catholic Theologian Alfonso Tostado on the Pentateuch Commentary of Isaac Abravanel*, by Solomon Gaon. Hoboken, N.J.: Ktav, 1993.

Introduction to *Sephardic Holiday Cooking*, by Gilda Angel. Mount Vernon, N.Y.: Decalogue Books 1986.

Introduction to *Spanish and Portuguese Jewry Before and After 1492*, by David Fintz Altabe. New York: Sepher-Hermon Press, 1993.

"The Jewish Poems of Emma Lazarus." *American Sephardi*, vol. 2 (1968), pp. 60–63.

Review of *The Parnas*, by Silvano Arieti. *Tradition*, vol. 18 (Fall 1980), pp. 310–313.

Review of *The Other Jews*, by Daniel Elazar. *Hadassah Magazine*, vol. 69 (November 1988), pp. 4–41.

Review of *A Treasury of Sephardic Laws*, by Herbert C. Dobrinsky. *Jewish Education*, vol. 55 (Fall 1987), p. 46.

"Roasted Pumpkin Seeds and Winding Roads of Memory." *National Jewish Monthly*, vol. 89 (October 1974), pp. 41–45.

Symposium response on Modern Orthodoxy, *Tradition*, vol. 20
    (Spring 1982), pp. 6–9.